V. E. SCHWAB
SHADES OF MAGIC
THE STEEL PRINCE
NIGHT of KNIVES

ARTIST
BUDI SETIAWAN

INKER
CHAPTER 1.
BUDI SETIAWAN

CHAPTER 2-4.
ANDREA OLIMPIERI

COLORIST
ENRICA EREN ANGIOLINI

COLOR ASSISTS
VIVIANA SPINELLI

LETTERING
ROB STEEN

TITAN
COMICS

V. E. SCHWAB
SHADES OF MAGIC
THE STEEL PRINCE
NIGHT of KNIVES

Introduction

"The Steel Prince," said Sol-in-Ar, and then, reading Maxim's expression:
"It surprises you, that the tales of your exploits reach beyond your own borders?"
The Faroan's fingers grazed the edge of the map. "The Steel Prince, who tore the heart
from the rebel army. The Steel Prince, who survived the night of knives.
The Steel Prince, who slayed the pirate queen."

Maxim finished his drink and set the glass aside.

"I suppose we never know the scale of our life's stories.
Which parts will survive, and which will die with us."

~A Conjuring of Light

Where is the line between truth and legend?

Maxim Maresh, royal and soldier, is learning that myths are not born – or stumbled across – but made, by actions embellished by time and distance into something far grander. And Maxim's own legend, as the Steel Prince, is beginning to take shape.

Defeating the Pirate Queen was a solid first step, but it will take far more for him to carve a place in the annals of history, especially when he doesn't even have the respect of his own soldiers, or the citizens of Verose.

Eager to prove himself, Maxim decides to enter the Night of Knives, a series of four grueling trials held in tunnels beneath the town. The rules are simple: enter alone, carrying whatever you like. Stop after the first, or the second, or the third, if you like. But once each door is opened, the only way out is through. And no one has ever survived the entire Night.

CAST OF CHARACTERS

MAXIM MARESH

Crown Prince of Arnes. Magically gifted with the ability to bend steel to his will. He is known to be a talented fighter and soldier who has led troops at the forefront of the Arnesian army, but he desires to do more.

NOKIL MARESH

King of Arnes. Frustrated with his son's preoccupation with the other realms, he banishes Maxim to Verose. He hopes to redirect his son's attention toward matters in their own world and kingdom.

TIEREN SERENSE

Head Priest of the London Sanctuary and the adviser to the king. Wise and powerful in his own right, he has watched over and trained Maxim in magical combat and matters of leadership and statecraft.

ISRA

A royal guard serving in the Arnesian army base in Verose. Toughened by the harsh streets of the Blood Coast, she leads a matchless team with her loyal companions, Osili and Toro.

RIO

With his distinctive clown-like facial make-up, Rio is a psychotic magic blade for hire. Together with his gang of cutthoats, Rio stalks the back alleys and dark streets of Verose at night looking for easy targets and soldiers to mug and kill.

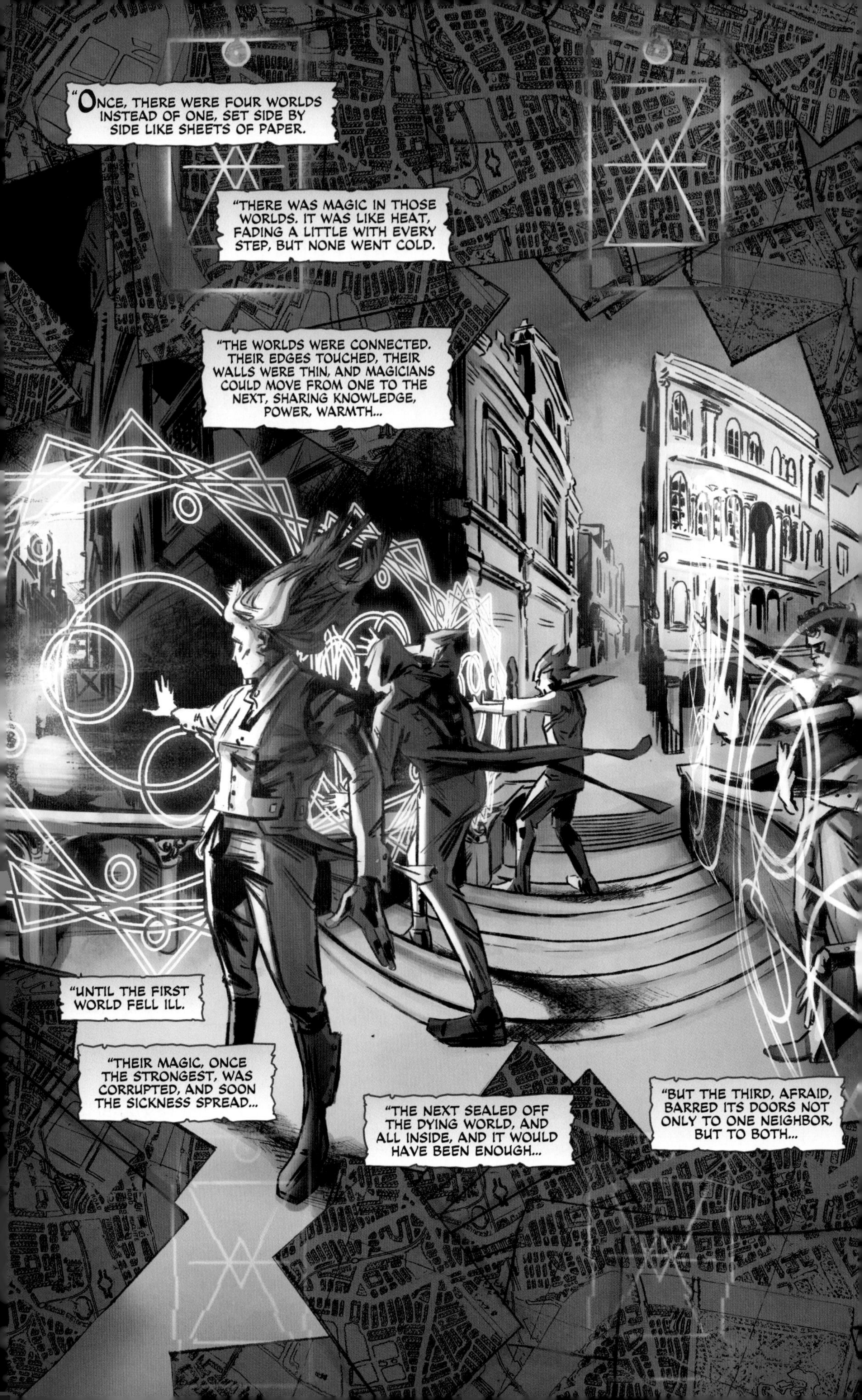
"ONCE, THERE WERE FOUR WORLDS INSTEAD OF ONE, SET SIDE BY SIDE LIKE SHEETS OF PAPER.
"THERE WAS MAGIC IN THOSE WORLDS. IT WAS LIKE HEAT, FADING A LITTLE WITH EVERY STEP, BUT NONE WENT COLD.
"THE WORLDS WERE CONNECTED. THEIR EDGES TOUCHED, THEIR WALLS WERE THIN, AND MAGICIANS COULD MOVE FROM ONE TO THE NEXT, SHARING KNOWLEDGE, POWER, WARMTH...
"UNTIL THE FIRST WORLD FELL ILL.
"THEIR MAGIC, ONCE THE STRONGEST, WAS CORRUPTED, AND SOON THE SICKNESS SPREAD...
"THE NEXT SEALED OFF THE DYING WORLD, AND ALL INSIDE, AND IT WOULD HAVE BEEN ENOUGH...
"BUT THE THIRD, AFRAID, BARRED ITS DOORS NOT ONLY TO ONE NEIGHBOR, BUT TO BOTH...

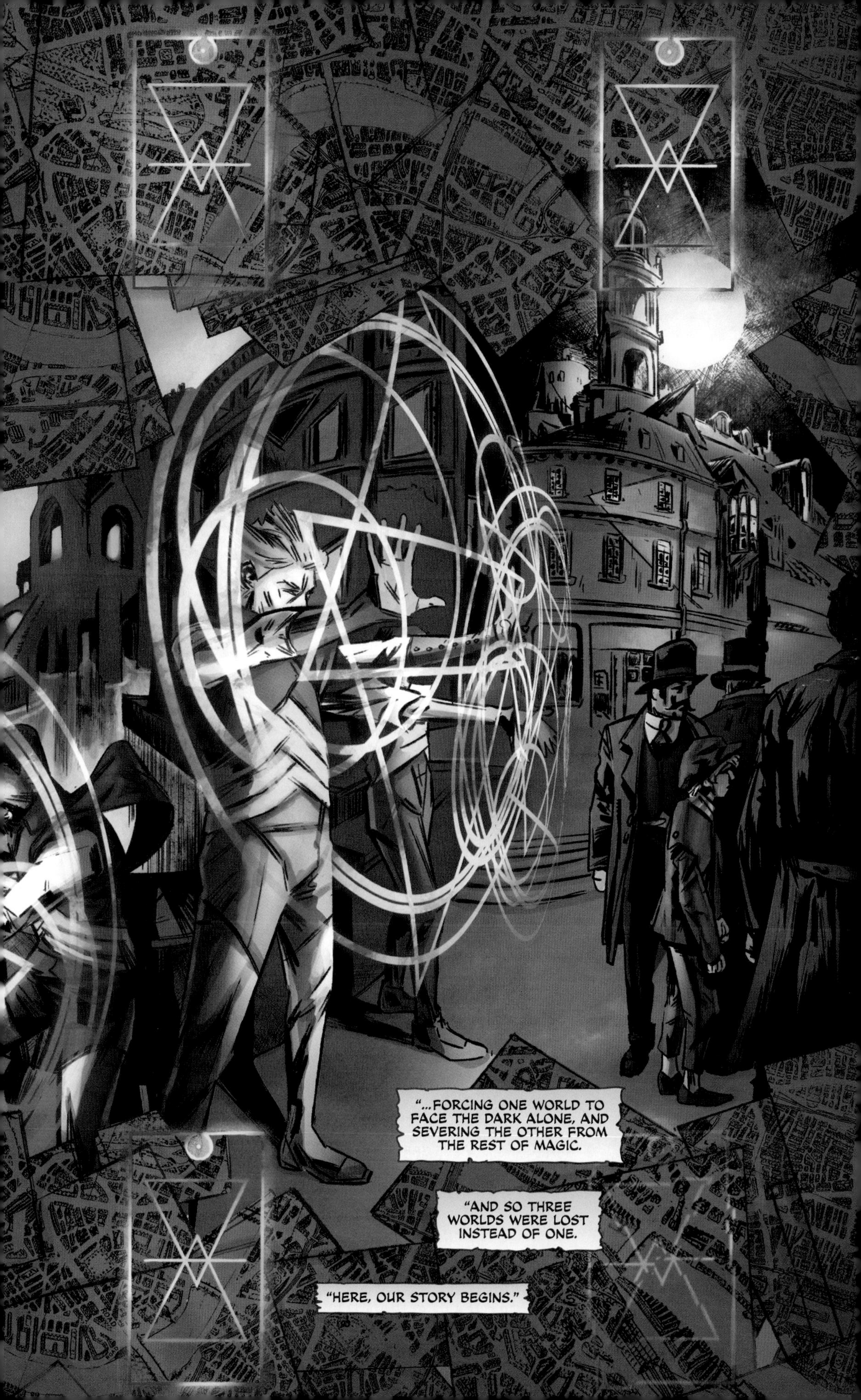
"...FORCING ONE WORLD TO FACE THE DARK ALONE, AND SEVERING THE OTHER FROM THE REST OF MAGIC.
"AND SO THREE WORLDS WERE LOST INSTEAD OF ONE.
"HERE, OUR STORY BEGINS."

#1

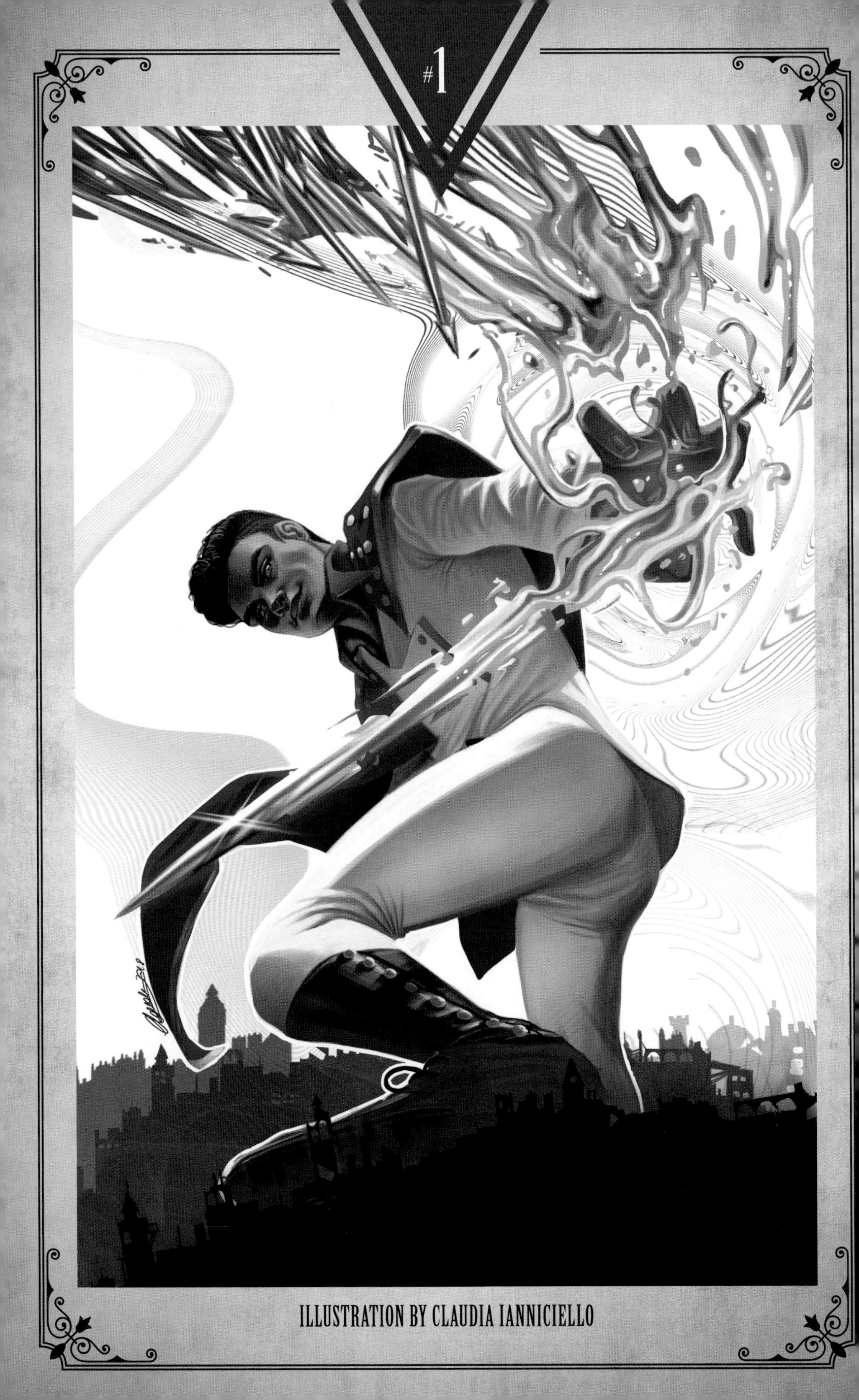

ILLUSTRATION BY CLAUDIA IANNICIELLO

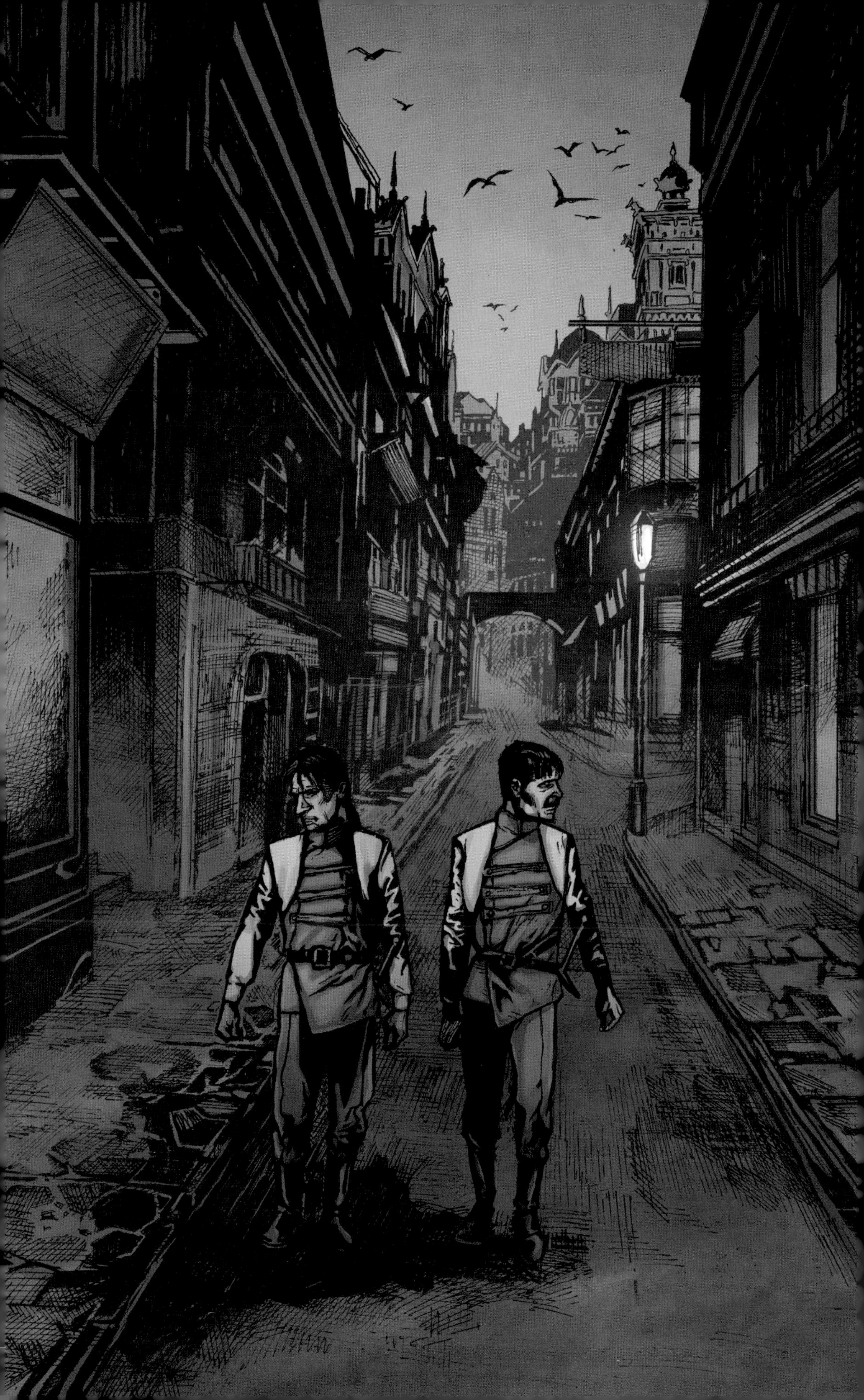

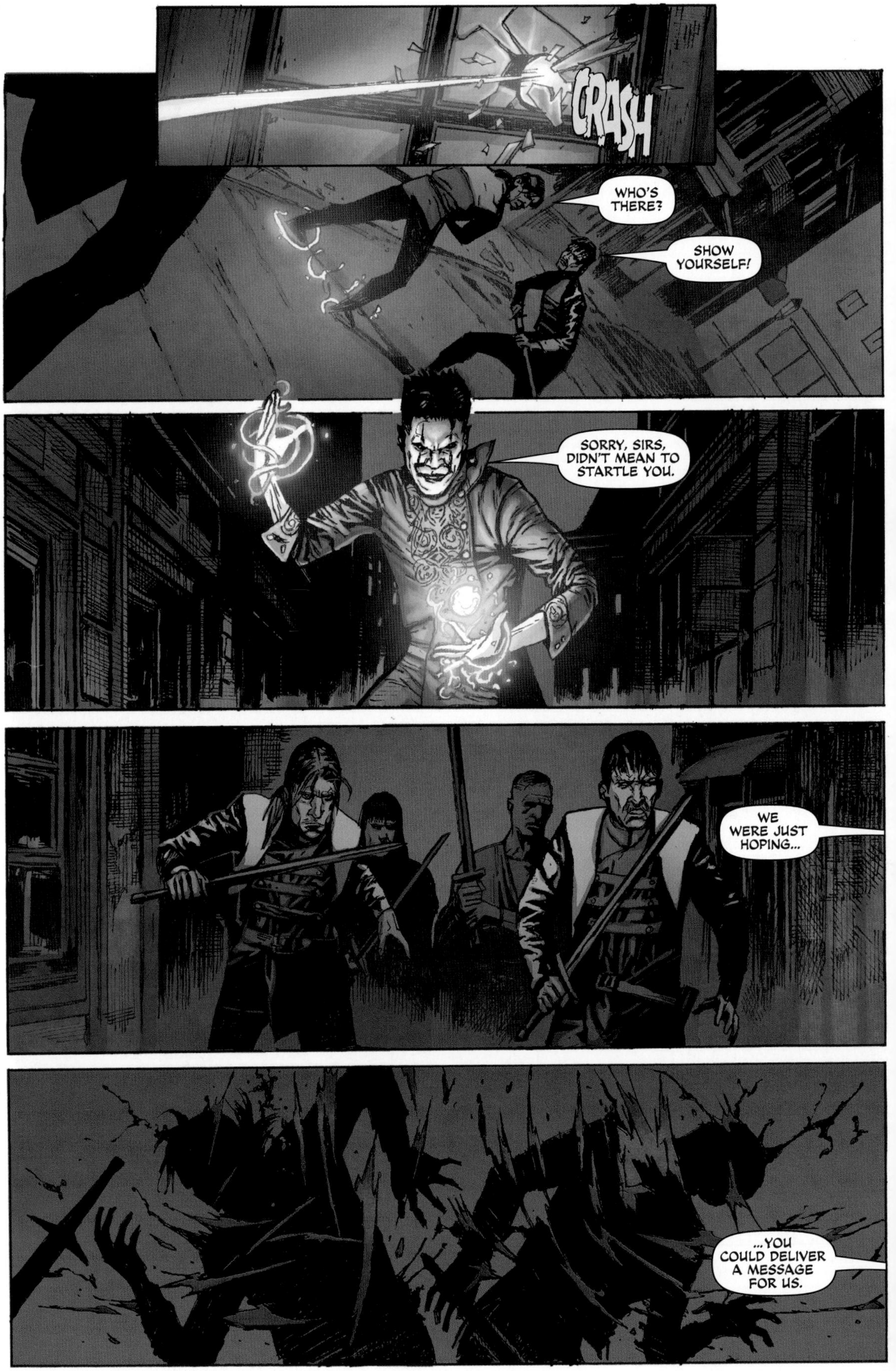
CRASH
WHO'S THERE?
SHOW YOURSELF!
SORRY, SIRS, DIDN'T MEAN TO STARTLE YOU.
WE WERE JUST HOPING...
...YOU COULD DELIVER A MESSAGE FOR US.

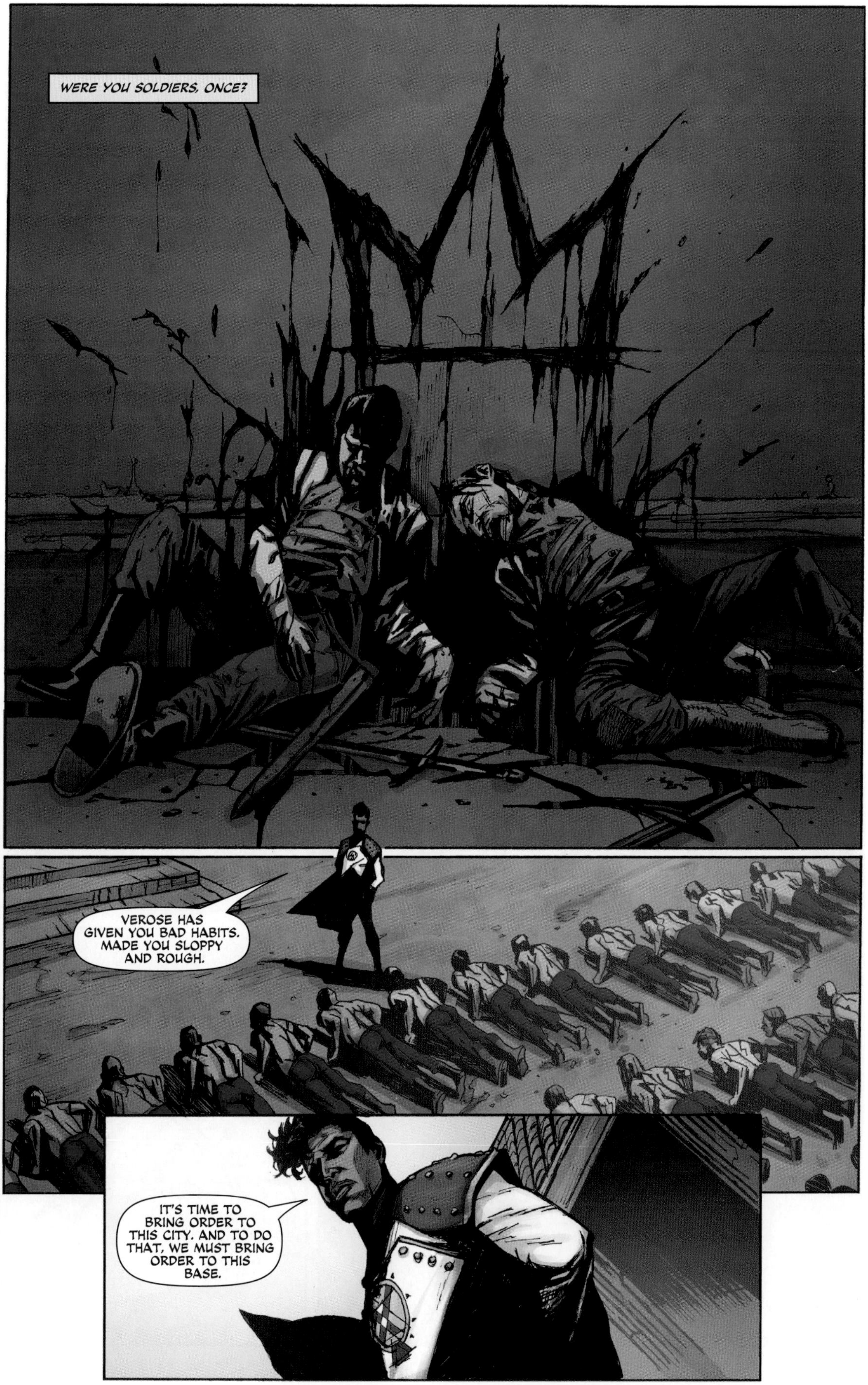
WERE YOU SOLDIERS, ONCE?
VEROSE HAS GIVEN YOU BAD HABITS. MADE YOU SLOPPY AND ROUGH.
IT'S TIME TO BRING ORDER TO THIS CITY. AND TO DO THAT, WE MUST BRING ORDER TO THIS BASE.

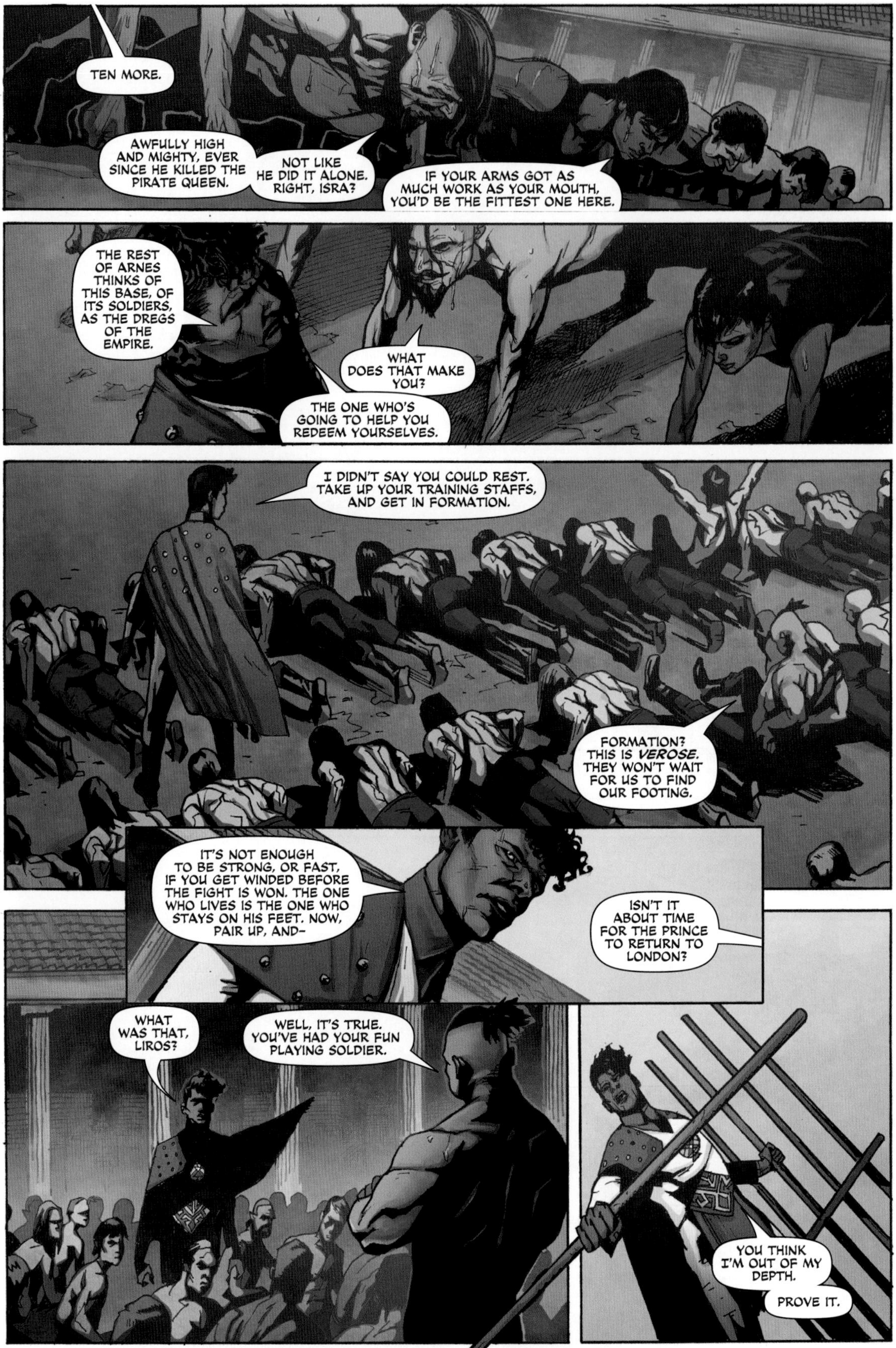
TEN MORE.
AWFULLY HIGH AND MIGHTY, EVER SINCE HE KILLED THE PIRATE QUEEN.
NOT LIKE HE DID IT ALONE. RIGHT, ISRA?
IF YOUR ARMS GOT AS MUCH WORK AS YOUR MOUTH, YOU'D BE THE FITTEST ONE HERE.
THE REST OF ARNES THINKS OF THIS BASE, OF ITS SOLDIERS, AS THE DREGS OF THE EMPIRE.
WHAT DOES THAT MAKE YOU?
THE ONE WHO'S GOING TO HELP YOU REDEEM YOURSELVES.
I DIDN'T SAY YOU COULD REST. TAKE UP YOUR TRAINING STAFFS, AND GET IN FORMATION.
FORMATION? THIS IS *VEROSE*. THEY WON'T WAIT FOR US TO FIND OUR FOOTING.
IT'S NOT ENOUGH TO BE STRONG, OR FAST, IF YOU GET WINDED BEFORE THE FIGHT IS WON. THE ONE WHO LIVES IS THE ONE WHO STAYS ON HIS FEET. NOW, PAIR UP, AND–
ISN'T IT ABOUT TIME FOR THE PRINCE TO RETURN TO LONDON?
WHAT WAS THAT, LIROS?
WELL, IT'S TRUE. YOU'VE HAD YOUR FUN PLAYING SOLDIER.
YOU THINK I'M OUT OF MY DEPTH.
PROVE IT.

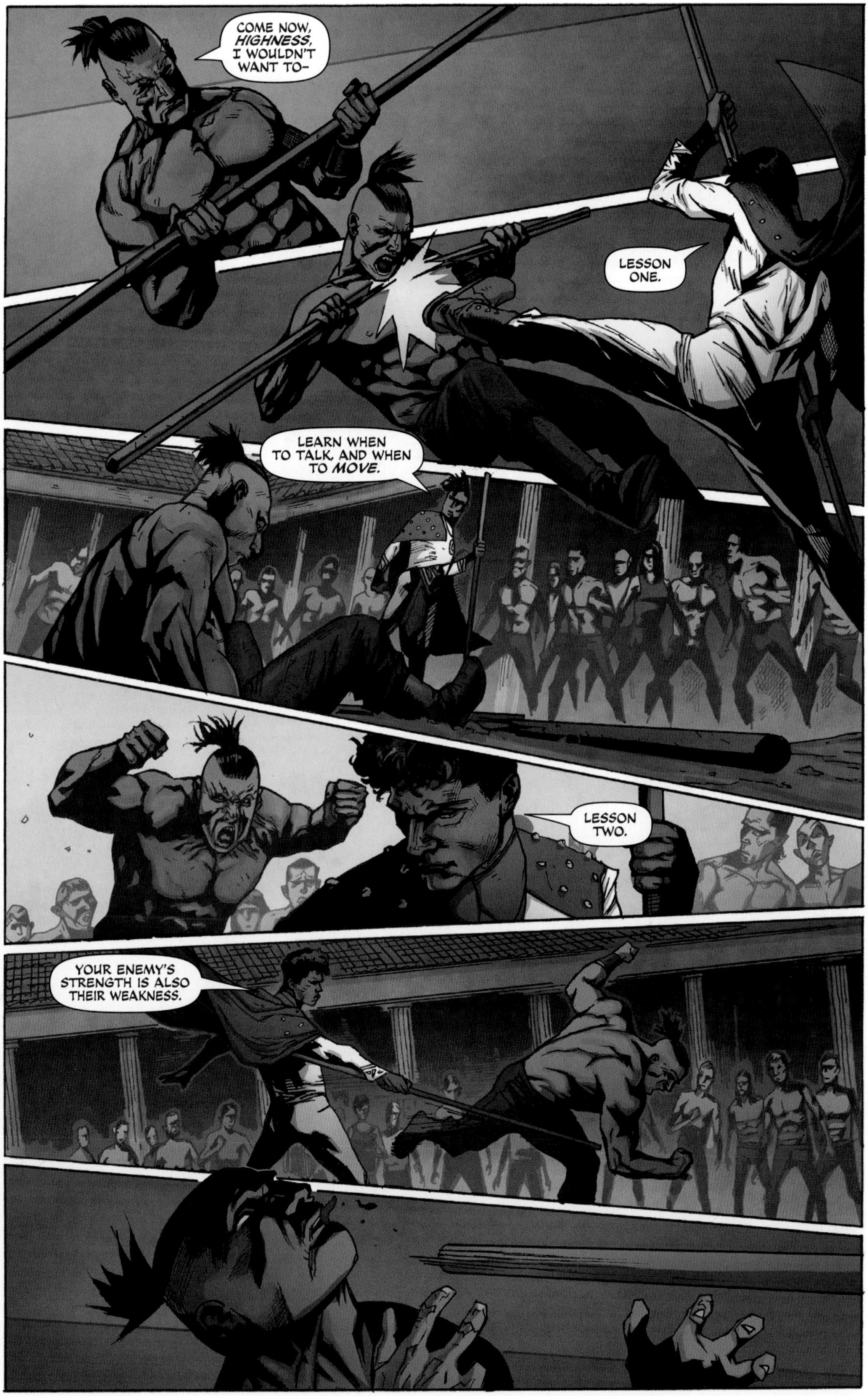
COME NOW, *HIGHNESS*, I WOULDN'T WANT TO-
LESSON ONE.
LEARN WHEN TO TALK, AND WHEN TO *MOVE*.
LESSON TWO.
YOUR ENEMY'S STRENGTH IS ALSO THEIR WEAKNESS.

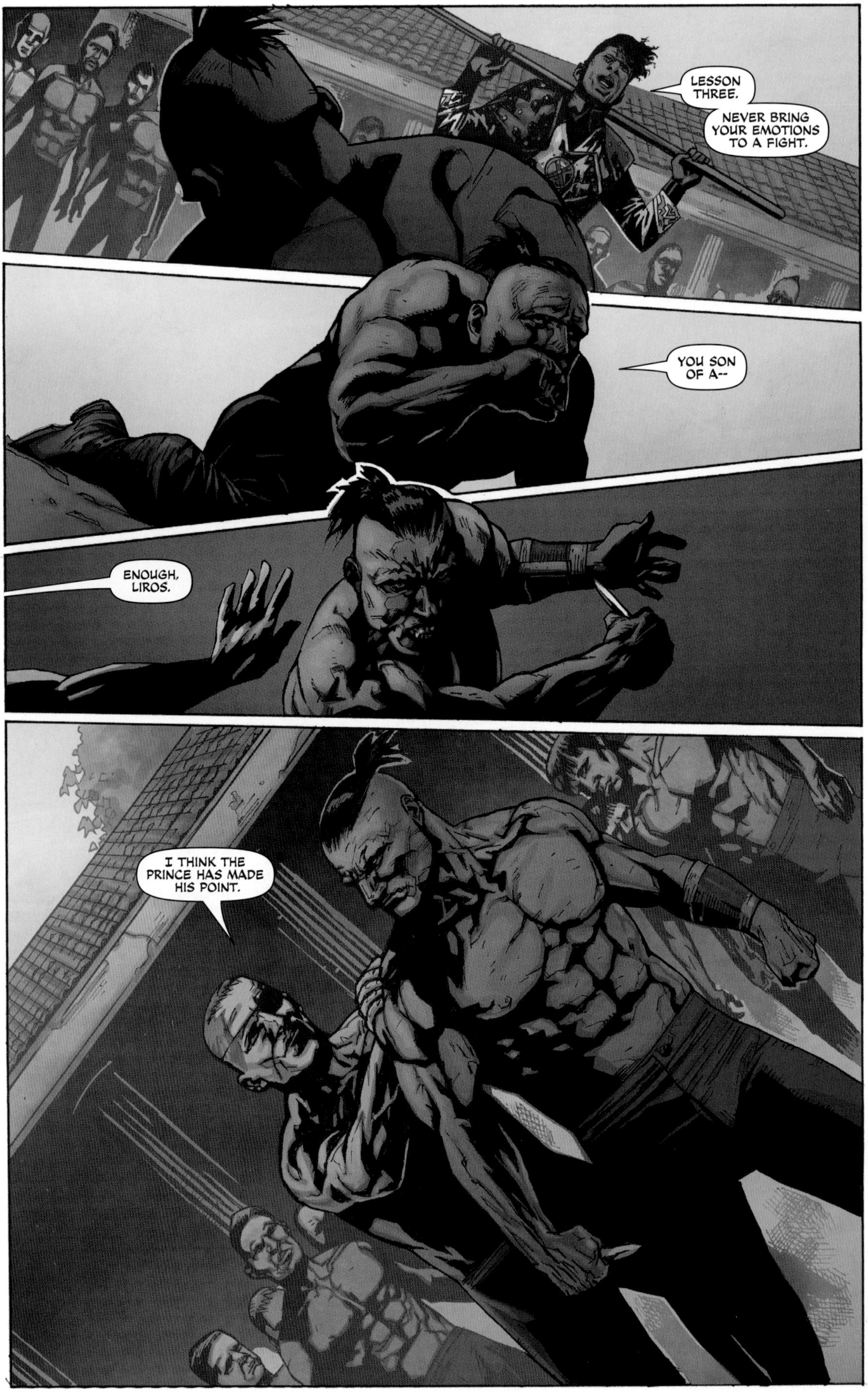
LESSON THREE.
NEVER BRING YOUR EMOTIONS TO A FIGHT.
YOU SON OF A--
ENOUGH, LIROS.
I THINK THE PRINCE HAS MADE HIS POINT.

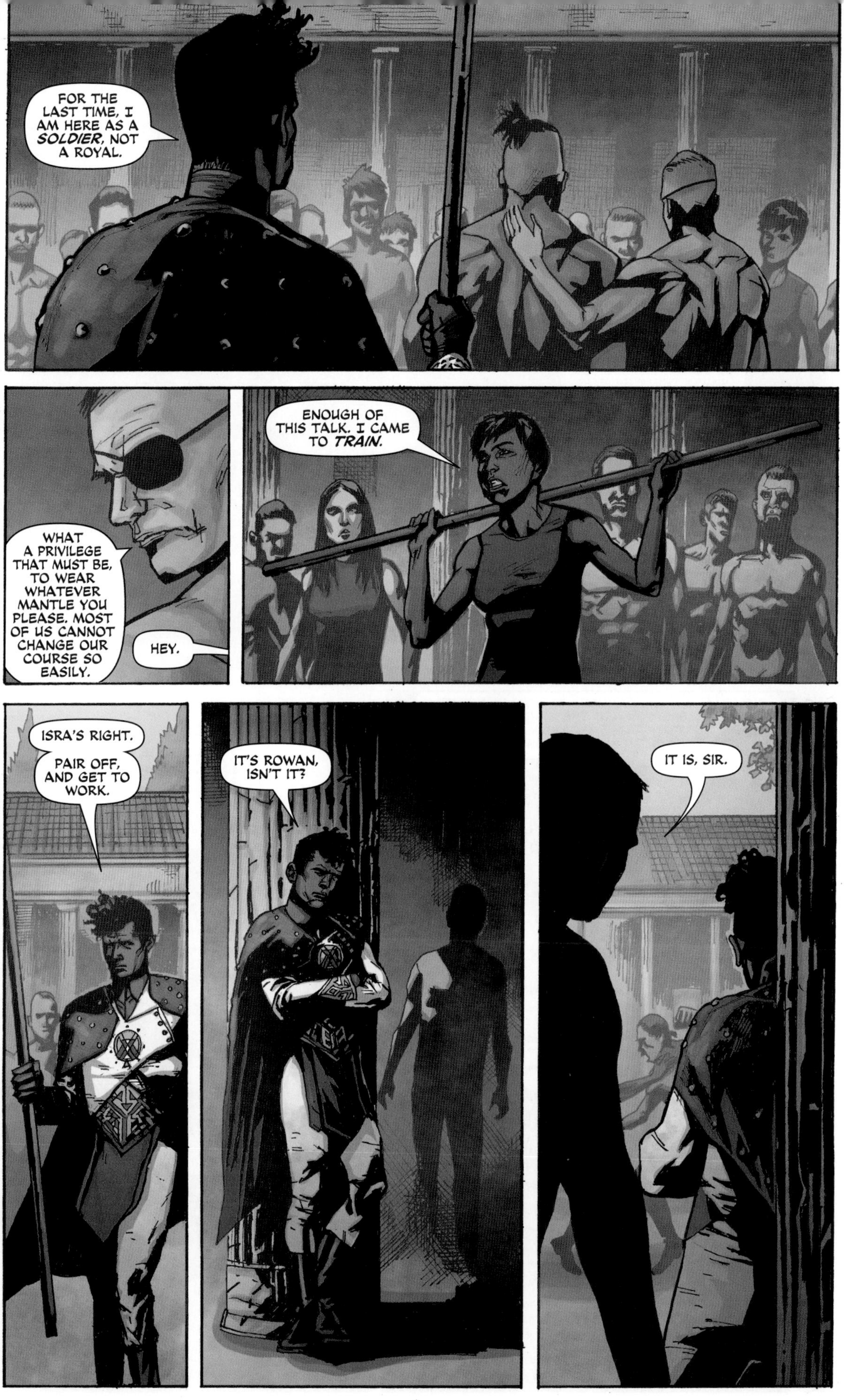
FOR THE LAST TIME, I AM HERE AS A *SOLDIER*, NOT A ROYAL.
WHAT A PRIVILEGE THAT MUST BE, TO WEAR WHATEVER MANTLE YOU PLEASE. MOST OF US CANNOT CHANGE OUR COURSE SO EASILY.
HEY.
ENOUGH OF THIS TALK. I CAME TO *TRAIN*.
ISRA'S RIGHT.
PAIR OFF, AND GET TO WORK.
IT'S ROWAN, ISN'T IT?
IT IS, SIR.

MAY I SPEAK PLAINLY?

LET ME GUESS, YOU DO NOT CARE FOR ME.

CARE HAS NOTHING TO DO WITH IT, SIR. YOU SIMPLY DON'T BELONG HERE.

WATCH YOUR WORDS, ROWAN. I MAY BE A PRINCE, BUT I *AM* A SOLDIER, TOO.

YOU DON'T SEEM TO UNDERSTAND.

YOU CANNOT BE THEIR BETTER *AND* THEIR EQUAL.

YOU TALK OF THE DANGERS IN VEROSE, YET TO THESE SOLDIERS, YOU ARE THE GREATEST THREAT. *YOU* ARE THE TARGET ON THEIR BACKS. THE BURDEN THEY MUST SHOULDER.

THE BEST THING YOU CAN DO FOR THE SOLDIERS HERE...

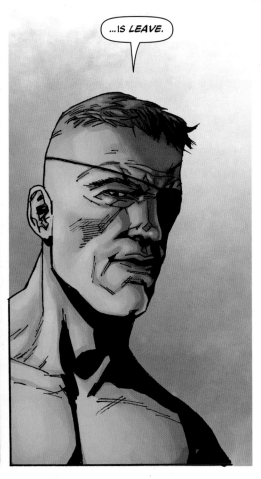

...IS *LEAVE*.

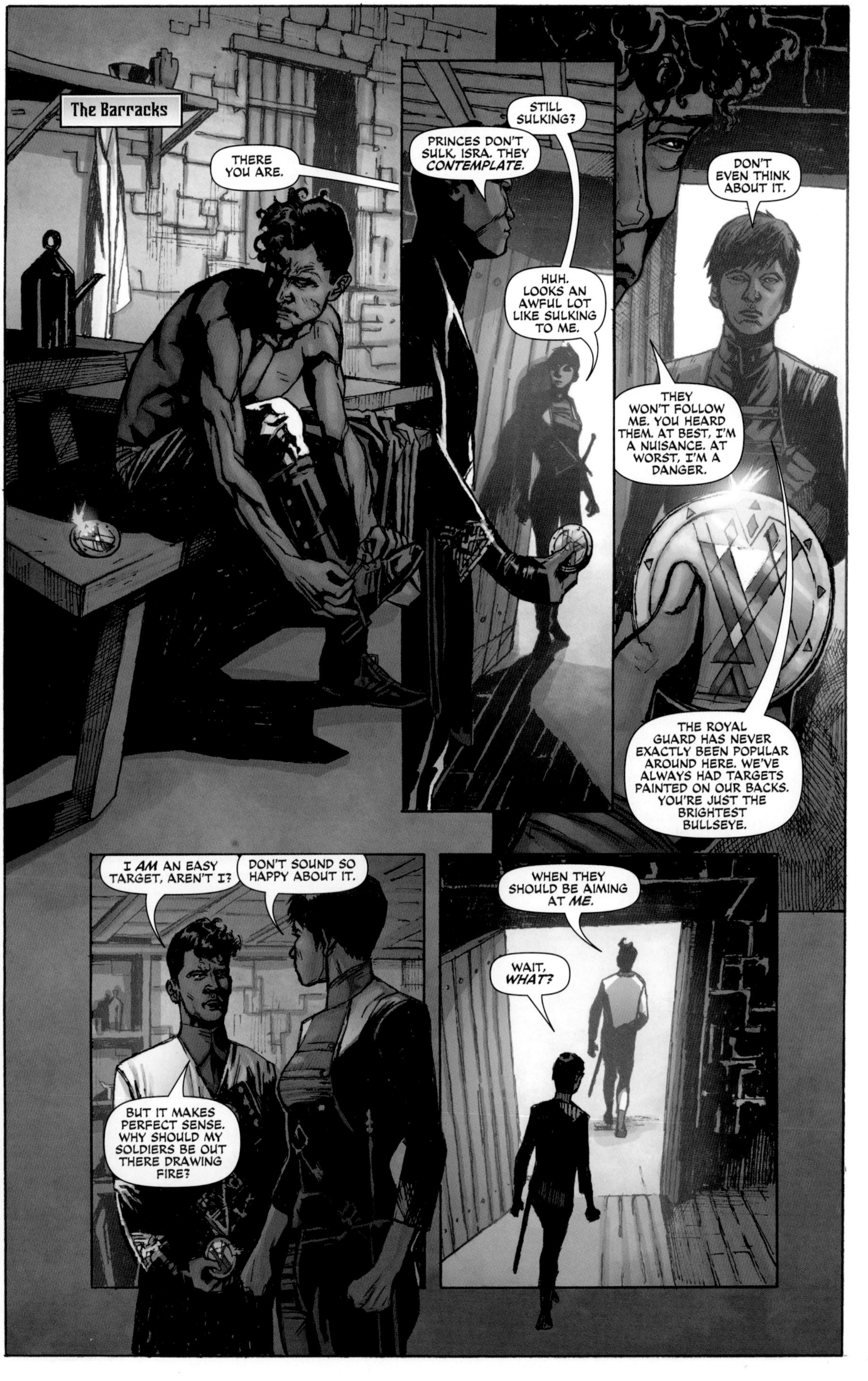
The Barracks
THERE YOU ARE.
STILL SULKING?
PRINCES DON'T SULK, ISRA. THEY *CONTEMPLATE*.
HUH. LOOKS AN AWFUL LOT LIKE SULKING TO ME.
DON'T EVEN THINK ABOUT IT.
THEY WON'T FOLLOW ME. YOU HEARD THEM. AT BEST, I'M A NUISANCE. AT WORST, I'M A DANGER.
THE ROYAL GUARD HAS NEVER EXACTLY BEEN POPULAR AROUND HERE. WE'VE ALWAYS HAD TARGETS PAINTED ON OUR BACKS. YOU'RE JUST THE BRIGHTEST BULLSEYE.
I *AM* AN EASY TARGET, AREN'T I?
DON'T SOUND SO HAPPY ABOUT IT.
BUT IT MAKES PERFECT SENSE. WHY SHOULD MY SOLDIERS BE OUT THERE DRAWING FIRE?
WHEN THEY SHOULD BE AIMING AT *ME*.
WAIT, *WHAT*?

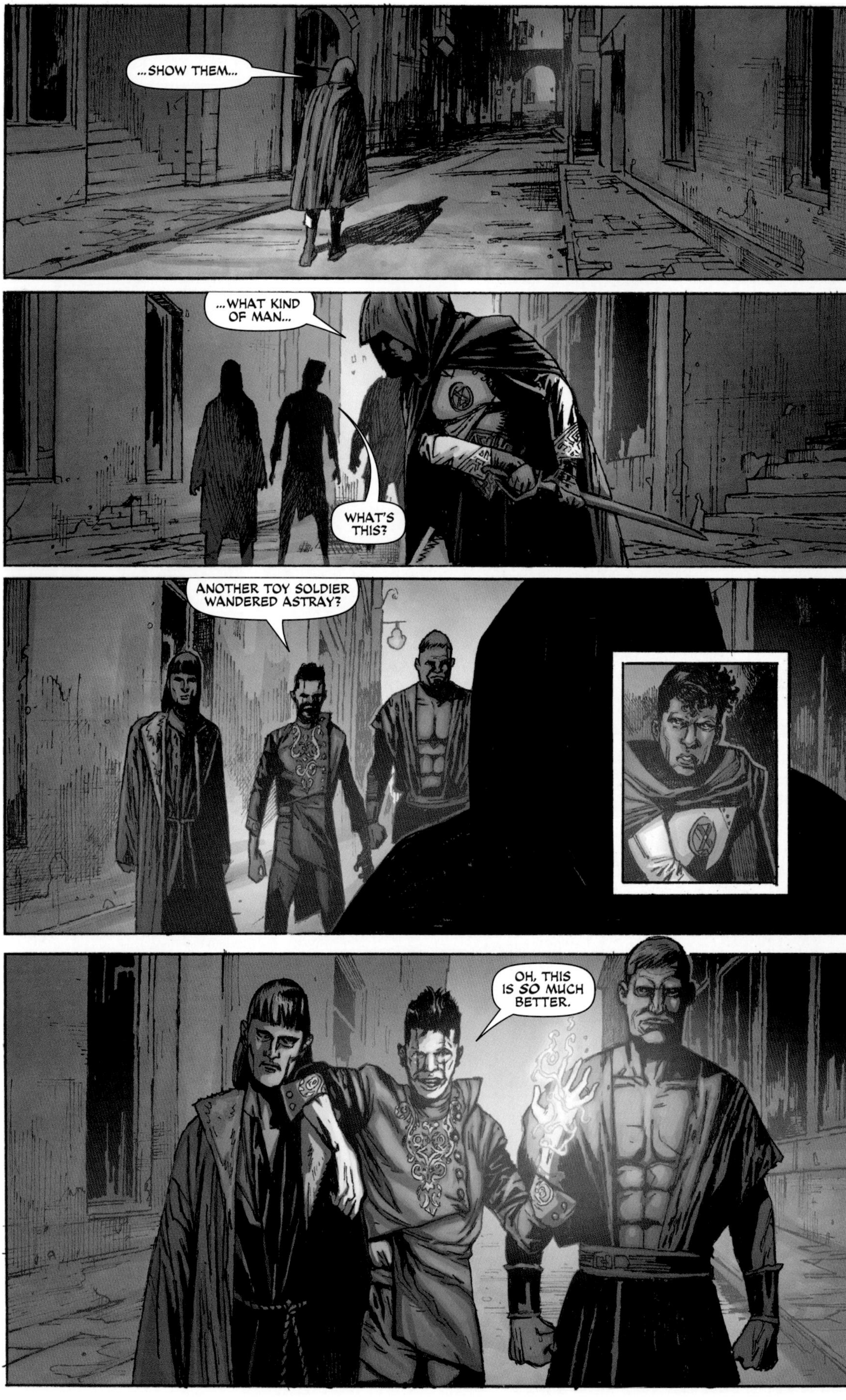
...SHOW THEM...
...WHAT KIND OF MAN...
WHAT'S THIS?
ANOTHER TOY SOLDIER WANDERED ASTRAY?
OH, THIS IS SO MUCH BETTER.

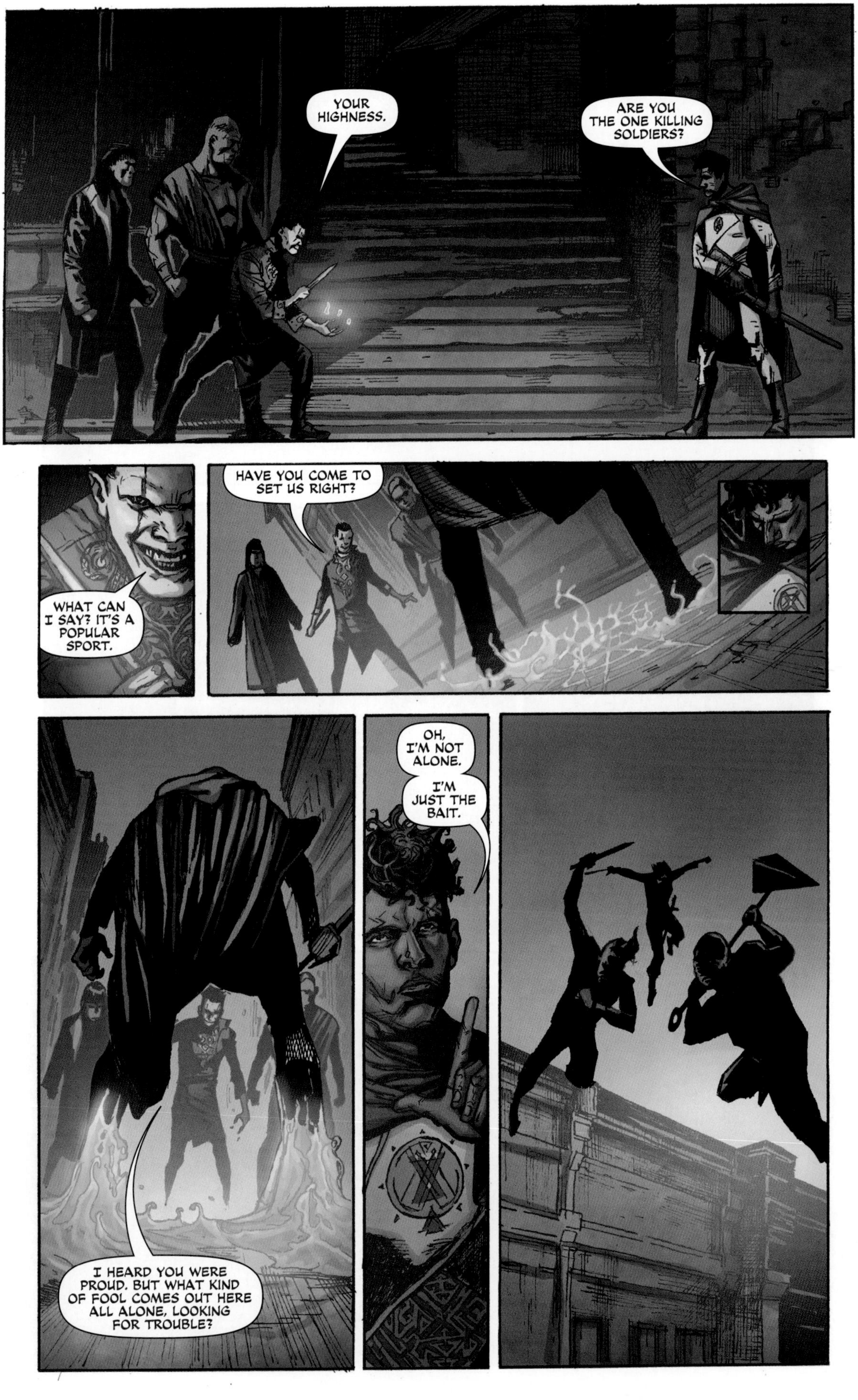
YOUR HIGHNESS.
ARE YOU THE ONE KILLING SOLDIERS?
WHAT CAN I SAY? IT'S A POPULAR SPORT.
HAVE YOU COME TO SET US RIGHT?
I HEARD YOU WERE PROUD. BUT WHAT KIND OF FOOL COMES OUT HERE ALL ALONE, LOOKING FOR TROUBLE?
OH, I'M NOT ALONE.
I'M JUST THE BAIT.

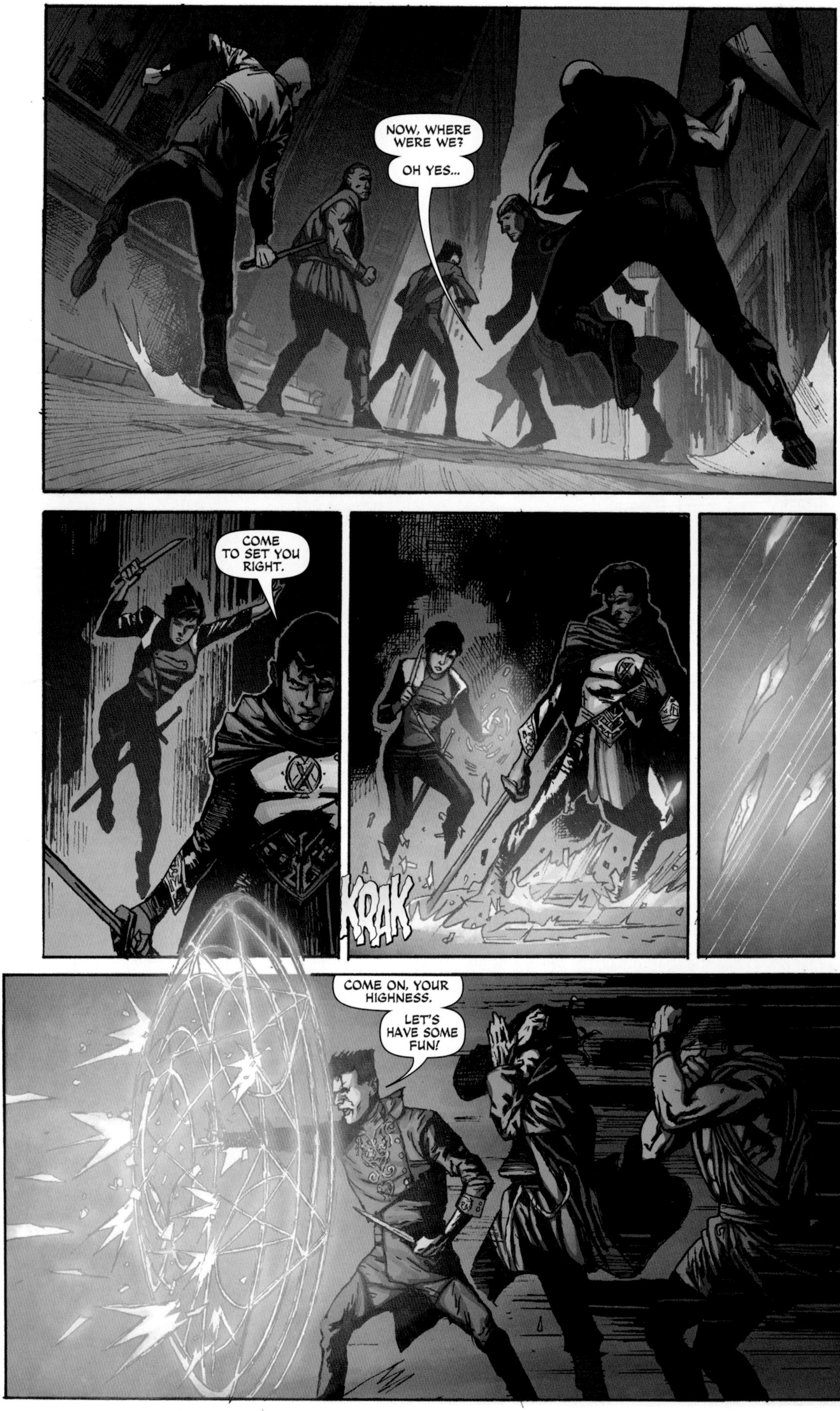
NOW, WHERE WERE WE?
OH YES...
COME TO SET YOU RIGHT.
KRAK
COME ON, YOUR HIGHNESS.
LET'S HAVE SOME FUN!

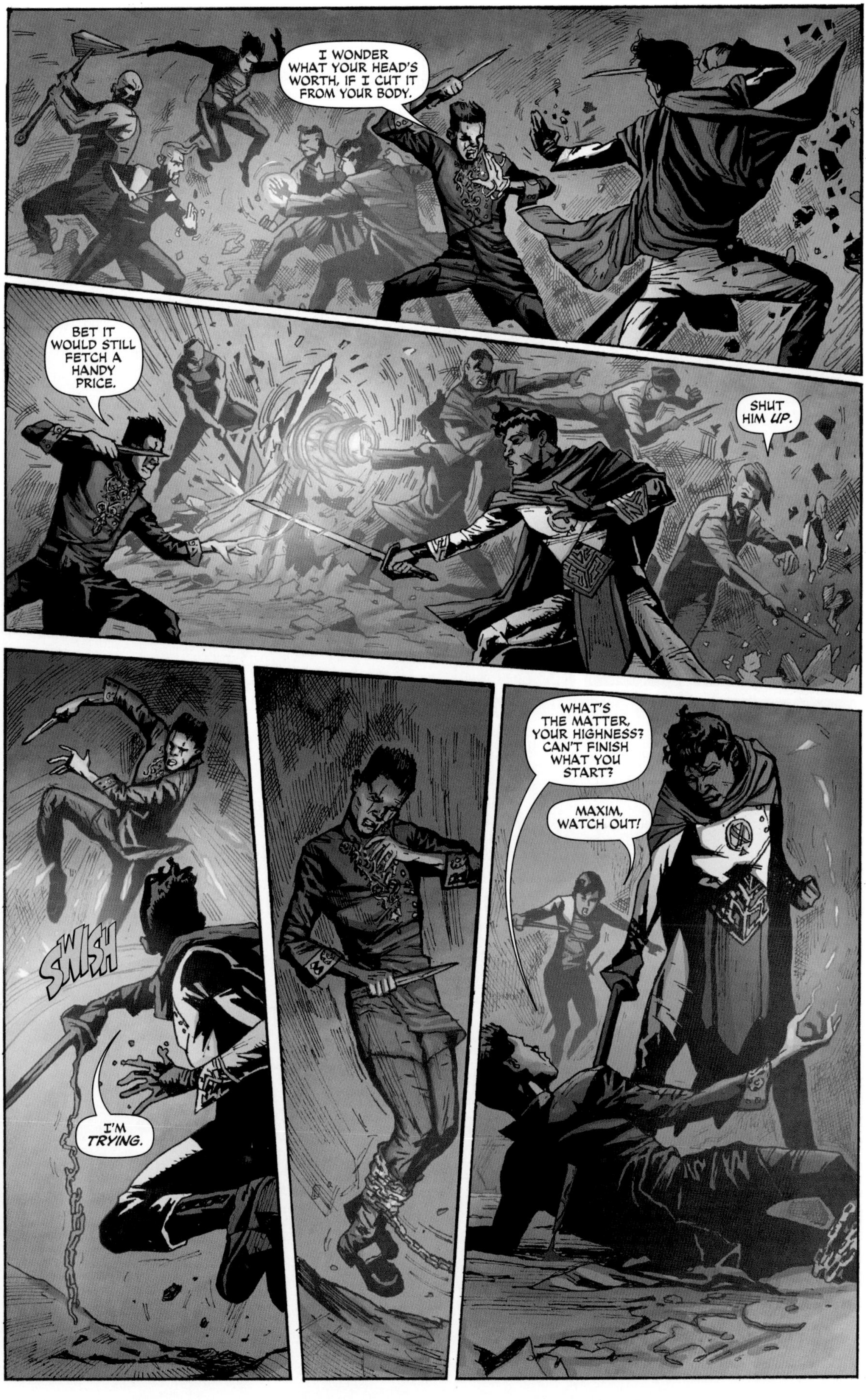
I WONDER WHAT YOUR HEAD'S WORTH, IF I CUT IT FROM YOUR BODY.
BET IT WOULD STILL FETCH A HANDY PRICE.
SHUT HIM *UP*.
SWISH
I'M *TRYING*.
WHAT'S THE MATTER, YOUR HIGHNESS? CAN'T FINISH WHAT YOU START?
MAXIM, WATCH OUT!

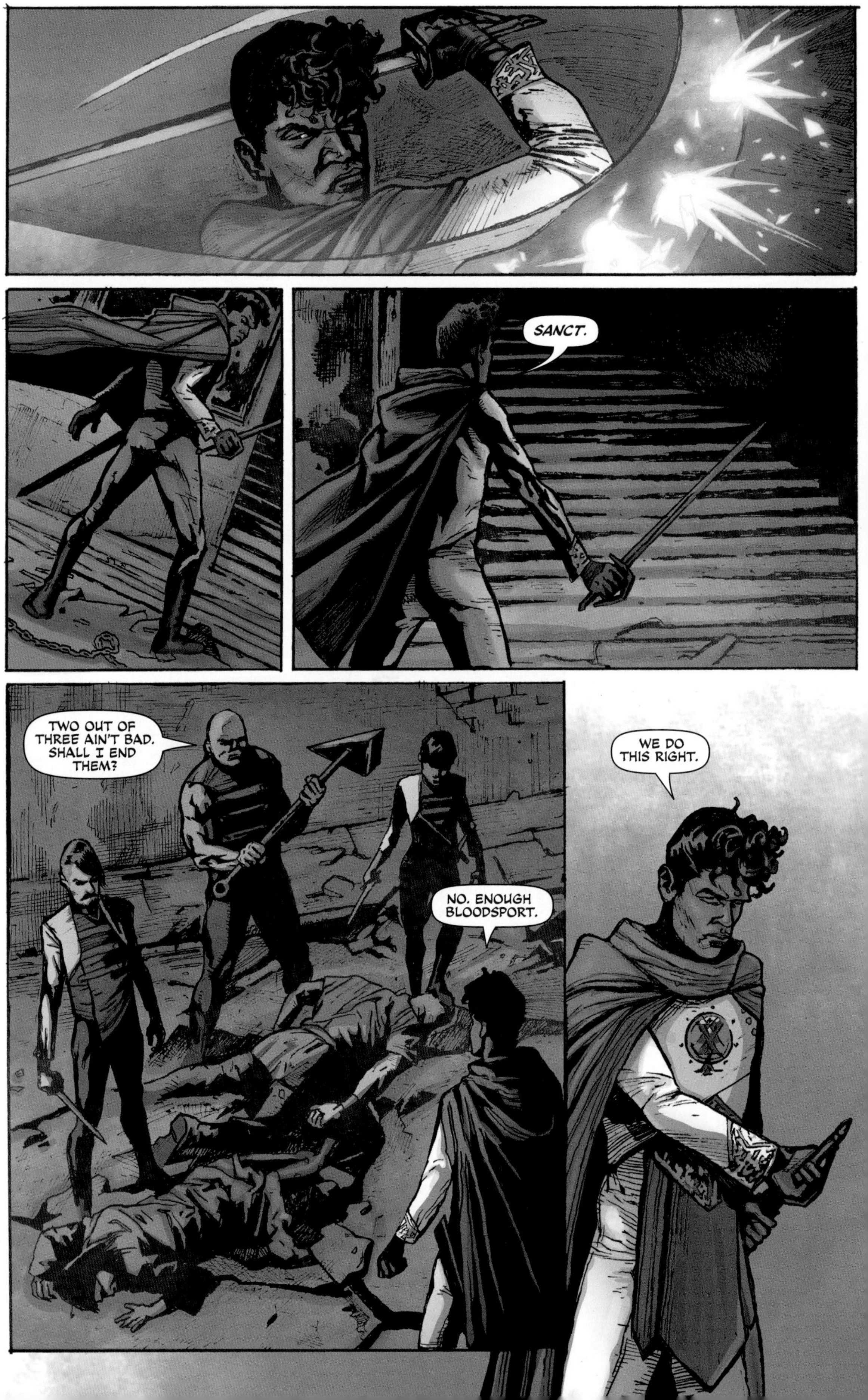
SANCT.
TWO OUT OF THREE AIN'T BAD. SHALL I END THEM?
WE DO THIS RIGHT.
NO. ENOUGH BLOODSPORT.

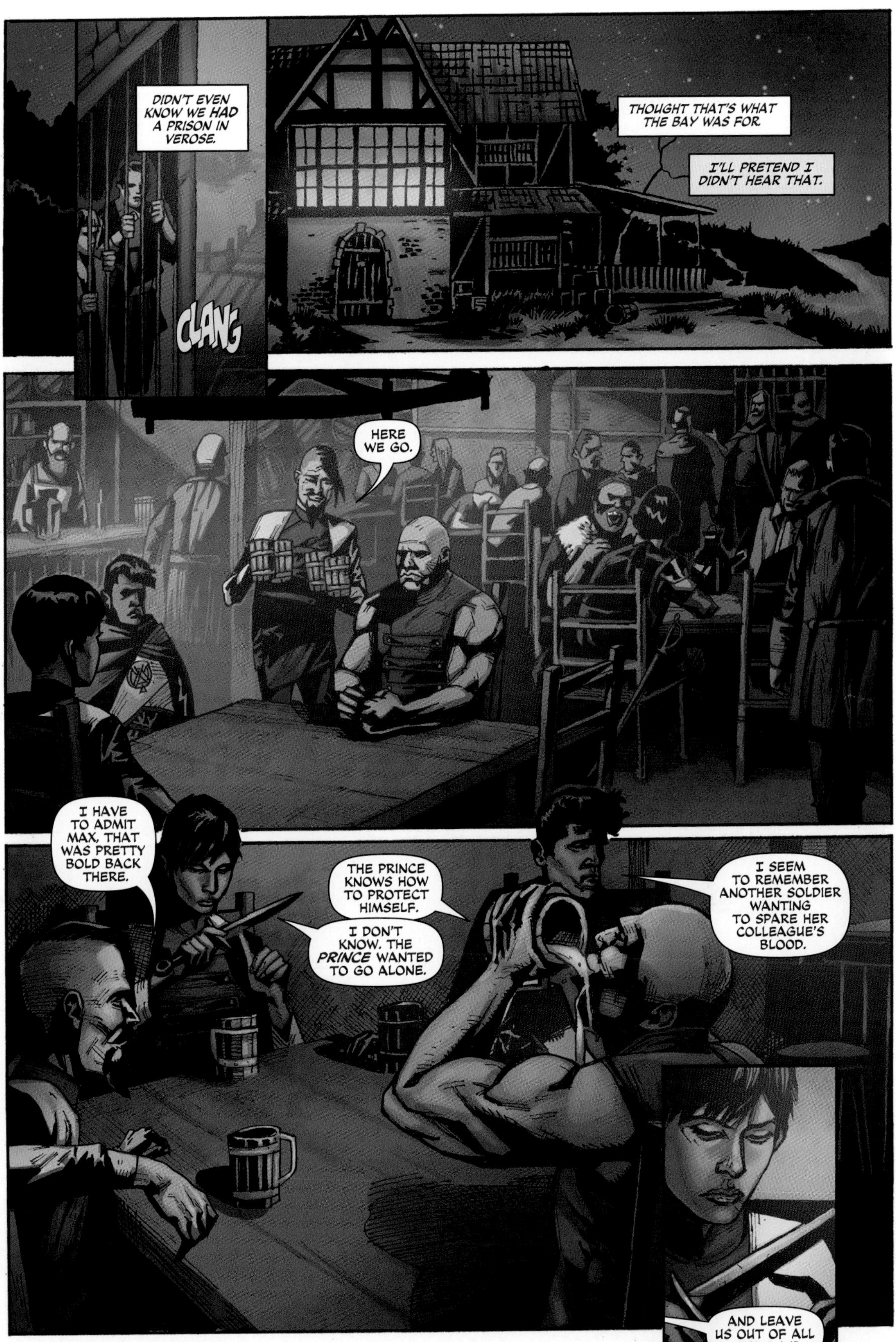
DIDN'T EVEN KNOW WE HAD A PRISON IN VEROSE.
CLANG
THOUGHT THAT'S WHAT THE BAY WAS FOR.
I'LL PRETEND I DIDN'T HEAR THAT.
HERE WE GO.
I HAVE TO ADMIT MAX, THAT WAS PRETTY BOLD BACK THERE.
THE PRINCE KNOWS HOW TO PROTECT HIMSELF.
I DON'T KNOW. THE PRINCE WANTED TO GO ALONE.
I SEEM TO REMEMBER ANOTHER SOLDIER WANTING TO SPARE HER COLLEAGUE'S BLOOD.
AND LEAVE US OUT OF ALL THE FUN?

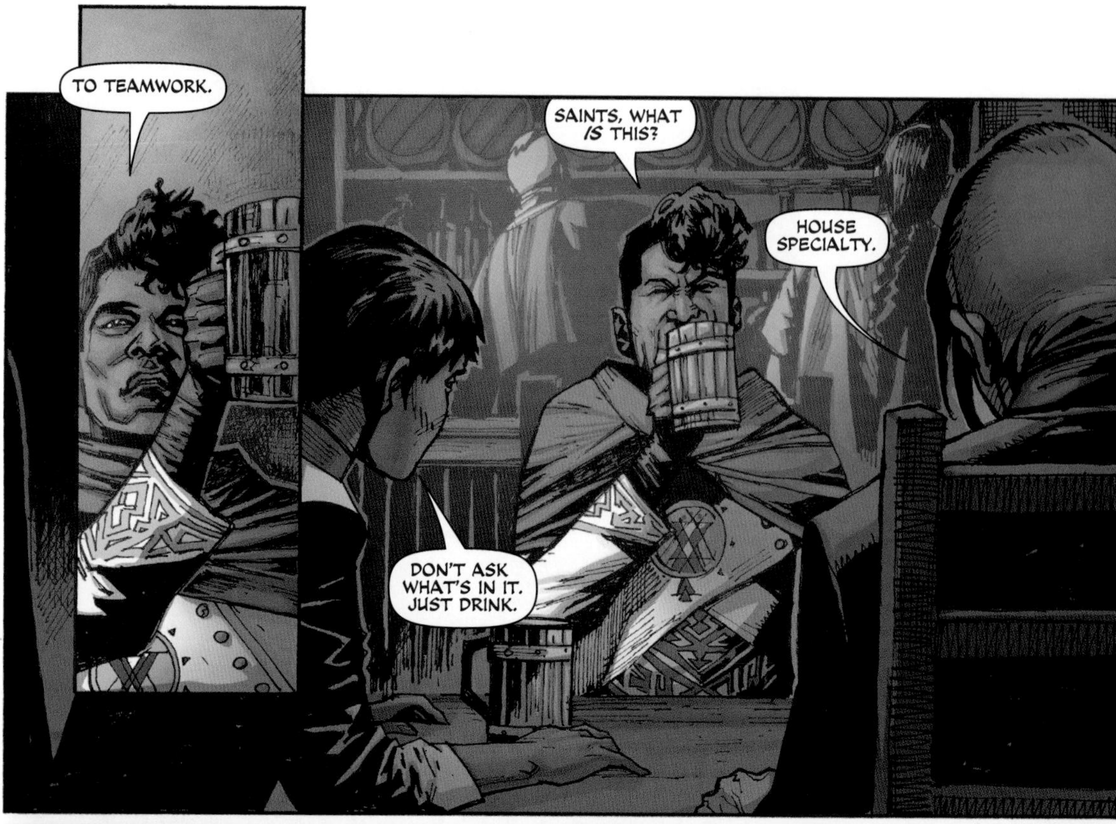
TO TEAMWORK.
SAINTS, WHAT *IS* THIS?
HOUSE SPECIALTY.
DON'T ASK WHAT'S IN IT. JUST DRINK.

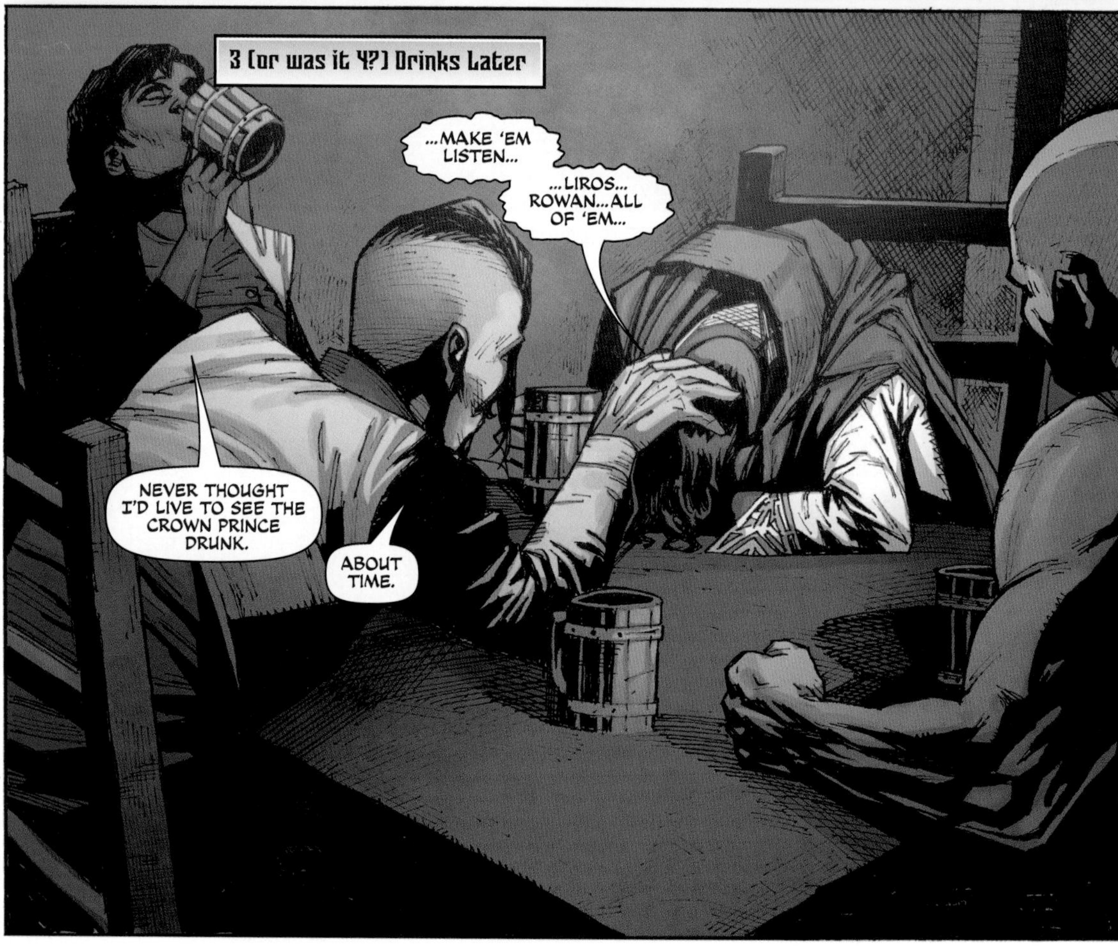
3 (or was it 4?) Drinks Later
...MAKE 'EM LISTEN...
...LIROS... ROWAN...ALL OF 'EM...
NEVER THOUGHT I'D LIVE TO SEE THE CROWN PRINCE DRUNK.
ABOUT TIME.

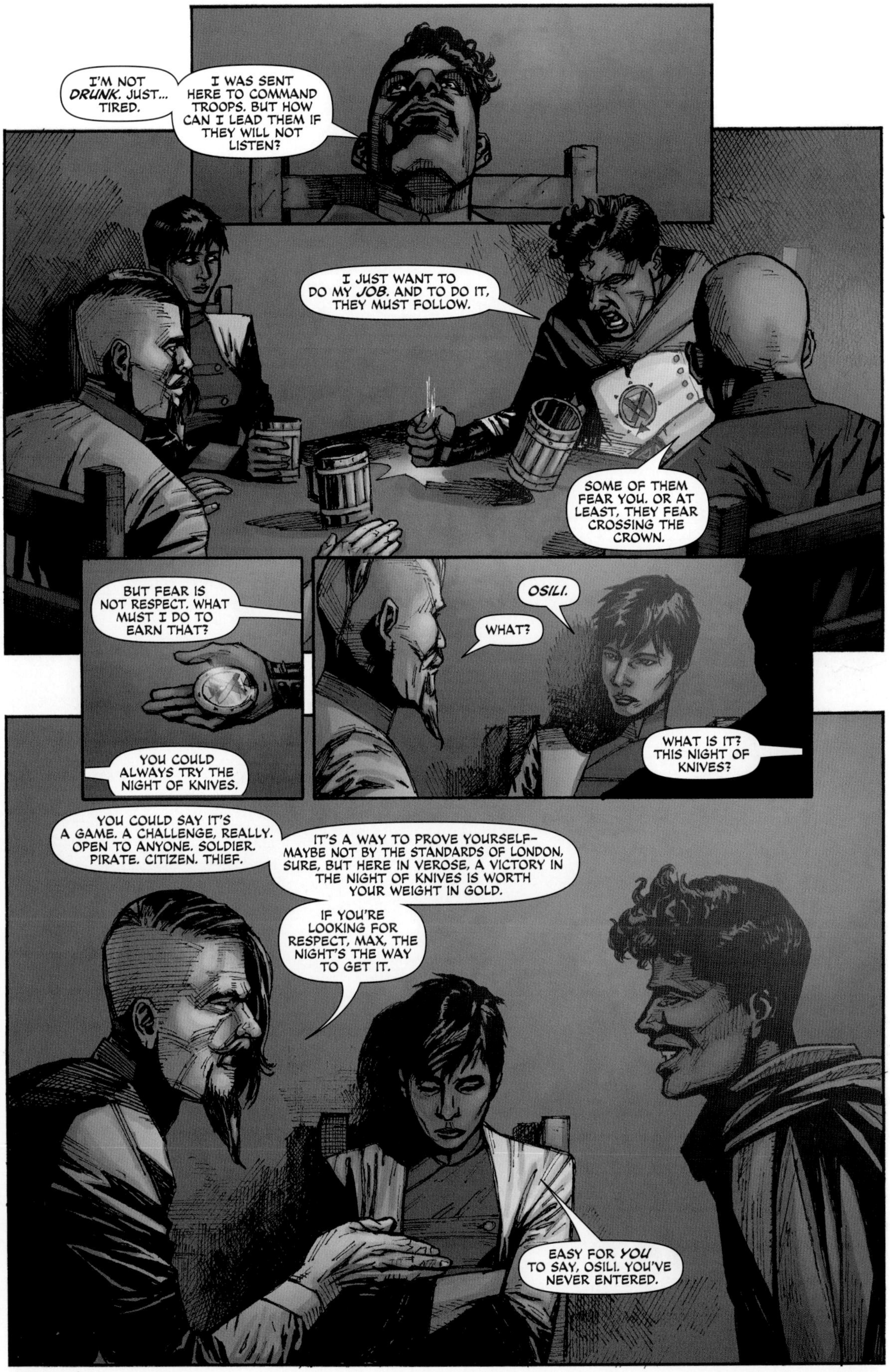
I'M NOT DRUNK. JUST... TIRED.
I WAS SENT HERE TO COMMAND TROOPS. BUT HOW CAN I LEAD THEM IF THEY WILL NOT LISTEN?
I JUST WANT TO DO MY JOB. AND TO DO IT, THEY MUST FOLLOW.
SOME OF THEM FEAR YOU. OR AT LEAST, THEY FEAR CROSSING THE CROWN.
BUT FEAR IS NOT RESPECT. WHAT MUST I DO TO EARN THAT?
YOU COULD ALWAYS TRY THE NIGHT OF KNIVES.
OSILI.
WHAT?
WHAT IS IT? THIS NIGHT OF KNIVES?
YOU COULD SAY IT'S A GAME. A CHALLENGE, REALLY. OPEN TO ANYONE. SOLDIER. PIRATE. CITIZEN. THIEF.
IT'S A WAY TO PROVE YOURSELF-MAYBE NOT BY THE STANDARDS OF LONDON, SURE, BUT HERE IN VEROSE, A VICTORY IN THE NIGHT OF KNIVES IS WORTH YOUR WEIGHT IN GOLD.
IF YOU'RE LOOKING FOR RESPECT, MAX, THE NIGHT'S THE WAY TO GET IT.
EASY FOR YOU TO SAY, OSILI. YOU'VE NEVER ENTERED.

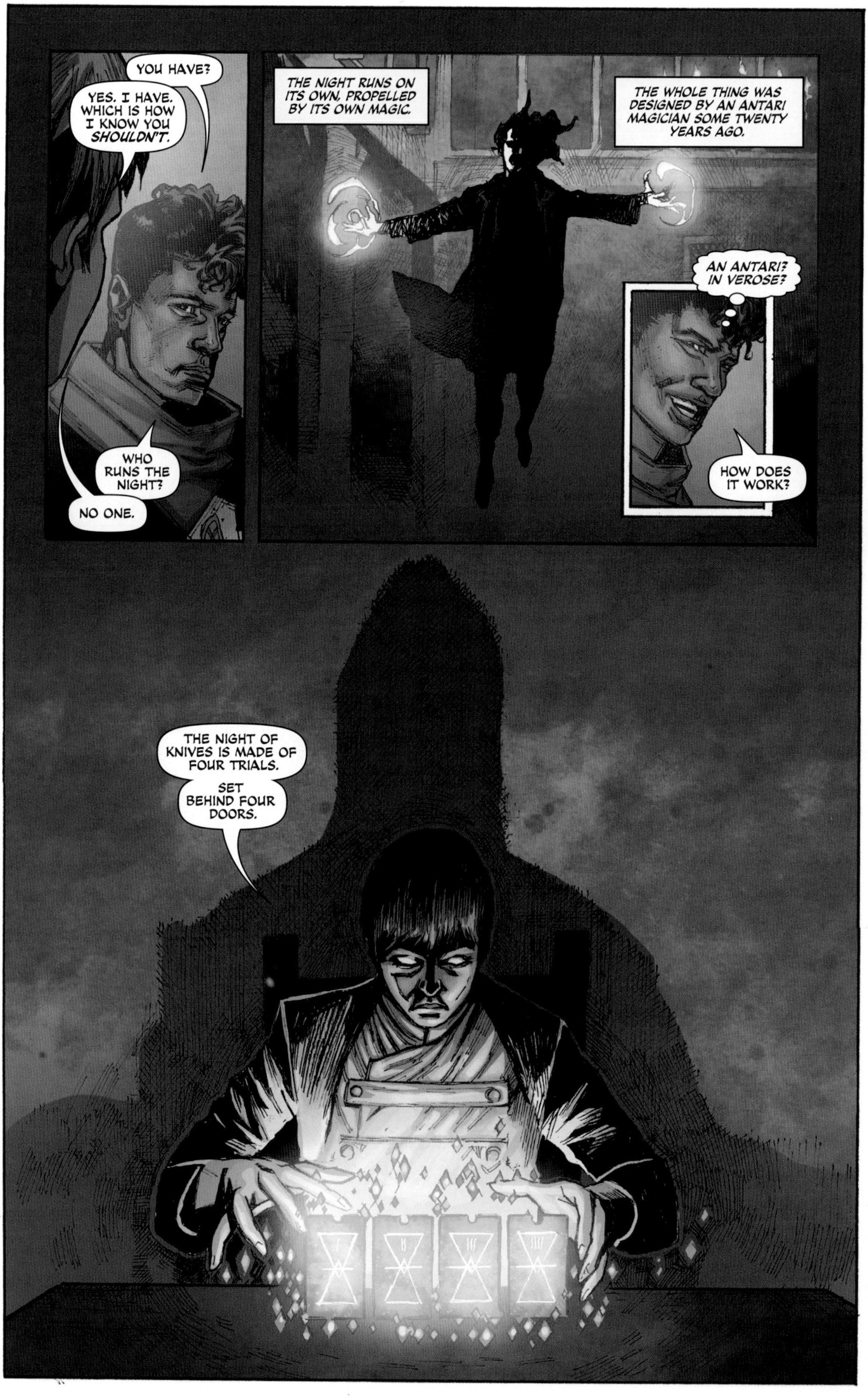
YOU HAVE?
YES. I HAVE. WHICH IS HOW I KNOW YOU *SHOULDN'T*.
WHO RUNS THE NIGHT?
NO ONE.
THE NIGHT RUNS ON ITS OWN, PROPELLED BY ITS OWN MAGIC.
THE WHOLE THING WAS DESIGNED BY AN ANTARI MAGICIAN SOME TWENTY YEARS AGO.
AN ANTARI? IN VEROSE?
HOW DOES IT WORK?
THE NIGHT OF KNIVES IS MADE OF FOUR TRIALS.
SET BEHIND FOUR DOORS.

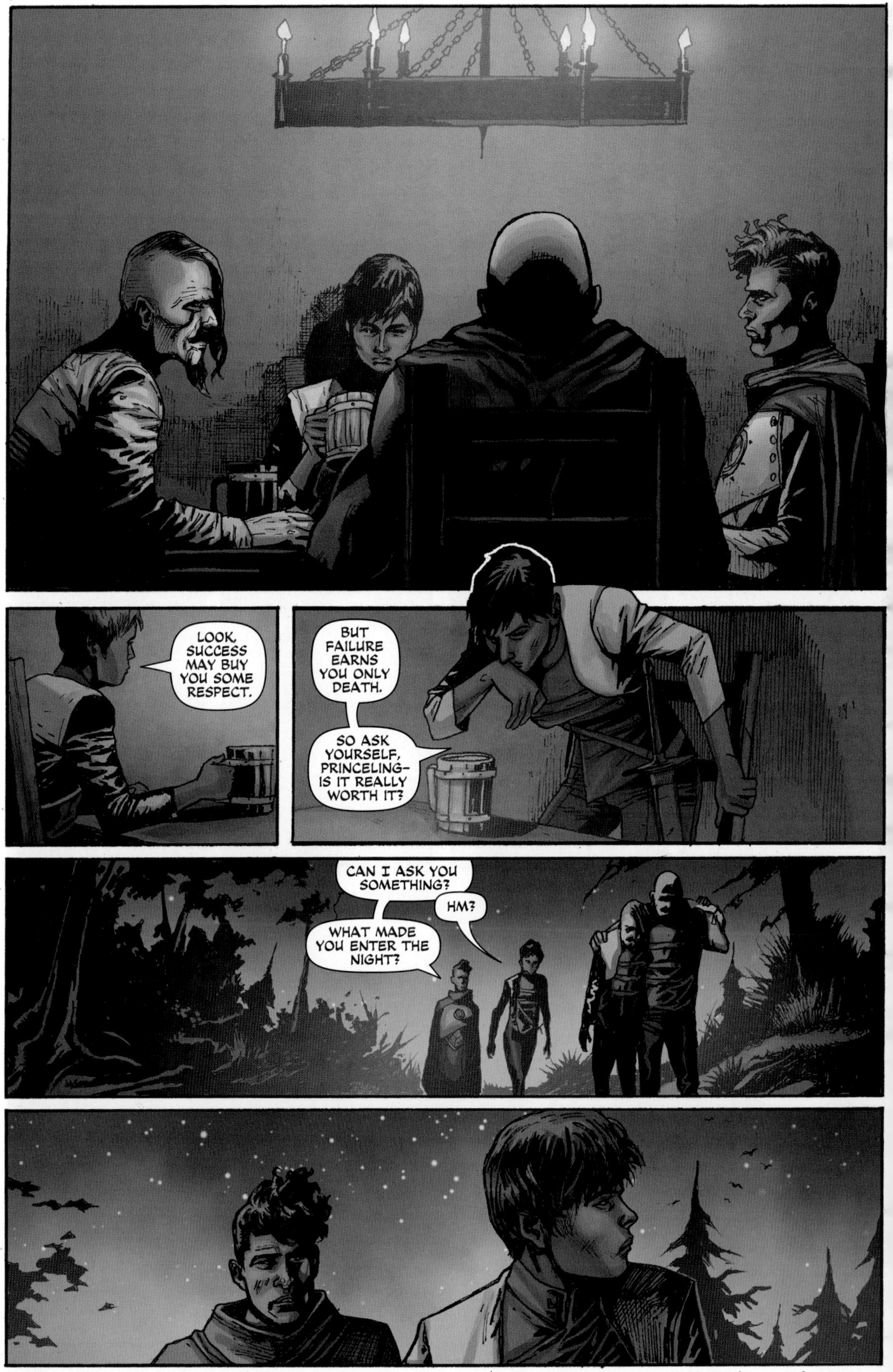
LOOK, SUCCESS MAY BUY YOU SOME RESPECT.
BUT FAILURE EARNS YOU ONLY DEATH.
SO ASK YOURSELF, PRINCELING-- IS IT REALLY WORTH IT?
CAN I ASK YOU SOMETHING?
HM?
WHAT MADE YOU ENTER THE NIGHT?

EACH ROOM IS DESIGNED TO CHALLENGE A DIFFERENT KIND OF STRENGTH.

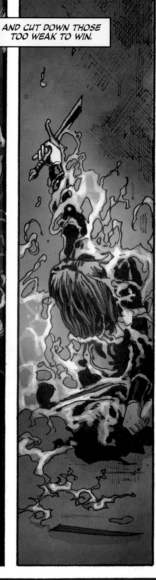

AND CUT DOWN THOSE TOO WEAK TO WIN.

YOU'D BE SURPRISED HOW MANY DIE.

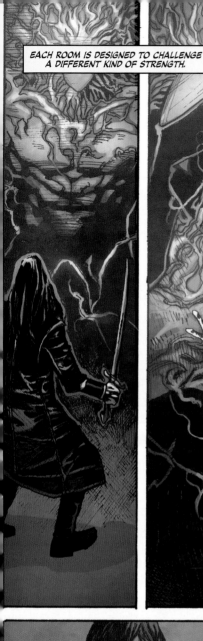

THAT'S BECAUSE NIGHT ISN'T JUST A TEST OF STRENGTH.

IT'S A BATTLE BETWEEN EGO AND RESTRAINT.

ONCE YOU ENTER A TRIAL, THERE IS NO TURNING BACK.

YOU WIN, OR YOU DIE.

ARISA SPARED MY LIFE, AND SENT ME BACK TO THE BASE, STAINED WITH THE BLOOD OF FRIENDS.

SO YOU HAD SOMETHING TO PROVE.

THIS IS DIFFERENT.

IS IT? I CANNOT SUCCEED IN THIS LIFE WITHOUT THEIR LOYALTY. AND I CANNOT EARN IT WITHOUT THEIR RESPECT.

YOU'RE SERIOUSLY CONSIDERING THIS.

CUPS, I ENTER MY NAME. MOONS, I DON'T.

WAIT—

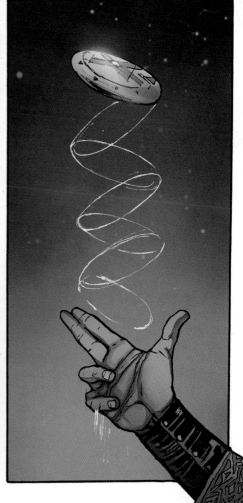

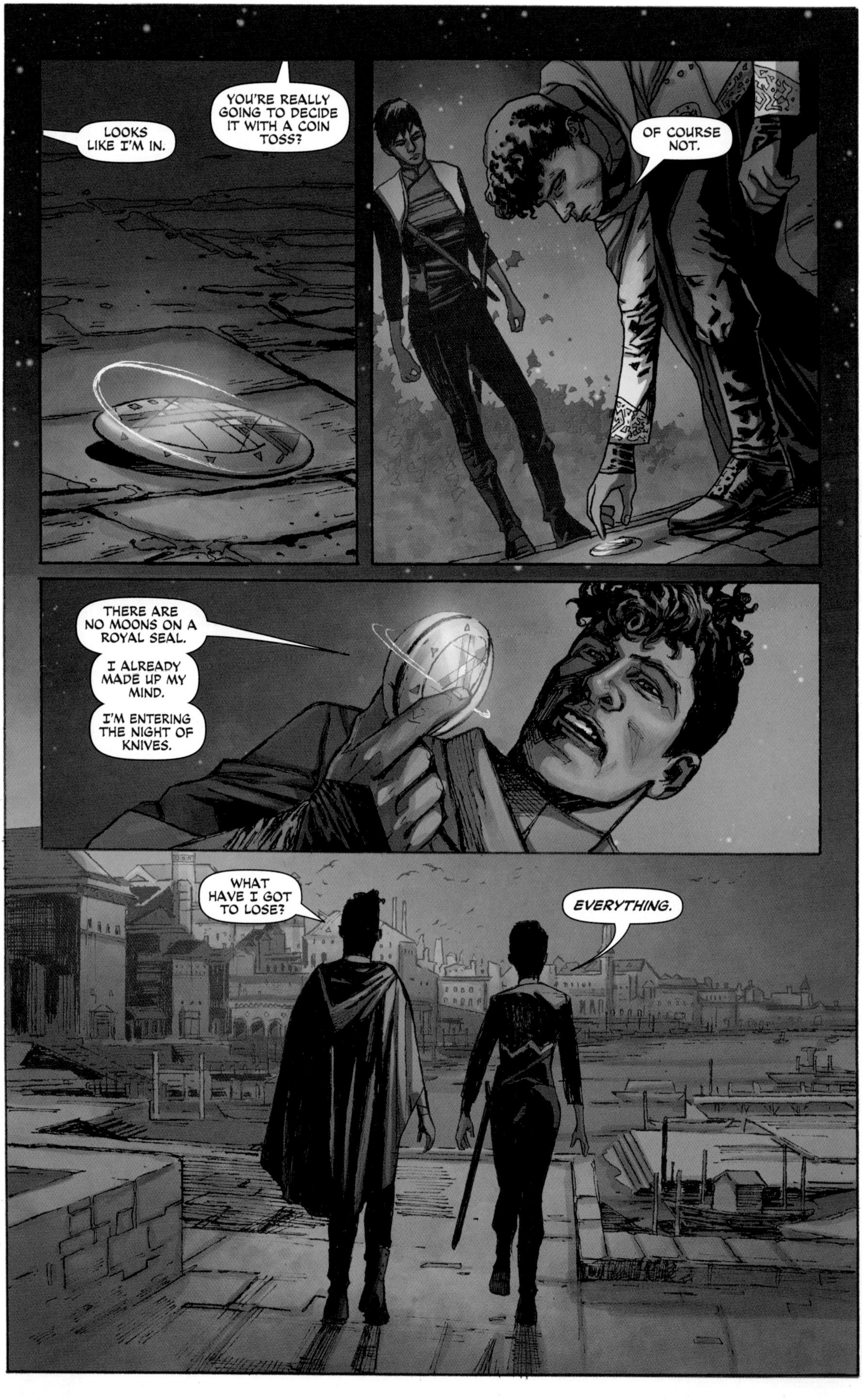
LOOKS LIKE I'M IN.
YOU'RE REALLY GOING TO DECIDE IT WITH A COIN TOSS?
OF COURSE NOT.
THERE ARE NO MOONS ON A ROYAL SEAL.
I ALREADY MADE UP MY MIND.
I'M ENTERING THE NIGHT OF KNIVES.
WHAT HAVE I GOT TO LOSE?
EVERYTHING.

#2

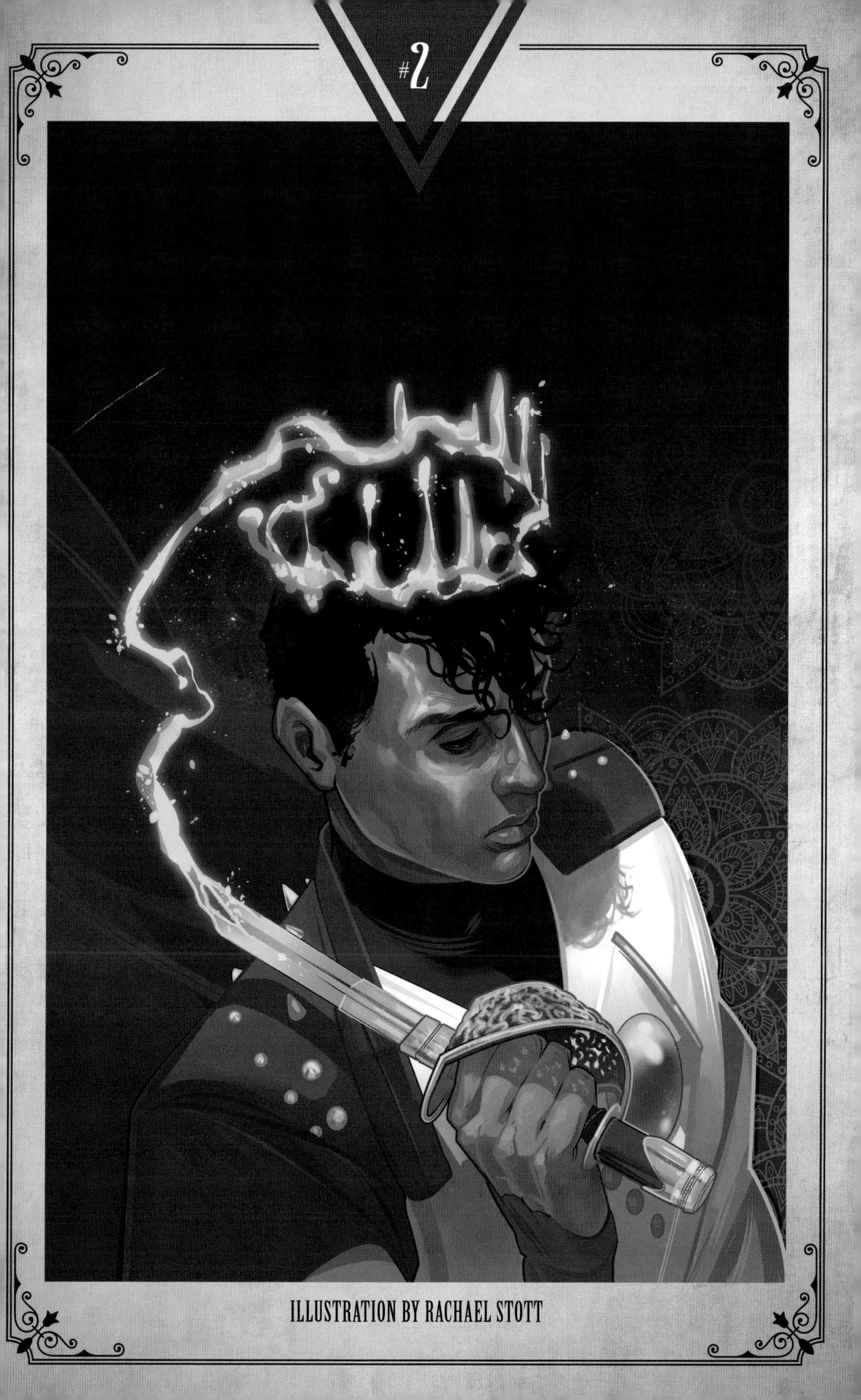

ILLUSTRATION BY RACHAEL STOTT

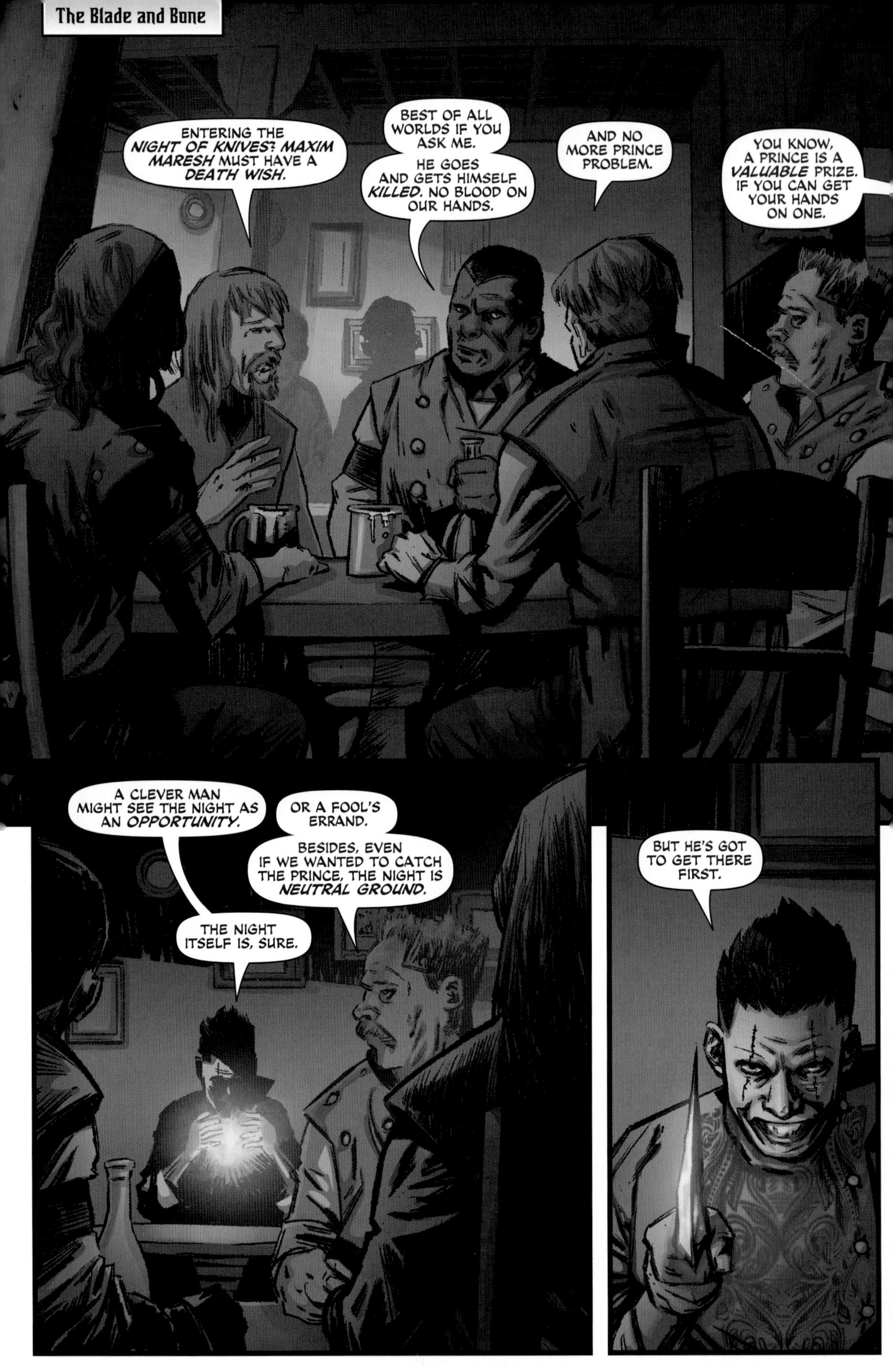
The Blade and Bone
ENTERING THE NIGHT OF KNIVES? MAXIM MARESH MUST HAVE A DEATH WISH.
BEST OF ALL WORLDS IF YOU ASK ME.
HE GOES AND GETS HIMSELF KILLED. NO BLOOD ON OUR HANDS.
AND NO MORE PRINCE PROBLEM.
YOU KNOW, A PRINCE IS A VALUABLE PRIZE. IF YOU CAN GET YOUR HANDS ON ONE.
A CLEVER MAN MIGHT SEE THE NIGHT AS AN OPPORTUNITY.
OR A FOOL'S ERRAND.
BESIDES, EVEN IF WE WANTED TO CATCH THE PRINCE, THE NIGHT IS NEUTRAL GROUND.
THE NIGHT ITSELF IS, SURE.
BUT HE'S GOT TO GET THERE FIRST.

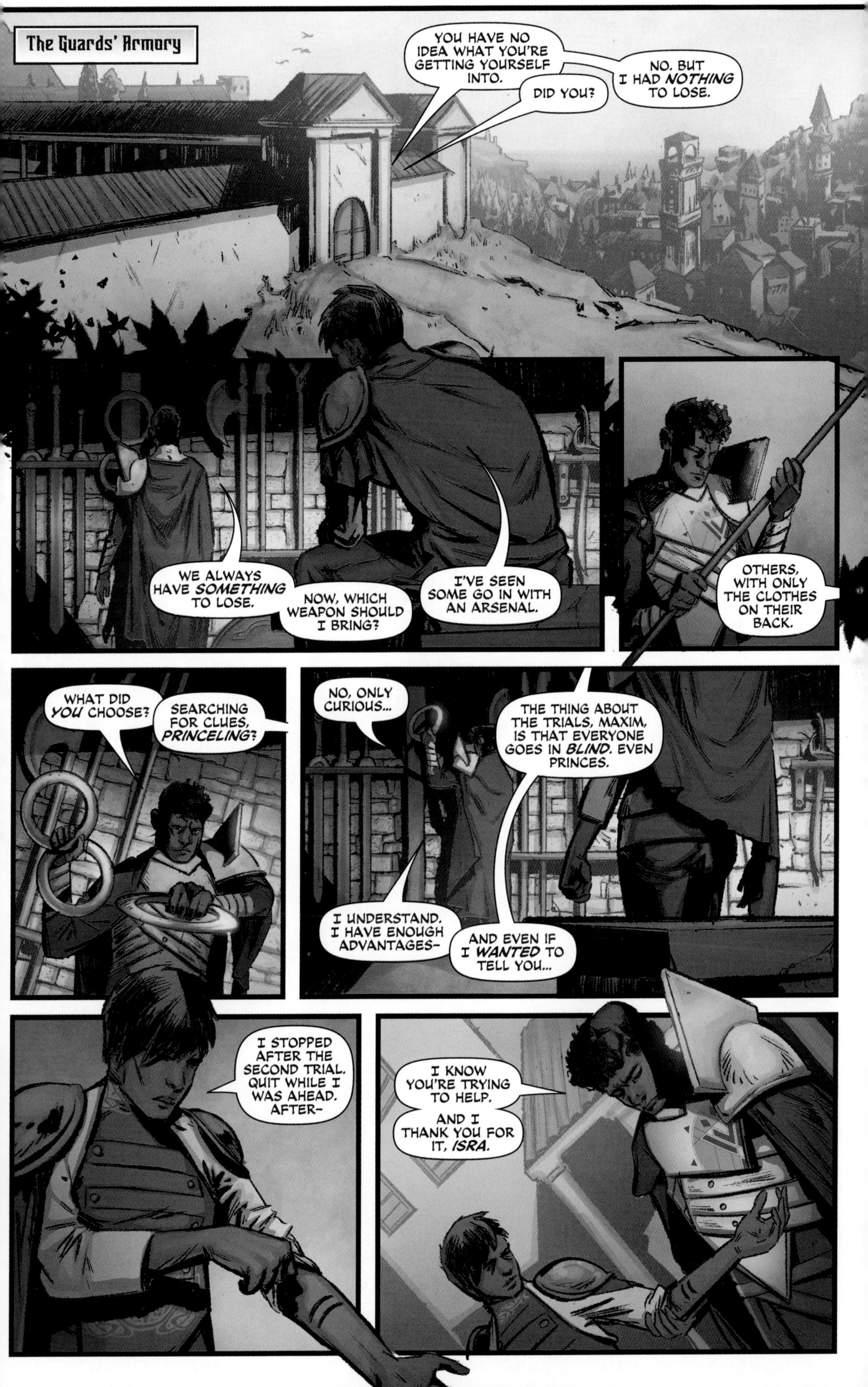

The Guards' Armory
YOU HAVE NO IDEA WHAT YOU'RE GETTING YOURSELF INTO.
DID YOU?
NO. BUT I HAD NOTHING TO LOSE.
WE ALWAYS HAVE SOMETHING TO LOSE.
NOW, WHICH WEAPON SHOULD I BRING?
I'VE SEEN SOME GO IN WITH AN ARSENAL.
OTHERS, WITH ONLY THE CLOTHES ON THEIR BACK.
WHAT DID YOU CHOOSE?
SEARCHING FOR CLUES, PRINCELING?
NO, ONLY CURIOUS...
THE THING ABOUT THE TRIALS, MAXIM, IS THAT EVERYONE GOES IN BLIND. EVEN PRINCES.
I UNDERSTAND. I HAVE ENOUGH ADVANTAGES-
AND EVEN IF I WANTED TO TELL YOU...
I STOPPED AFTER THE SECOND TRIAL. QUIT WHILE I WAS AHEAD. AFTER-
I KNOW YOU'RE TRYING TO HELP.
AND I THANK YOU FOR IT, ISRA.

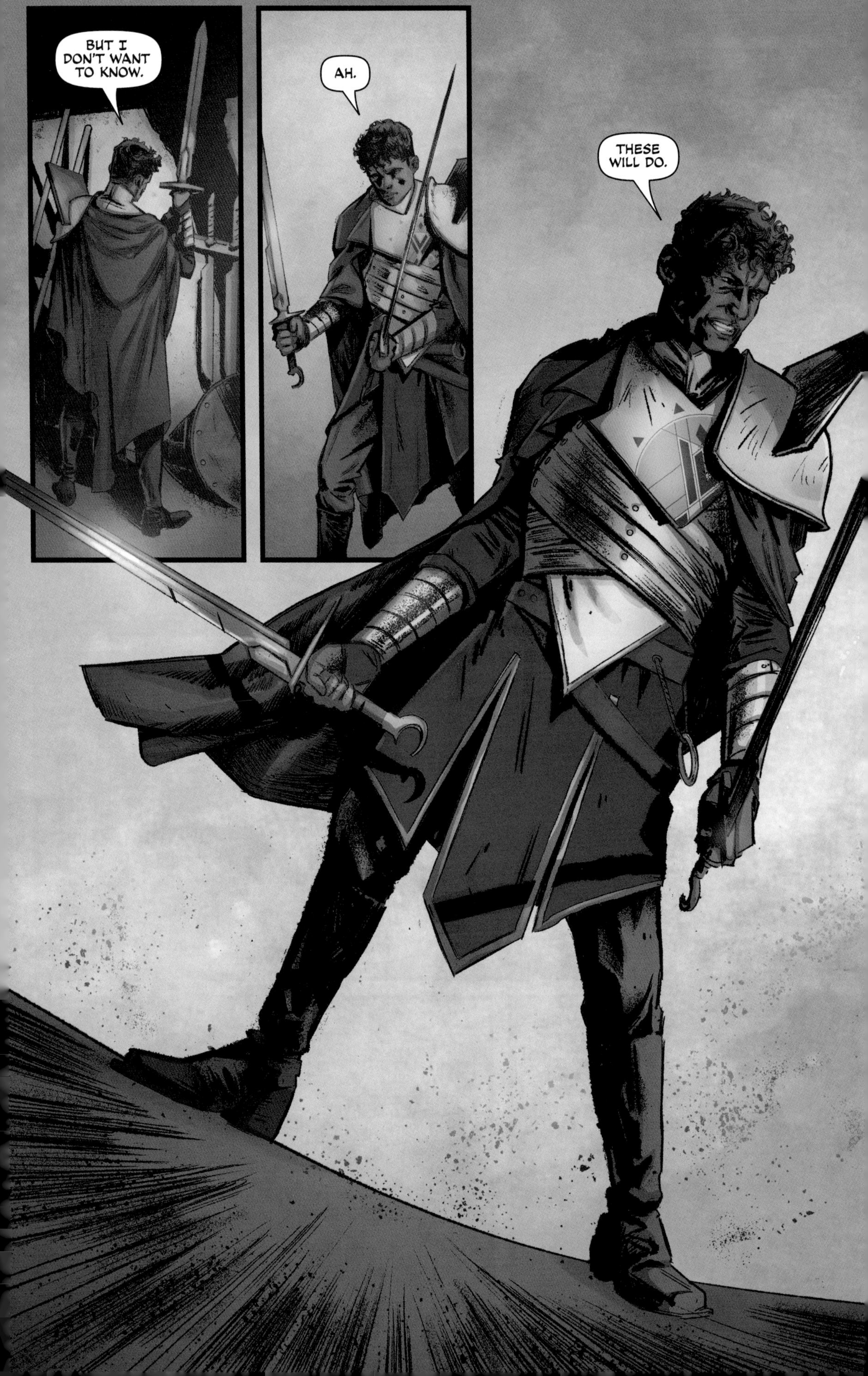
BUT I DON'T WANT TO KNOW.
AH.
THESE WILL DO.

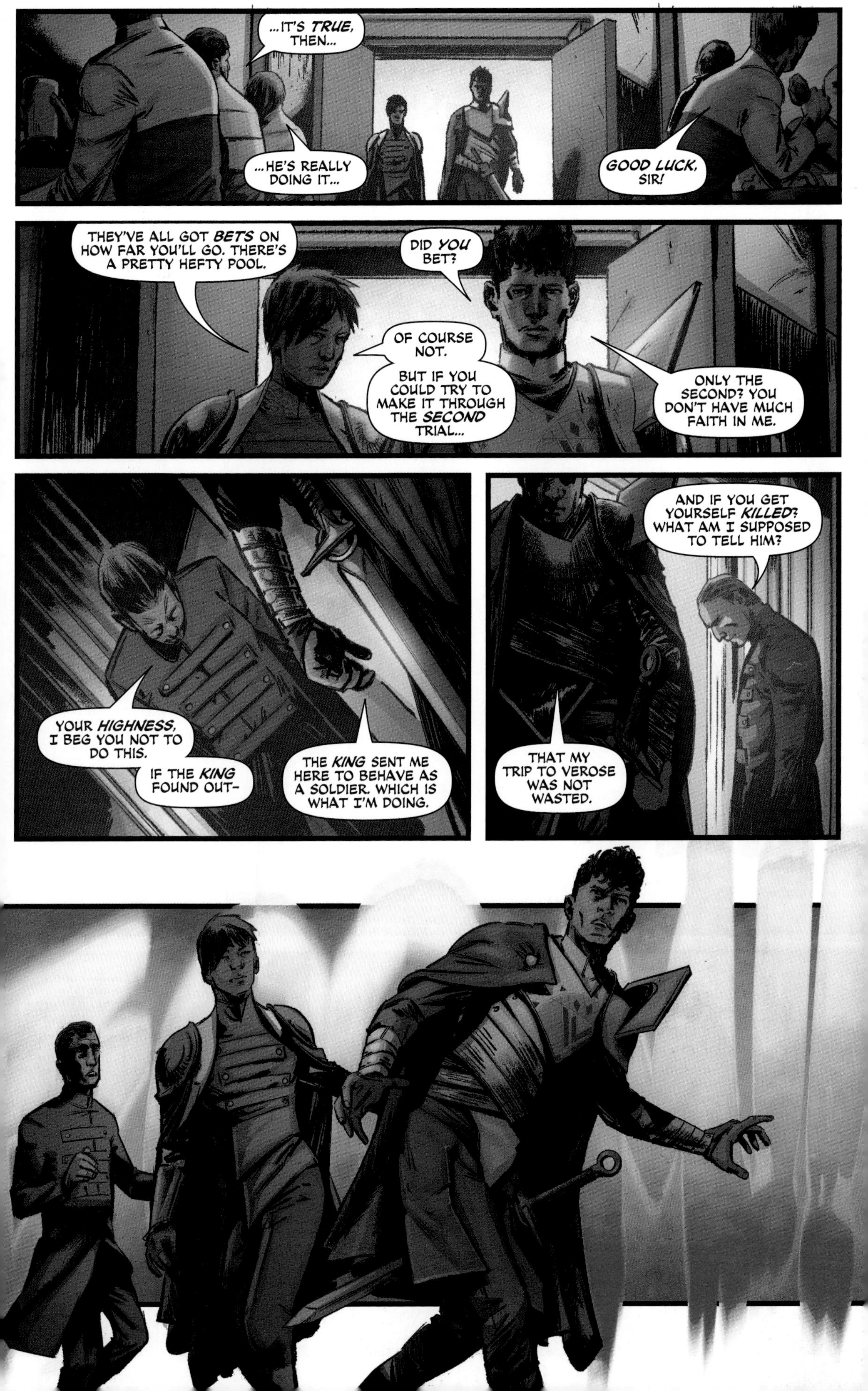
...IT'S TRUE, THEN...
...HE'S REALLY DOING IT...
GOOD LUCK, SIR!
THEY'VE ALL GOT BETS ON HOW FAR YOU'LL GO. THERE'S A PRETTY HEFTY POOL.
DID YOU BET?
OF COURSE NOT.
BUT IF YOU COULD TRY TO MAKE IT THROUGH THE SECOND TRIAL...
ONLY THE SECOND? YOU DON'T HAVE MUCH FAITH IN ME.
YOUR HIGHNESS, I BEG YOU NOT TO DO THIS.
IF THE KING FOUND OUT-
THE KING SENT ME HERE TO BEHAVE AS A SOLDIER. WHICH IS WHAT I'M DOING.
AND IF YOU GET YOURSELF KILLED? WHAT AM I SUPPOSED TO TELL HIM?
THAT MY TRIP TO VEROSE WAS NOT WASTED.

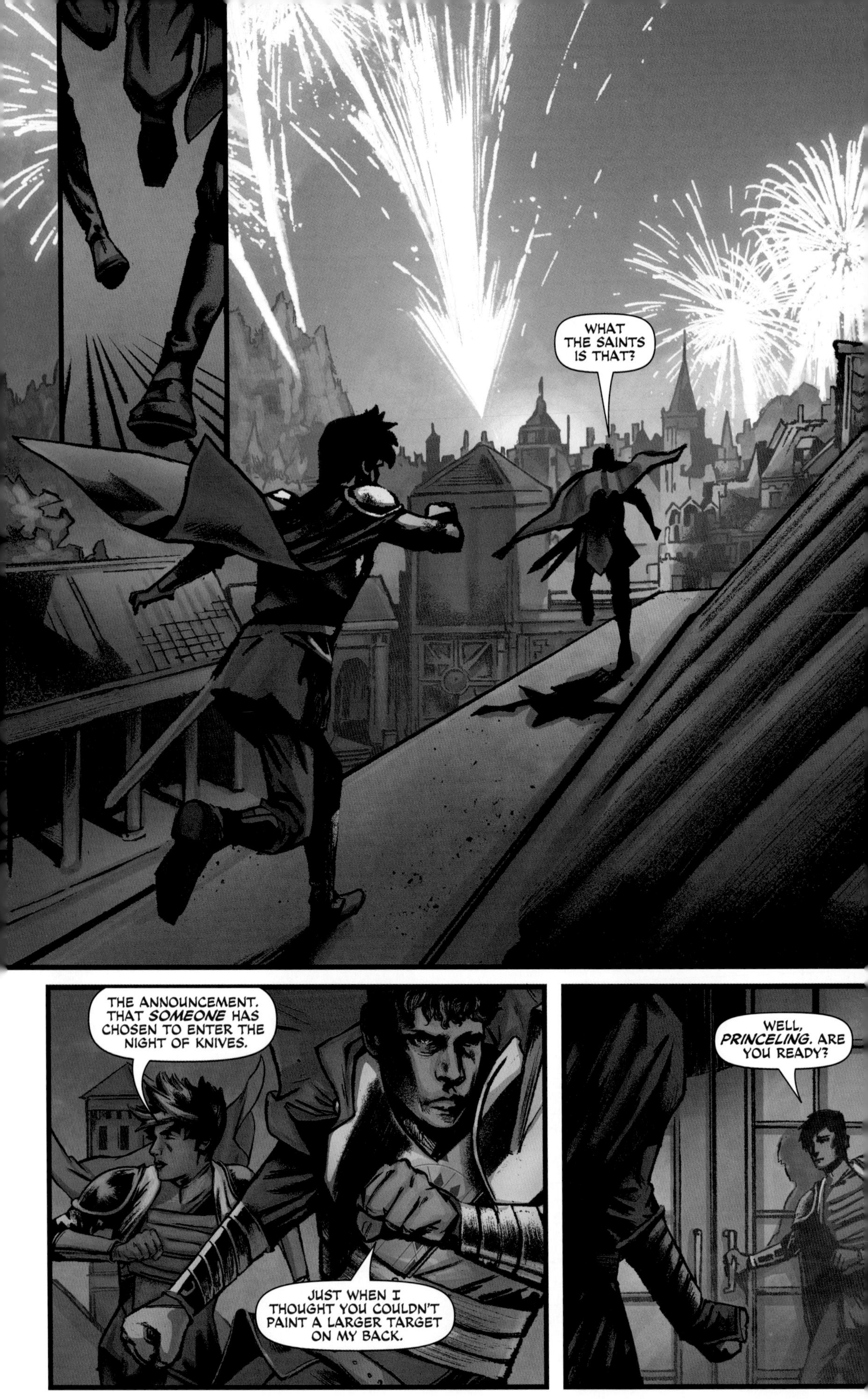
WHAT THE SAINTS IS THAT?
THE ANNOUNCEMENT. THAT *SOMEONE* HAS CHOSEN TO ENTER THE NIGHT OF KNIVES.
JUST WHEN I THOUGHT YOU COULDN'T PAINT A LARGER TARGET ON MY BACK.
WELL, *PRINCELING.* ARE YOU READY?

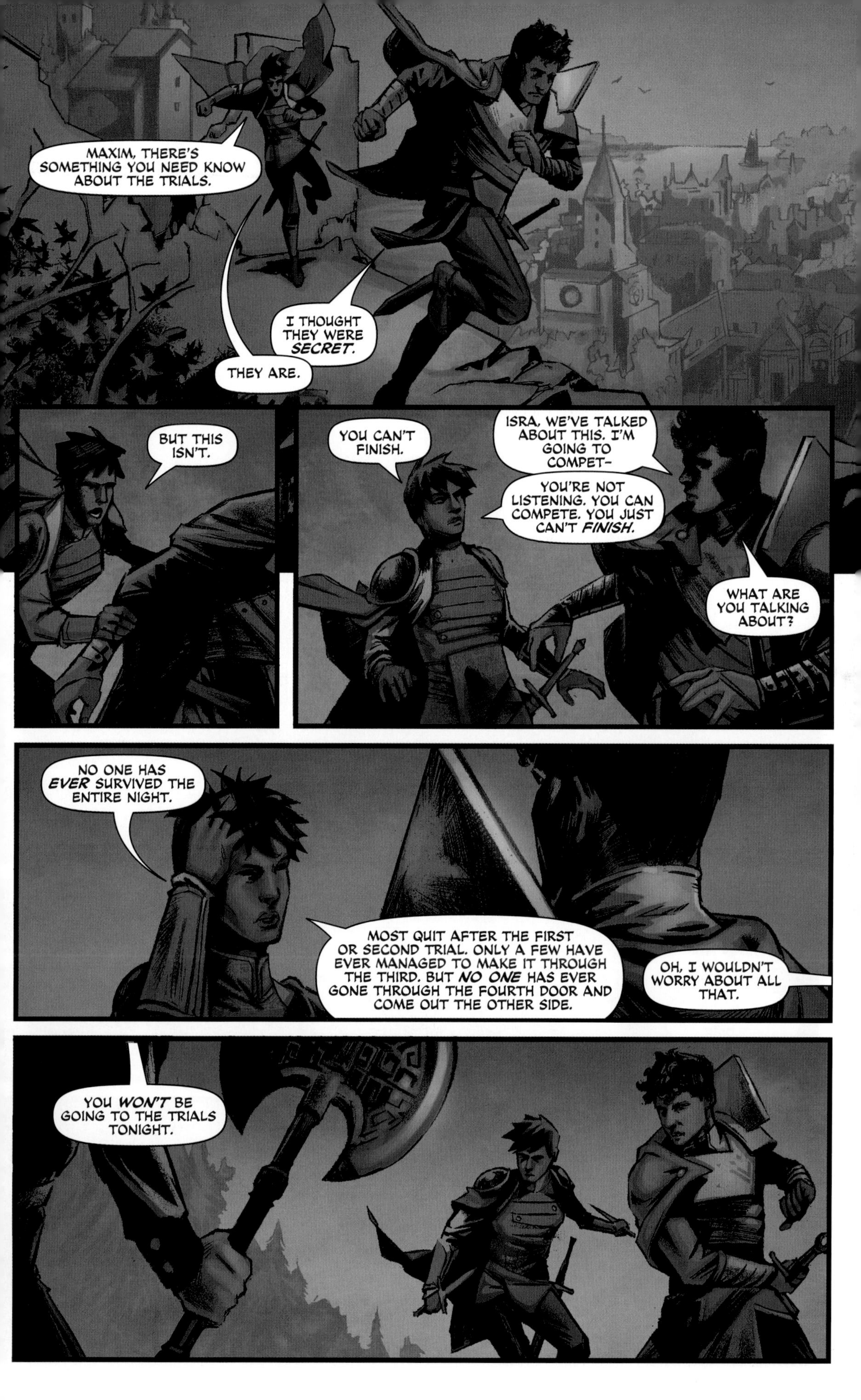
MAXIM, THERE'S SOMETHING YOU NEED KNOW ABOUT THE TRIALS.
I THOUGHT THEY WERE SECRET.
THEY ARE.
BUT THIS ISN'T.
YOU CAN'T FINISH.
ISRA, WE'VE TALKED ABOUT THIS. I'M GOING TO COMPET-
YOU'RE NOT LISTENING. YOU CAN COMPETE. YOU JUST CAN'T FINISH.
WHAT ARE YOU TALKING ABOUT?
NO ONE HAS EVER SURVIVED THE ENTIRE NIGHT.
MOST QUIT AFTER THE FIRST OR SECOND TRIAL. ONLY A FEW HAVE EVER MANAGED TO MAKE IT THROUGH THE THIRD. BUT NO ONE HAS EVER GONE THROUGH THE FOURTH DOOR AND COME OUT THE OTHER SIDE.
OH, I WOULDN'T WORRY ABOUT ALL THAT.
YOU WON'T BE GOING TO THE TRIALS TONIGHT.

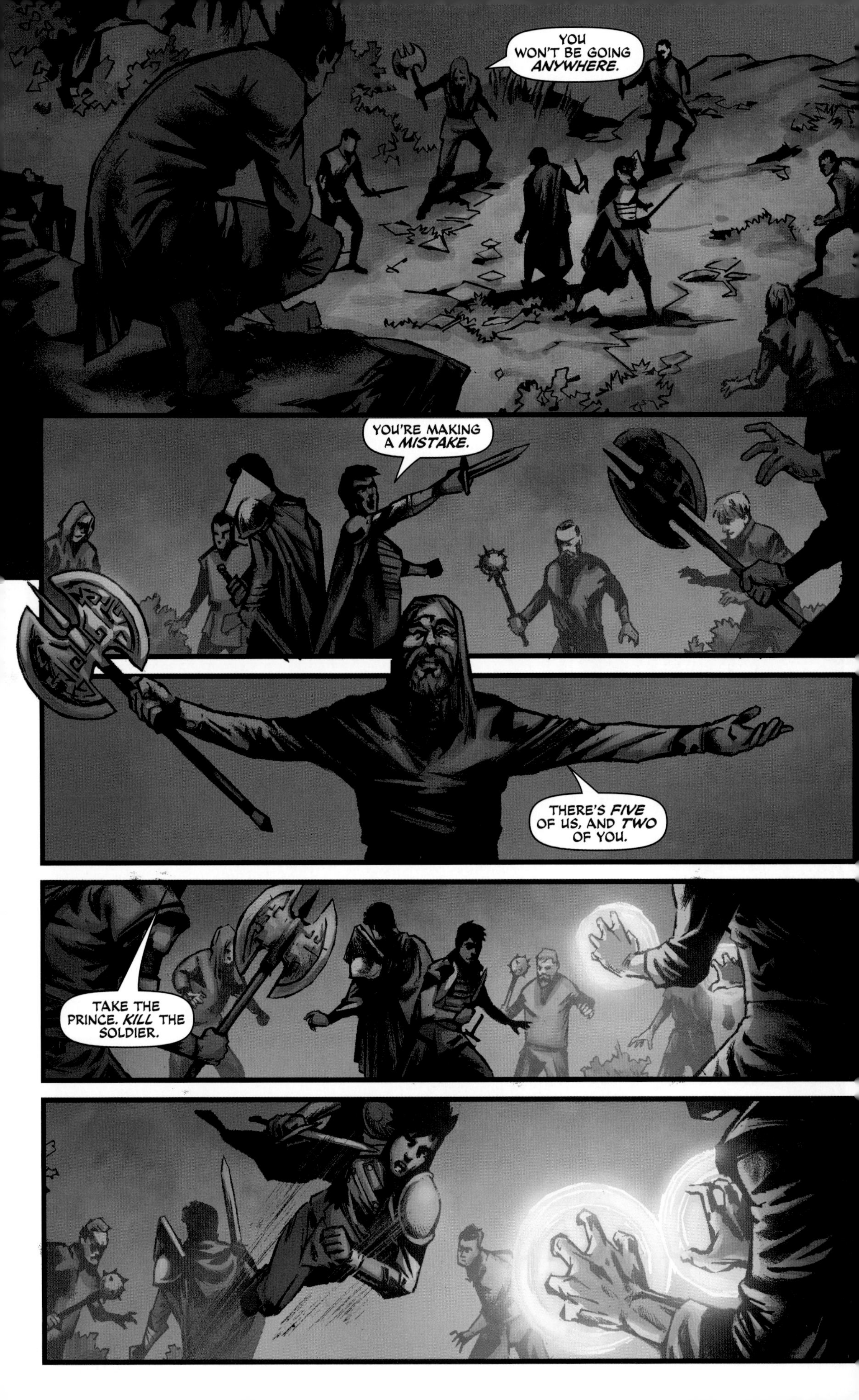
YOU WON'T BE GOING *ANYWHERE*.
YOU'RE MAKING A *MISTAKE*.
THERE'S *FIVE* OF US, AND *TWO* OF YOU.
TAKE THE PRINCE. *KILL* THE SOLDIER.

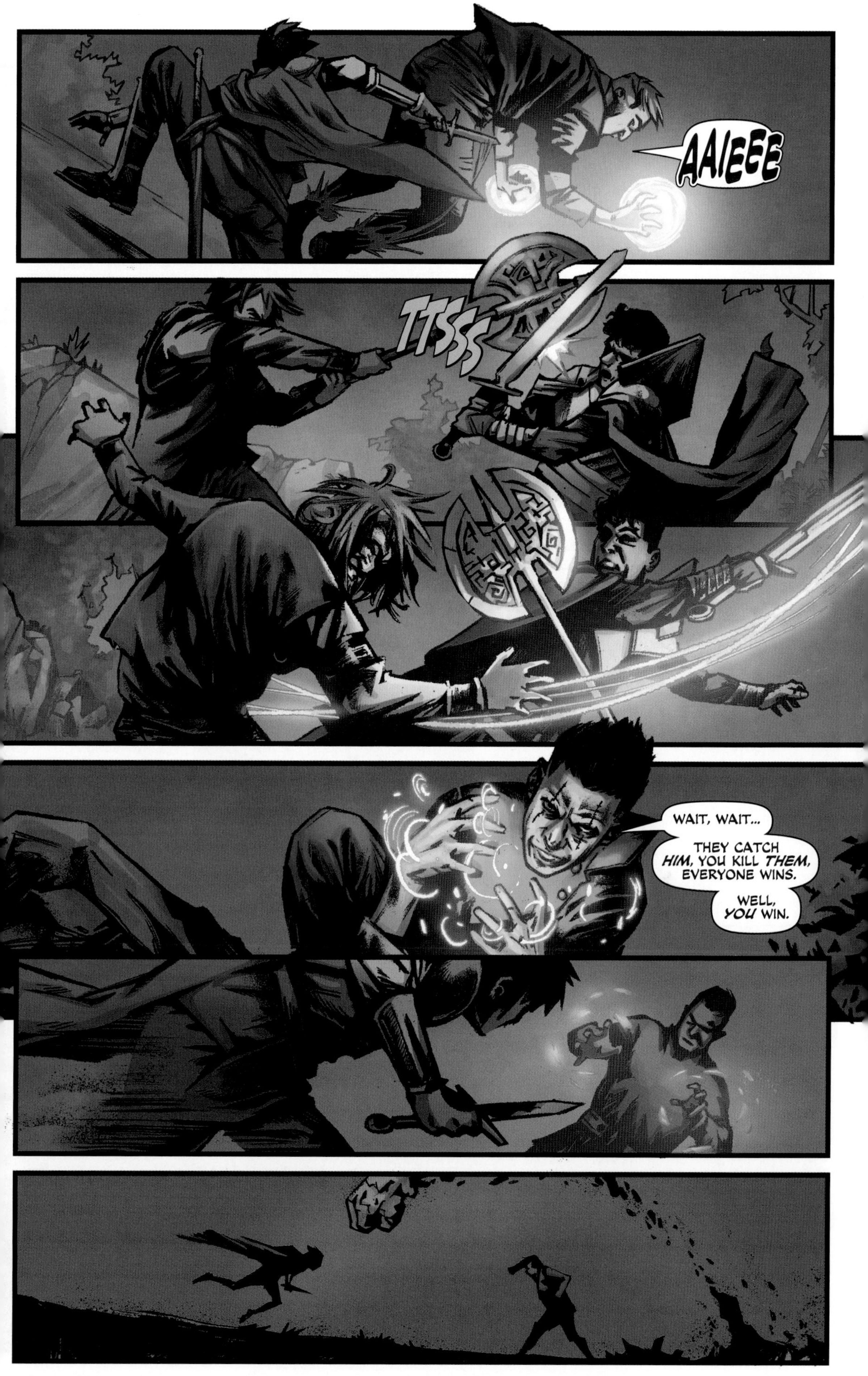
AAIEEE
TTSSS
WAIT, WAIT...
THEY CATCH *HIM*, YOU KILL *THEM*, EVERYONE WINS.
WELL, *YOU* WIN.

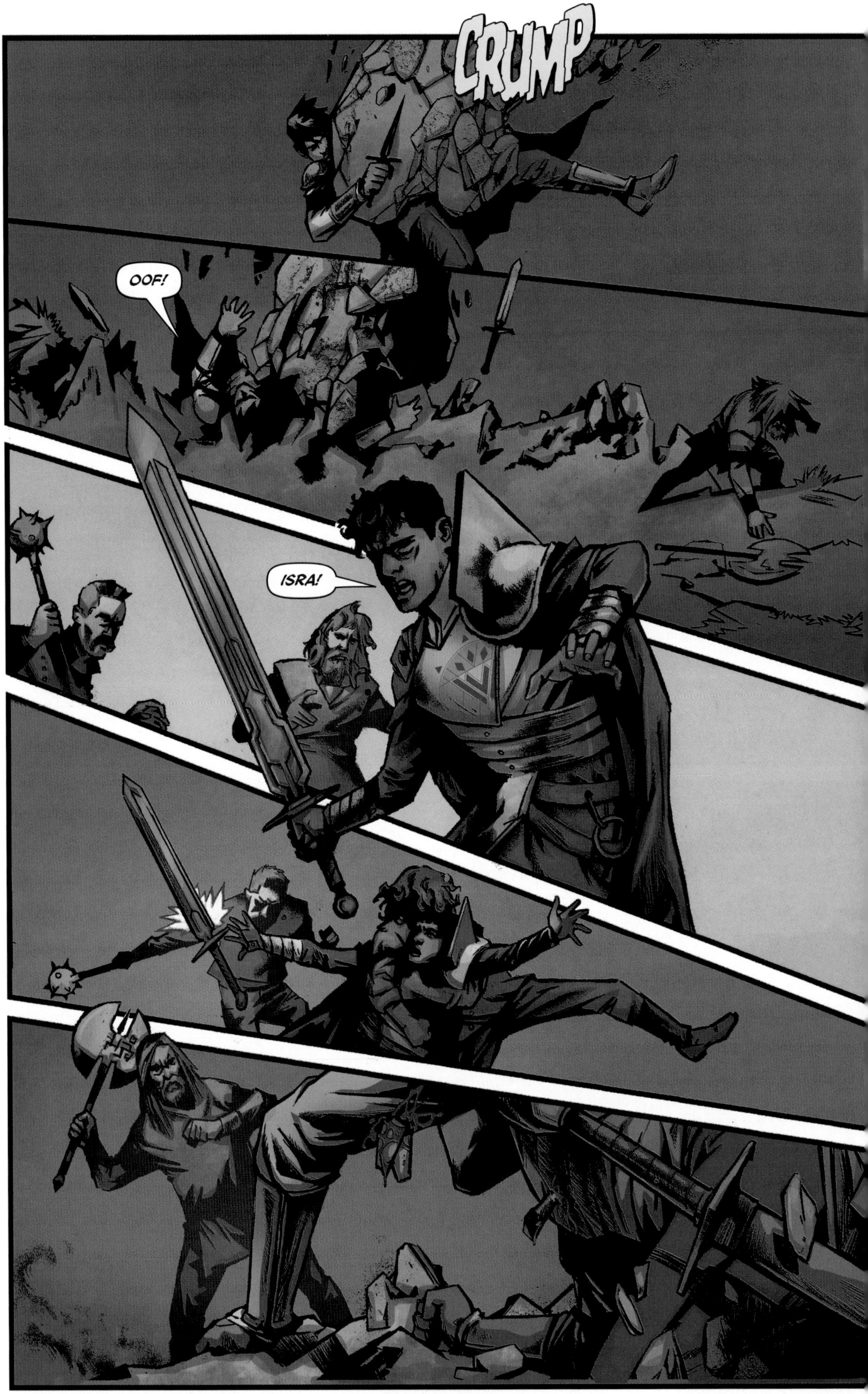
CRUMP
OOF!
ISRA!

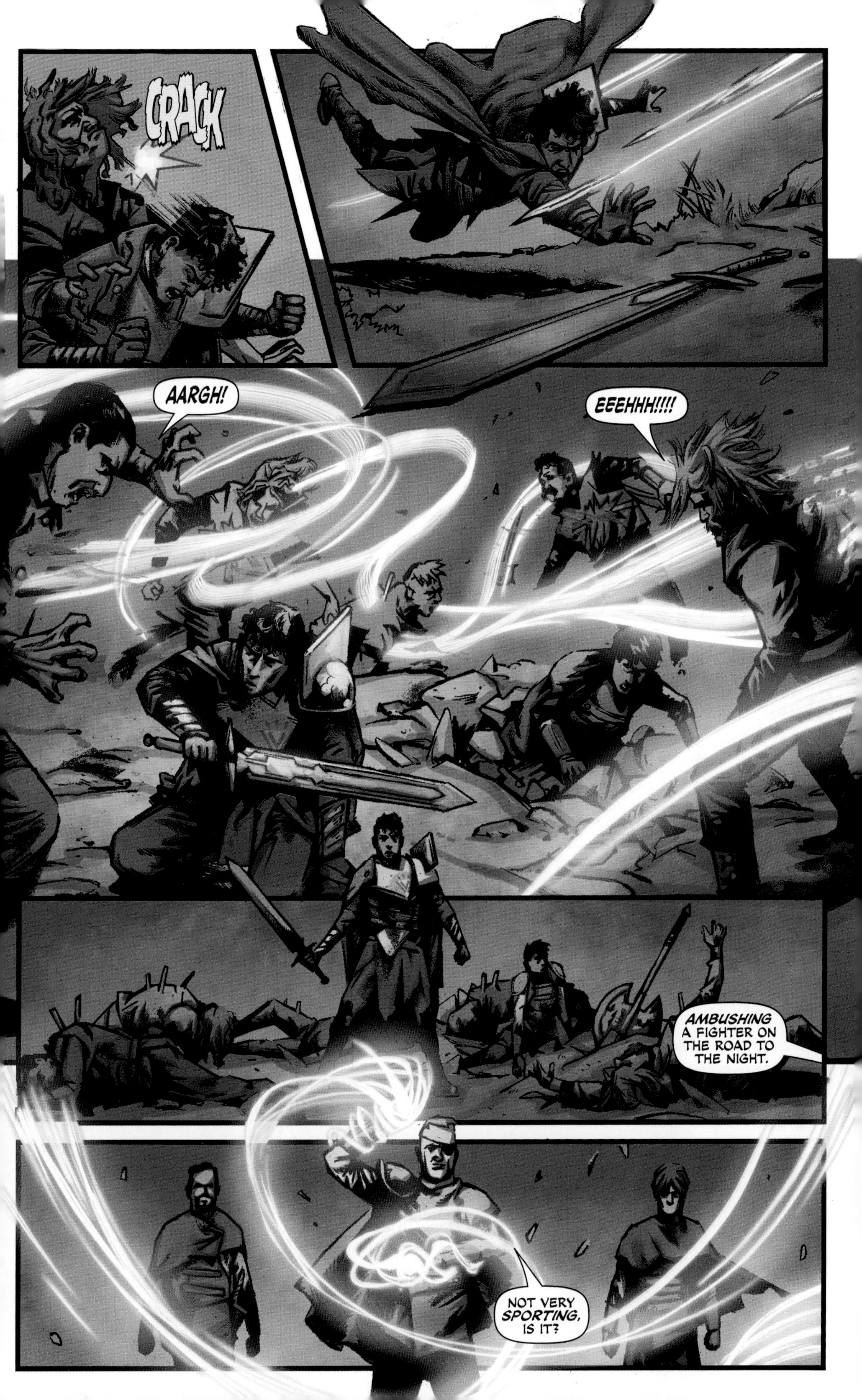
CRACK
AARGH!
EEEHHH!!!!
AMBUSHING A FIGHTER ON THE ROAD TO THE NIGHT.
NOT VERY SPORTING, IS IT?

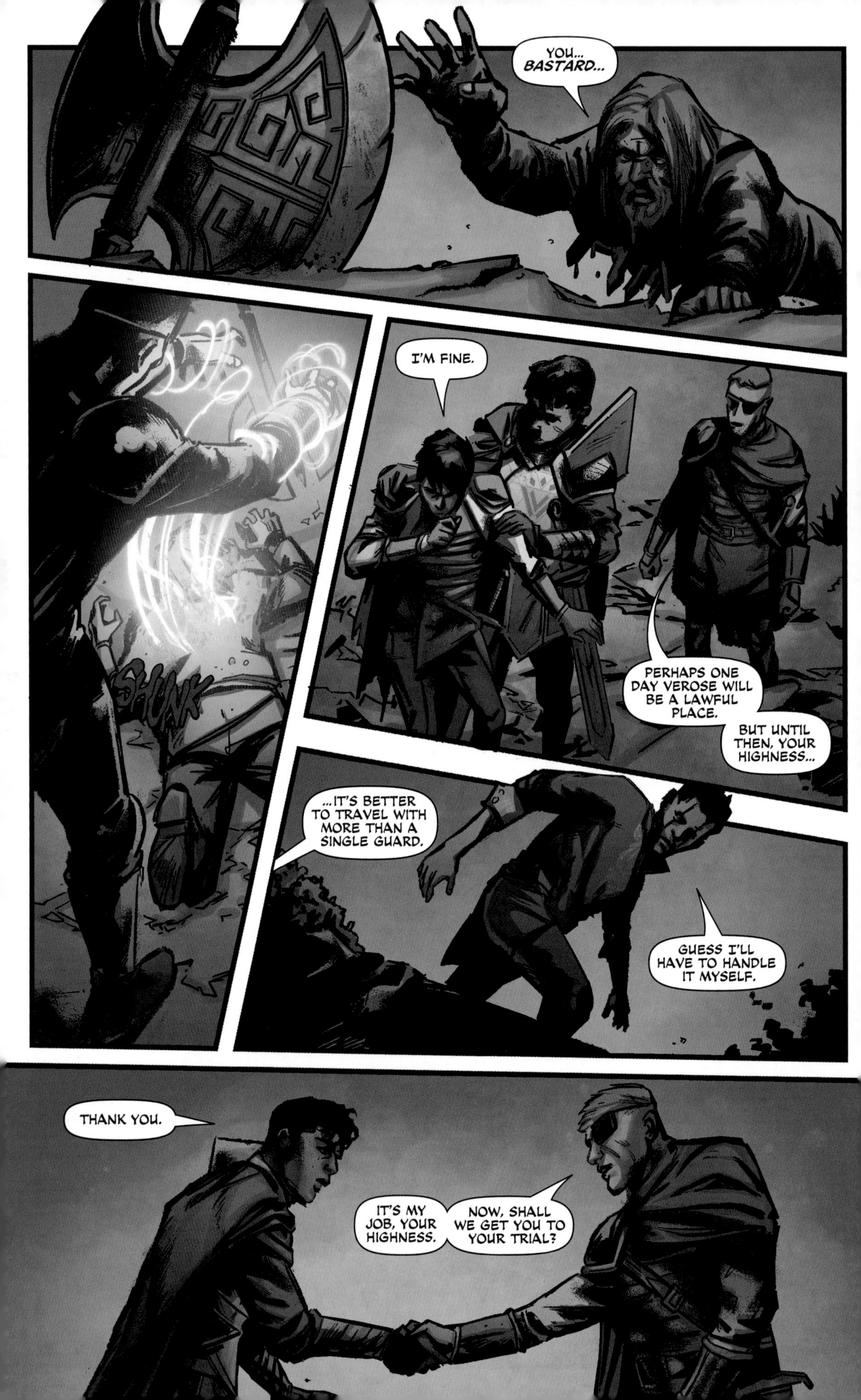
YOU... BASTARD...
SHUNK
I'M FINE.
PERHAPS ONE DAY VEROSE WILL BE A LAWFUL PLACE.
BUT UNTIL THEN, YOUR HIGHNESS...
...IT'S BETTER TO TRAVEL WITH MORE THAN A SINGLE GUARD.
GUESS I'LL HAVE TO HANDLE IT MYSELF.
THANK YOU.
IT'S MY JOB, YOUR HIGHNESS.
NOW, SHALL WE GET YOU TO YOUR TRIAL?

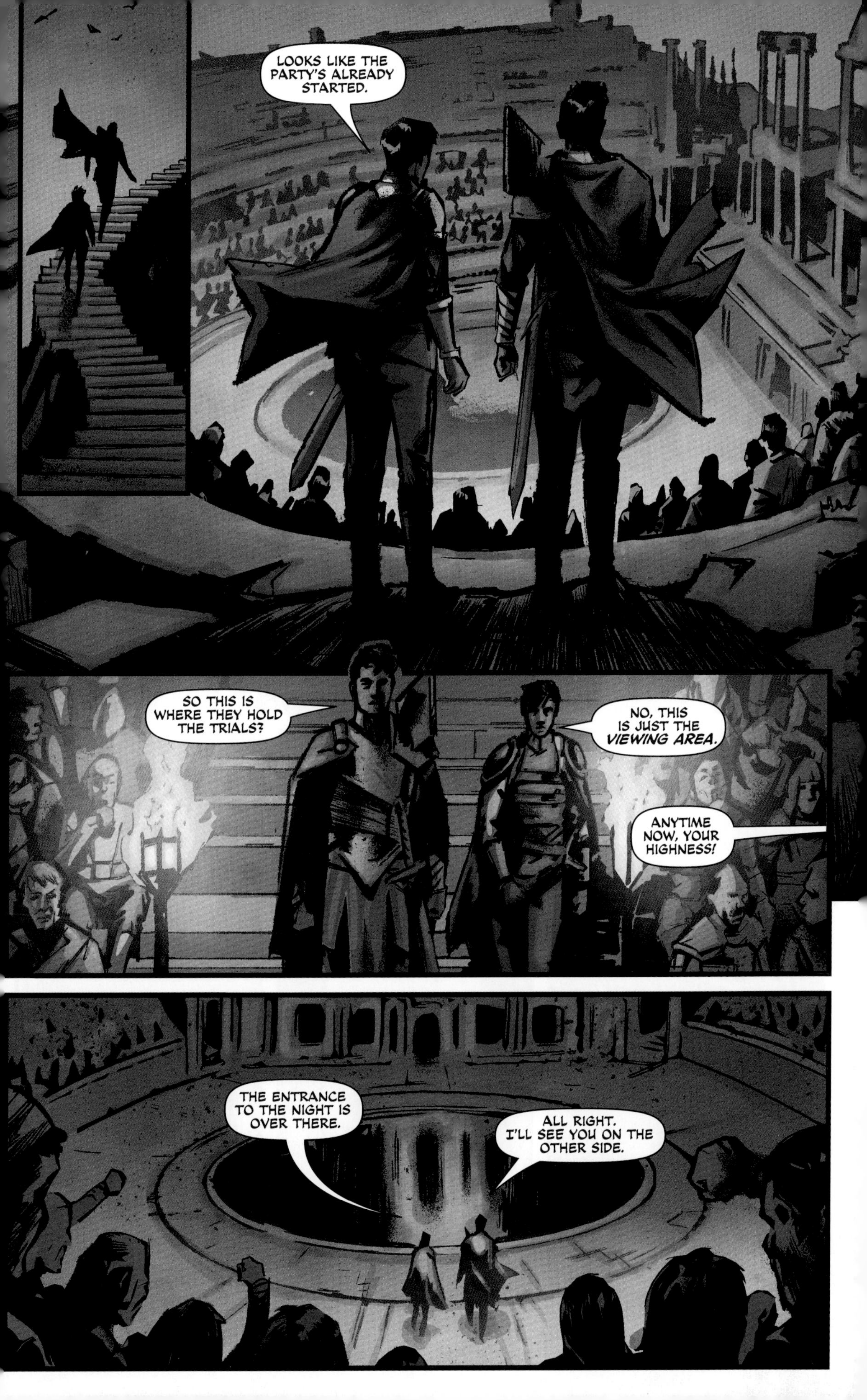
LOOKS LIKE THE PARTY'S ALREADY STARTED.
SO THIS IS WHERE THEY HOLD THE TRIALS?
NO, THIS IS JUST THE *VIEWING AREA*.
ANYTIME NOW, YOUR HIGHNESS!
THE ENTRANCE TO THE NIGHT IS OVER THERE.
ALL RIGHT. I'LL SEE YOU ON THE OTHER SIDE.

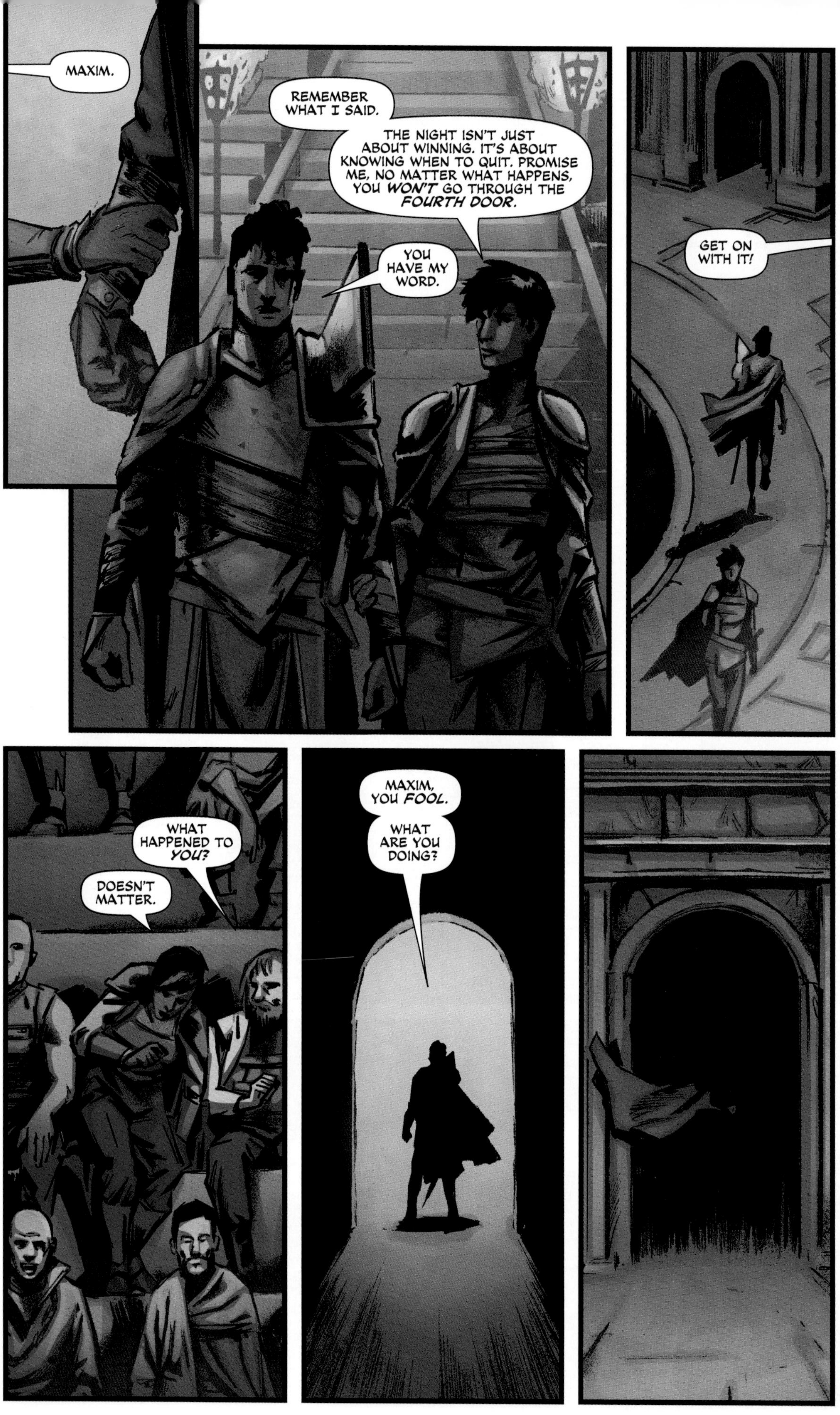
MAXIM.
REMEMBER WHAT I SAID.
THE NIGHT ISN'T JUST ABOUT WINNING. IT'S ABOUT KNOWING WHEN TO QUIT. PROMISE ME, NO MATTER WHAT HAPPENS, YOU WON'T GO THROUGH THE FOURTH DOOR.
YOU HAVE MY WORD.
GET ON WITH IT!
WHAT HAPPENED TO YOU?
DOESN'T MATTER.
MAXIM, YOU FOOL.
WHAT ARE YOU DOING?

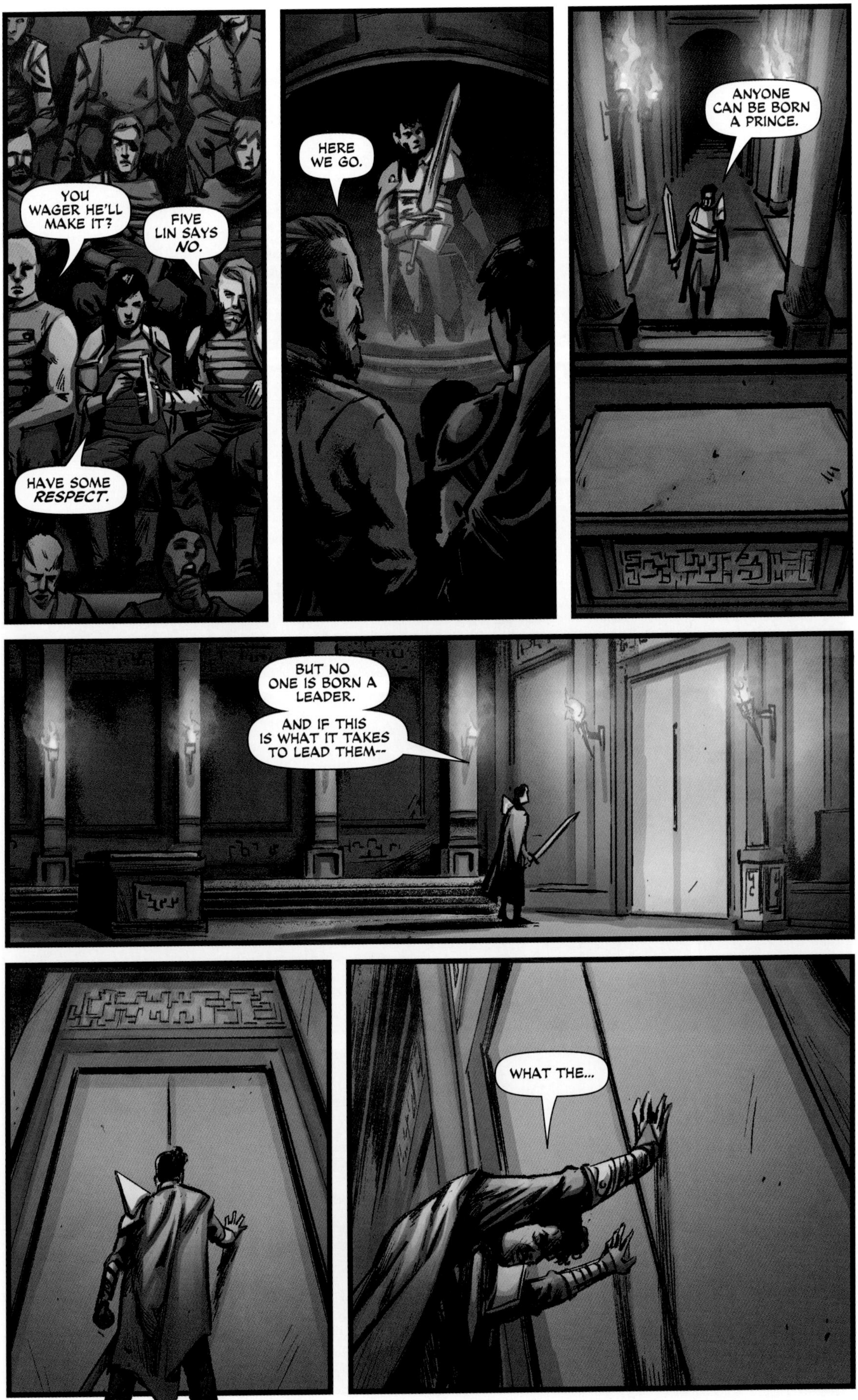

YOU WAGER HE'LL MAKE IT?
FIVE LIN SAYS *NO.*
HAVE SOME *RESPECT.*
HERE WE GO.
ANYONE CAN BE BORN A PRINCE.
BUT NO ONE IS BORN A LEADER.
AND IF THIS IS WHAT IT TAKES TO LEAD THEM--
WHAT THE...

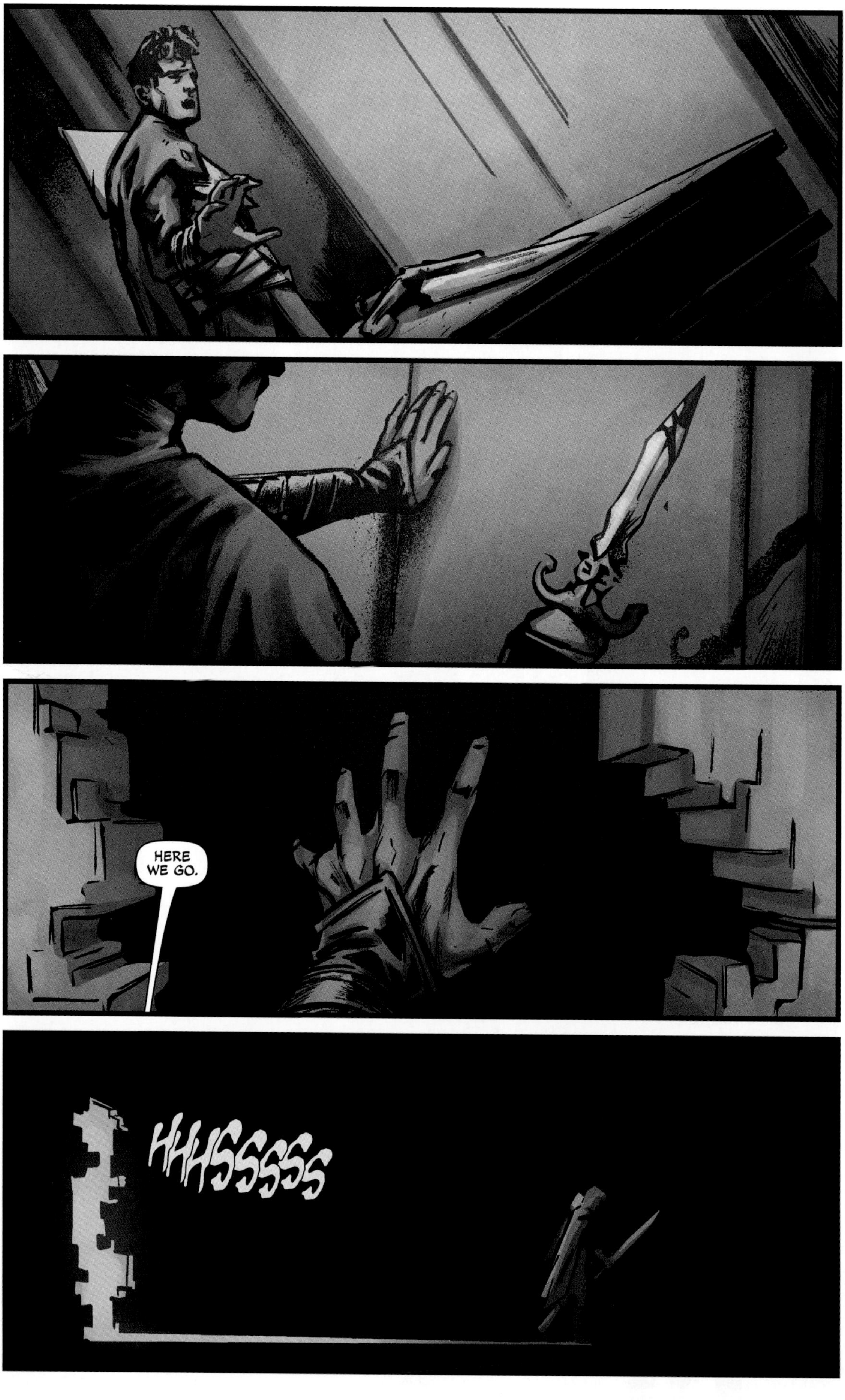
HERE WE GO.
HHHSSSSS

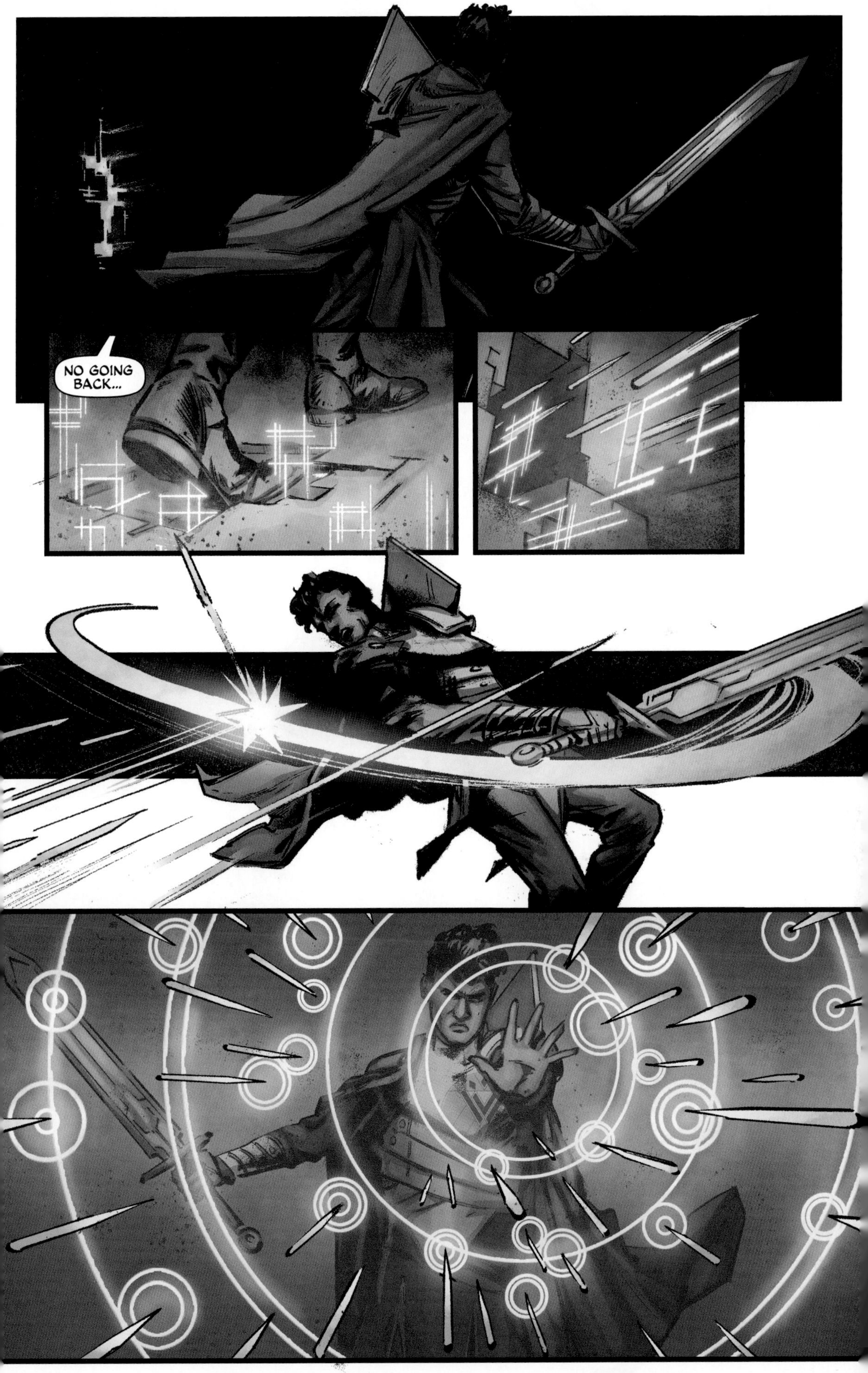
NO GOING BACK...

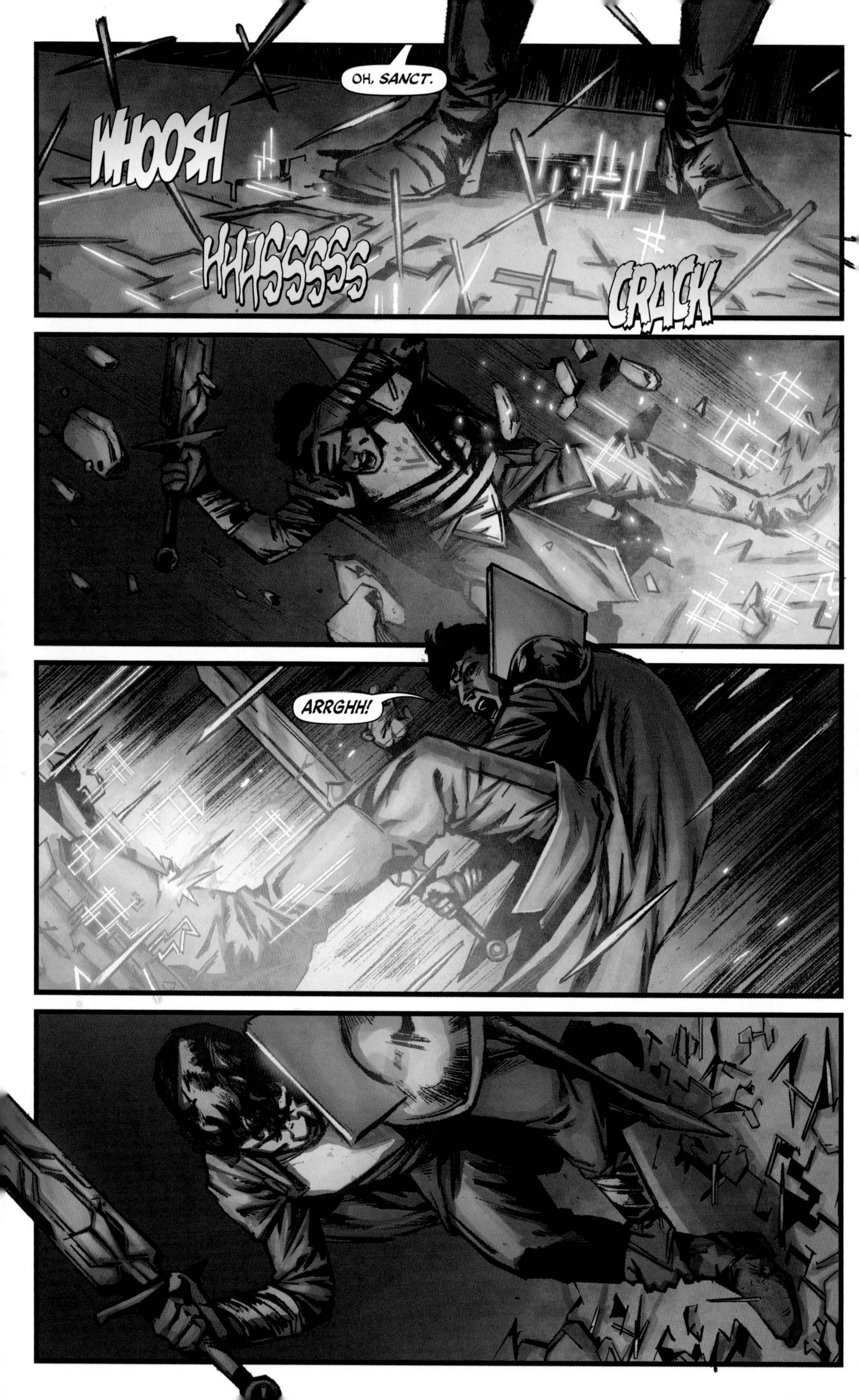
OH, SANCT.
WHOOSH
HHHSSSSSS
CRACK
ARRGHH!

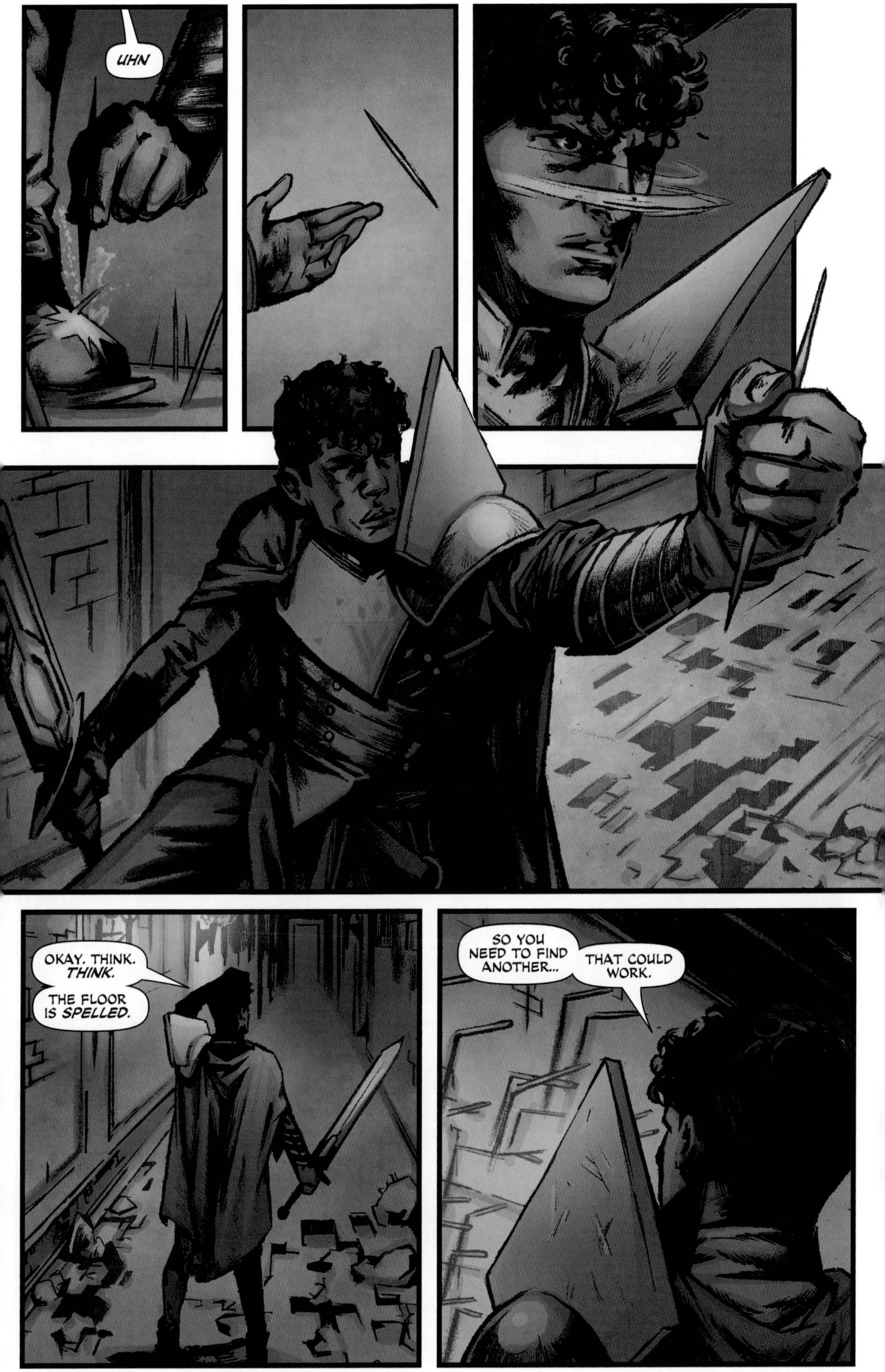
UHN
OKAY. THINK. THINK.
THE FLOOR IS SPELLED.
SO YOU NEED TO FIND ANOTHER...
THAT COULD WORK.

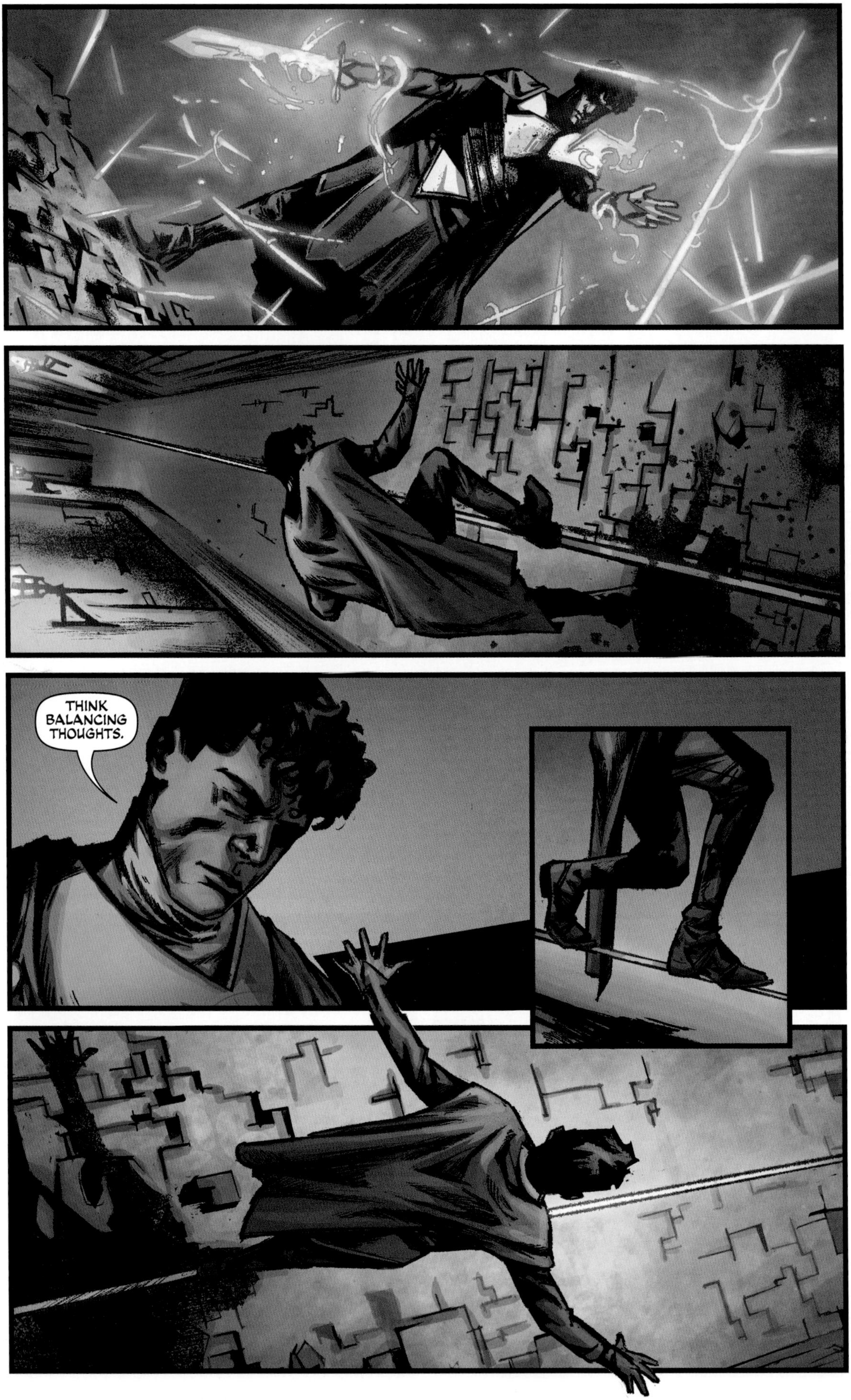
THINK BALANCING THOUGHTS.

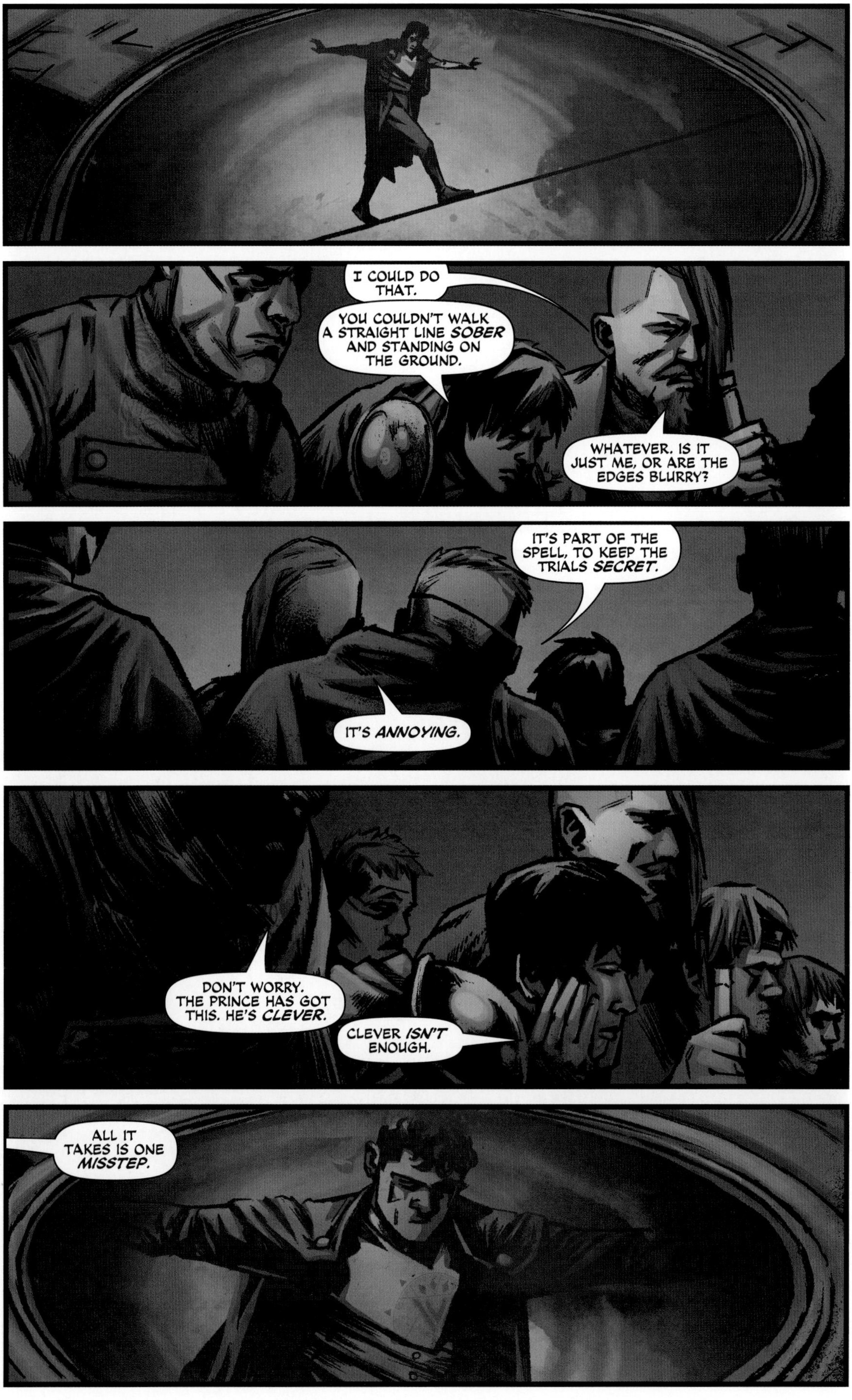
I COULD DO THAT.
YOU COULDN'T WALK A STRAIGHT LINE *SOBER* AND STANDING ON THE GROUND.
WHATEVER. IS IT JUST ME, OR ARE THE EDGES BLURRY?
IT'S PART OF THE SPELL, TO KEEP THE TRIALS *SECRET*.
IT'S *ANNOYING*.
DON'T WORRY. THE PRINCE HAS GOT THIS. HE'S *CLEVER*.
CLEVER *ISN'T* ENOUGH.
ALL IT TAKES IS ONE *MISSTEP*.

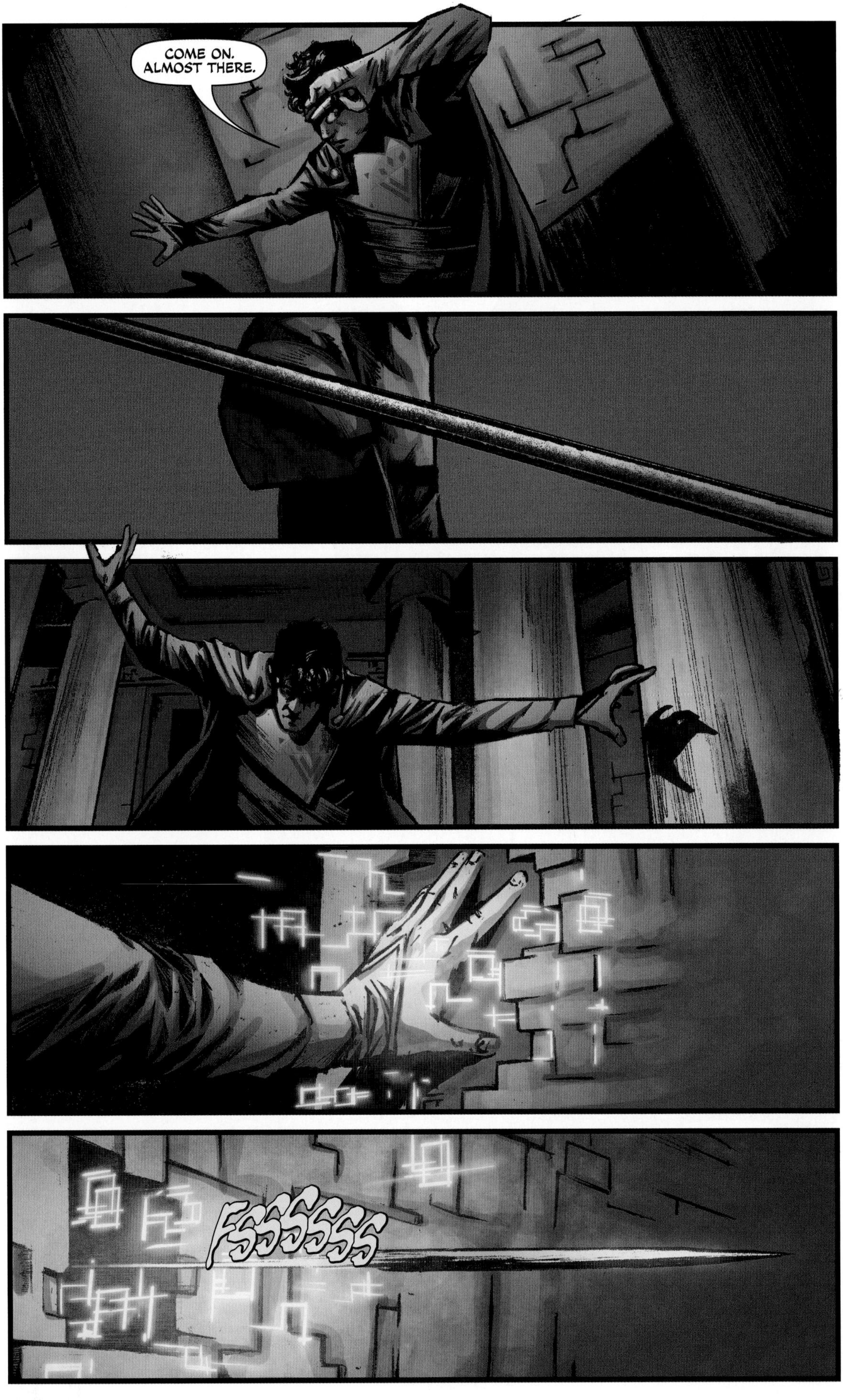
COME ON. ALMOST THERE.
FSSSSSSS

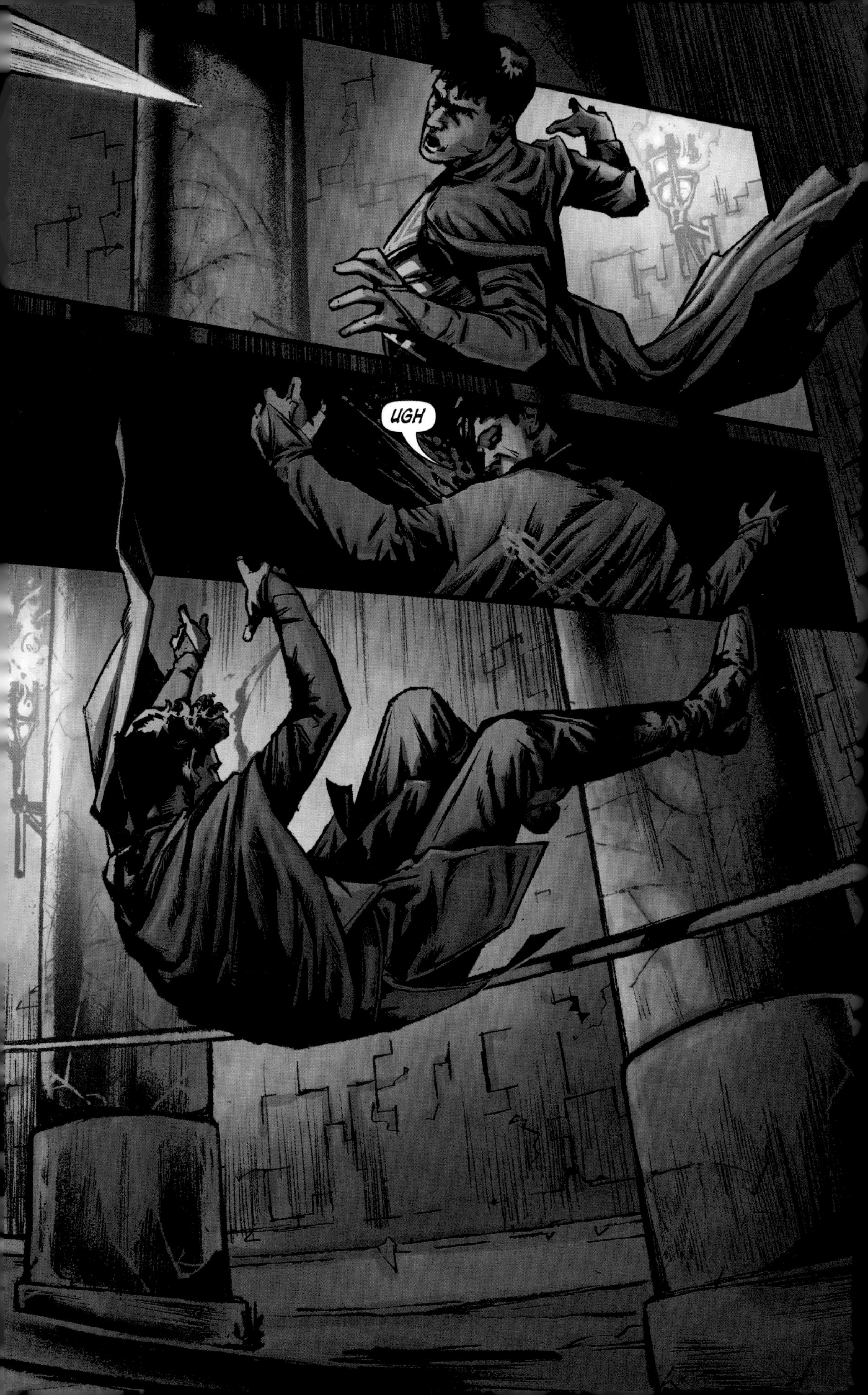
UGH

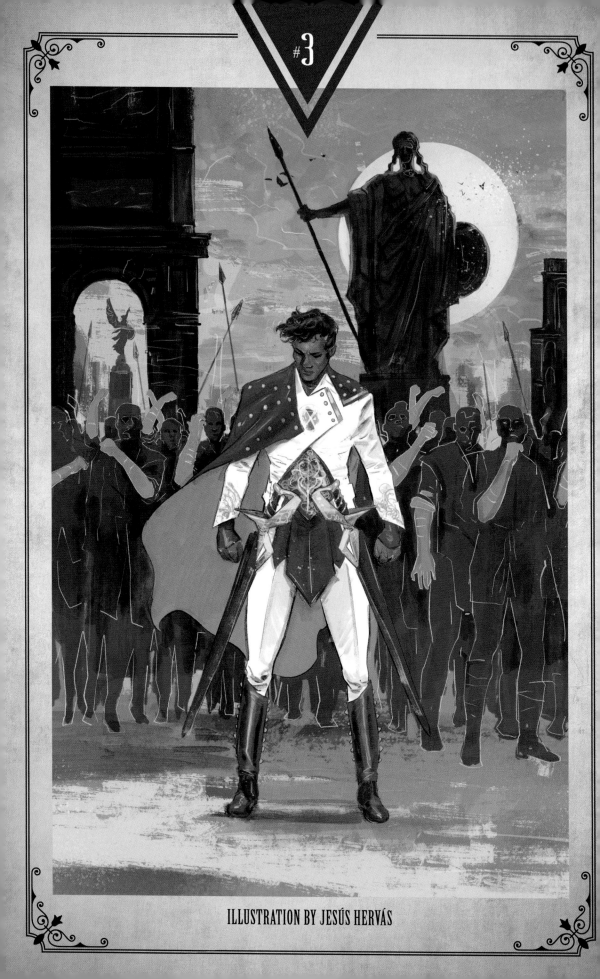

#3

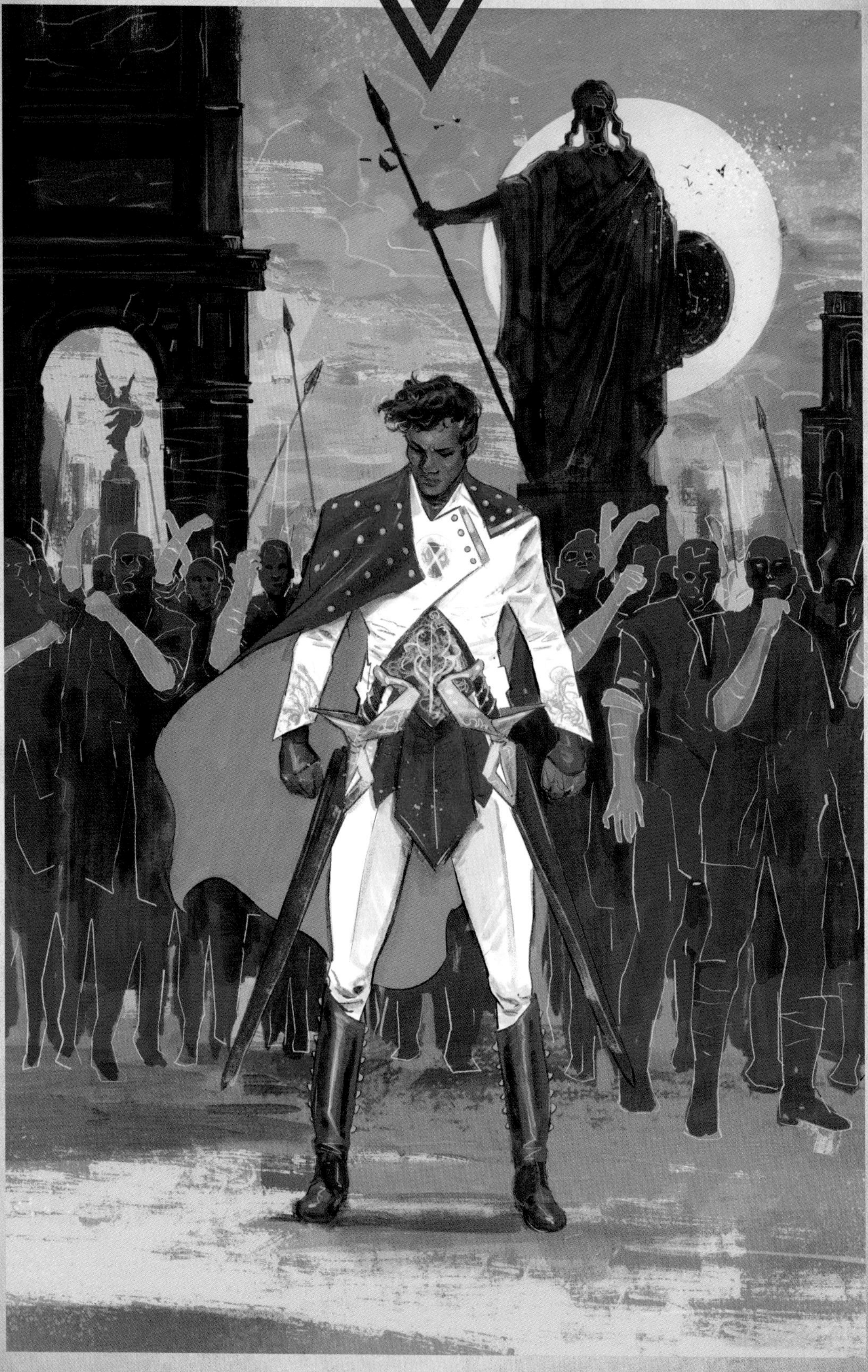

ILLUSTRATION BY JESÚS HERVÁS

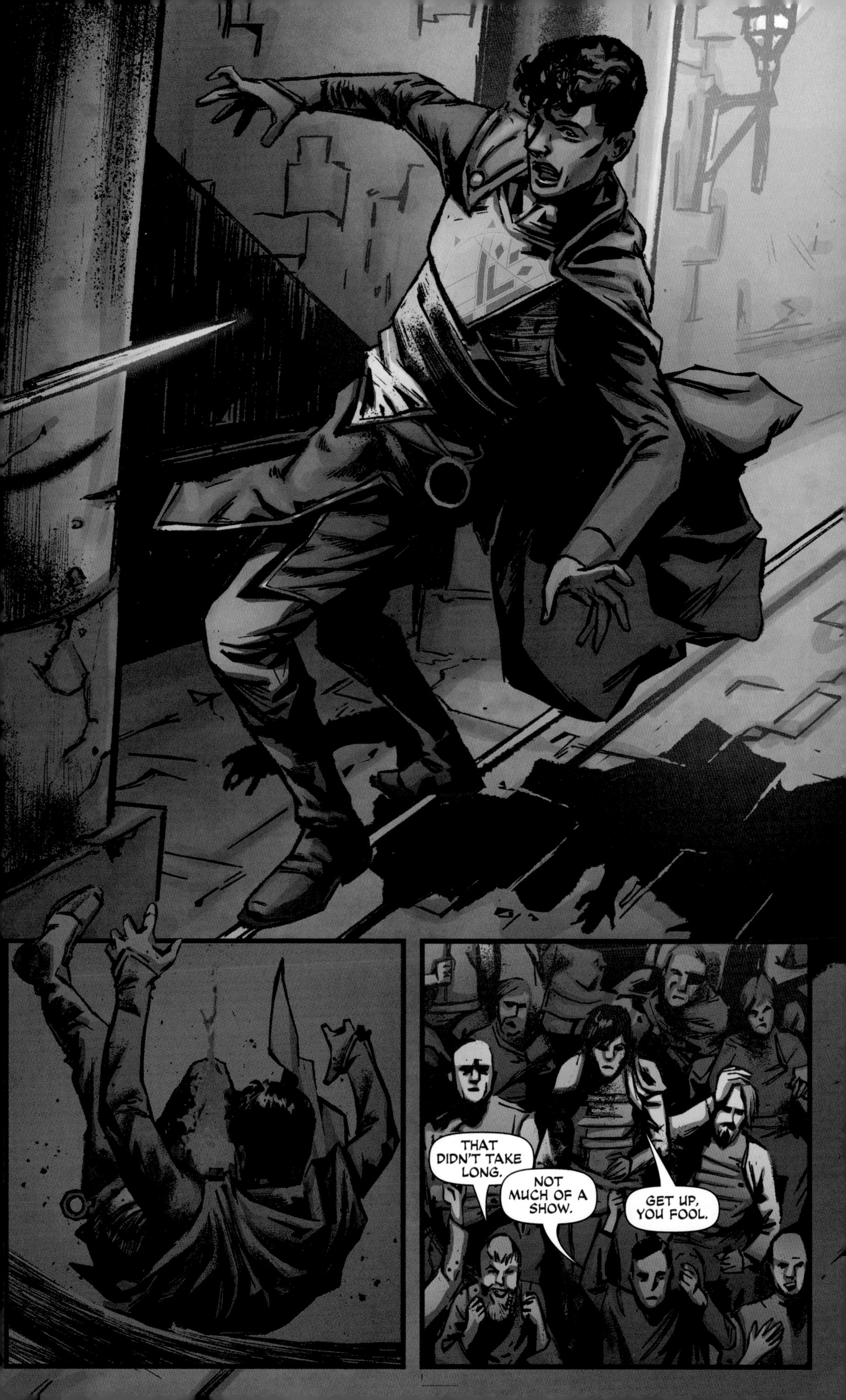
THAT DIDN'T TAKE LONG.
NOT MUCH OF A SHOW.
GET UP, YOU FOOL.

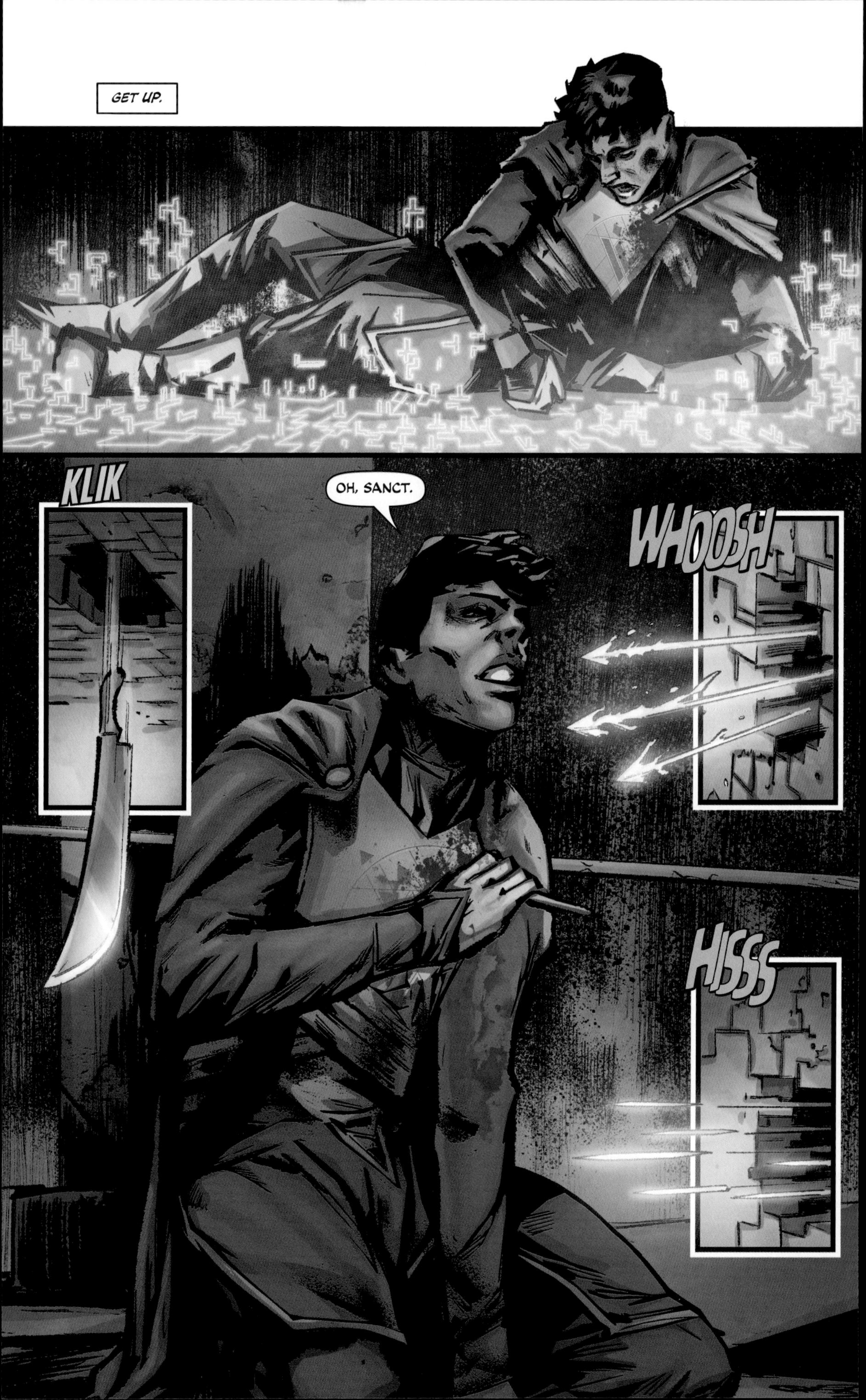
GET UP.
KLIK
OH, SANCT.
WHOOSH
HISSS

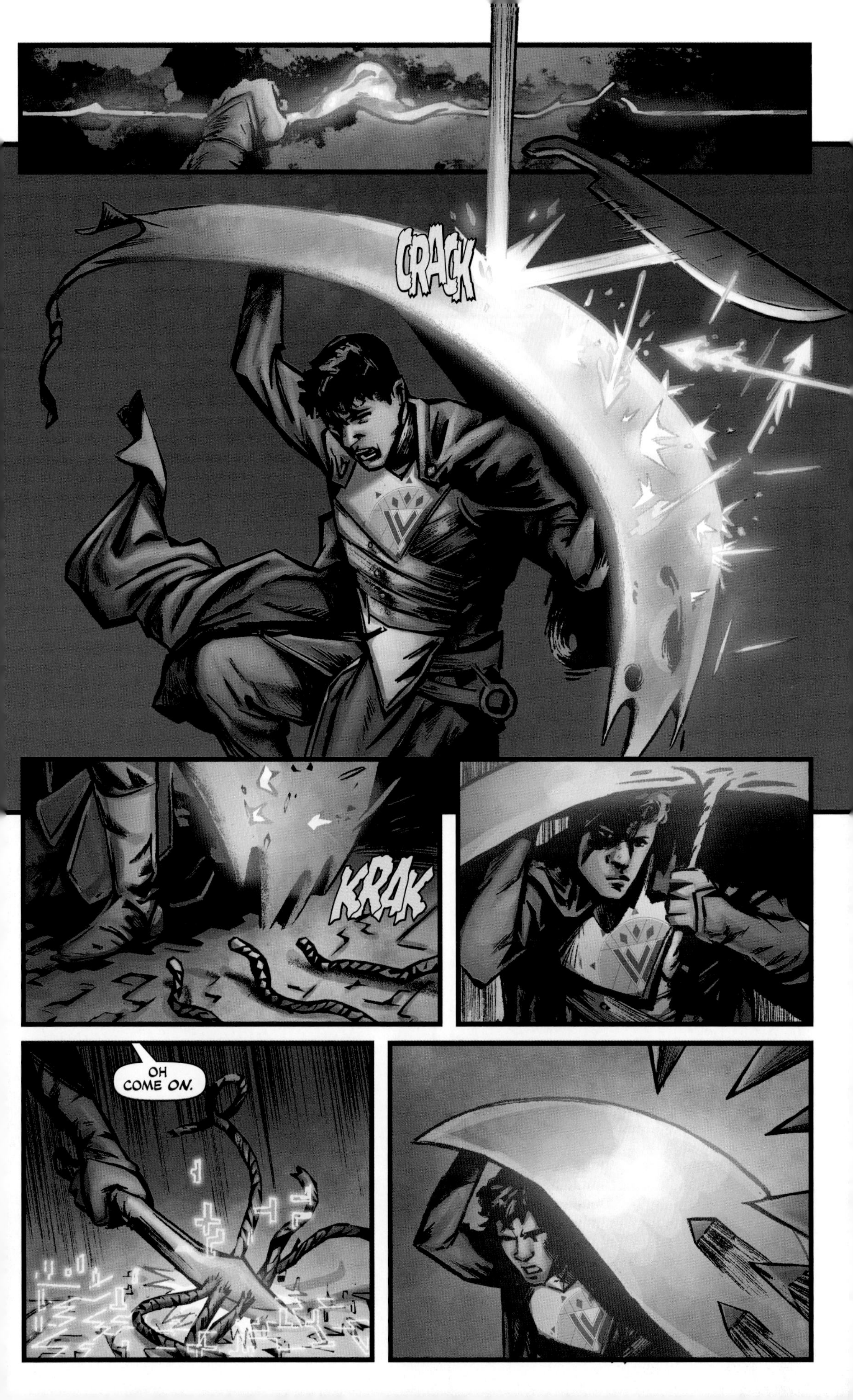
CRACK
KRAK
OH COME ON.

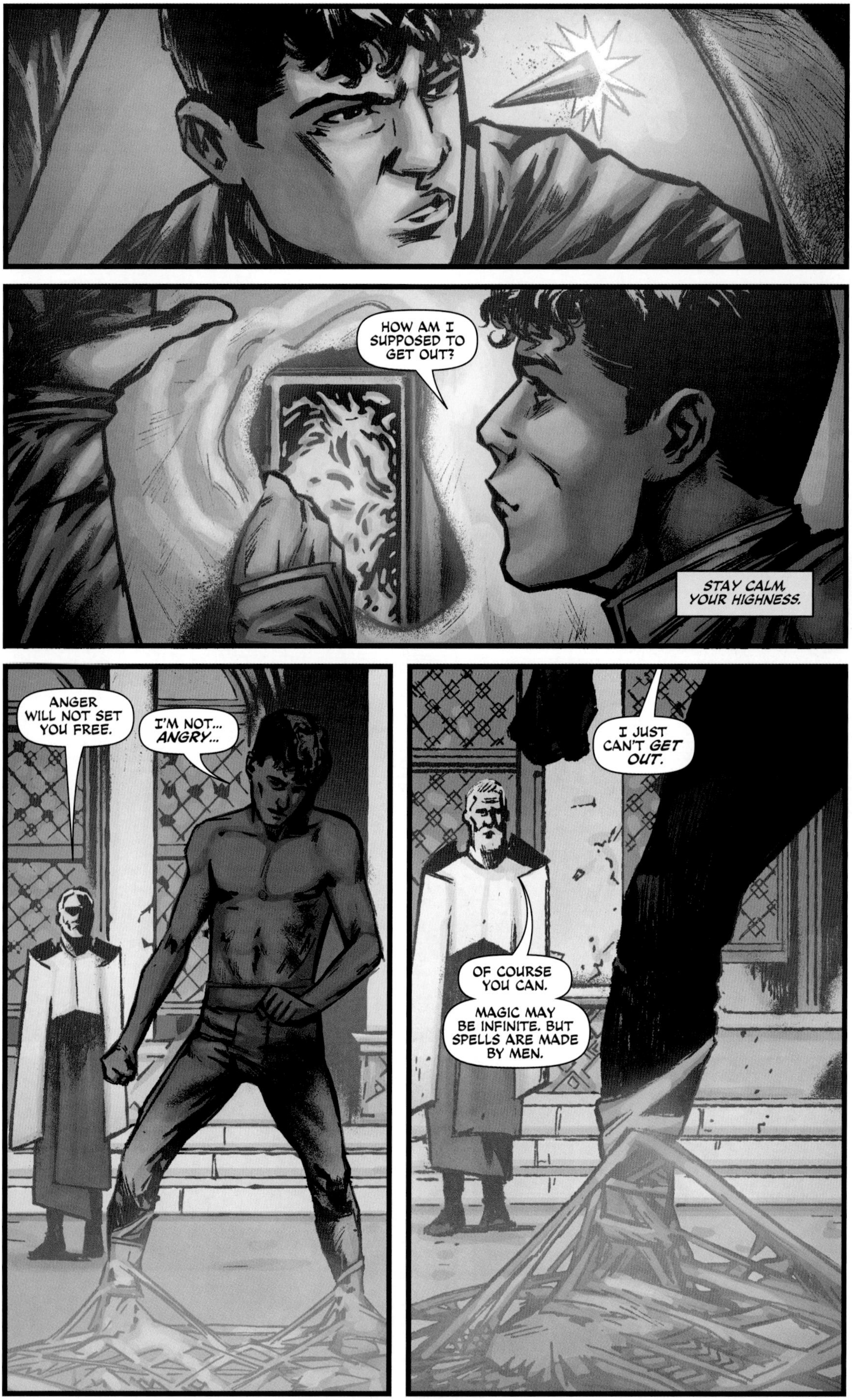
HOW AM I SUPPOSED TO GET OUT?
STAY CALM, YOUR HIGHNESS.
ANGER WILL NOT SET YOU FREE.
I'M NOT... ANGRY...
I JUST CAN'T GET OUT.
OF COURSE YOU CAN.
MAGIC MAY BE INFINITE. BUT SPELLS ARE MADE BY MEN.

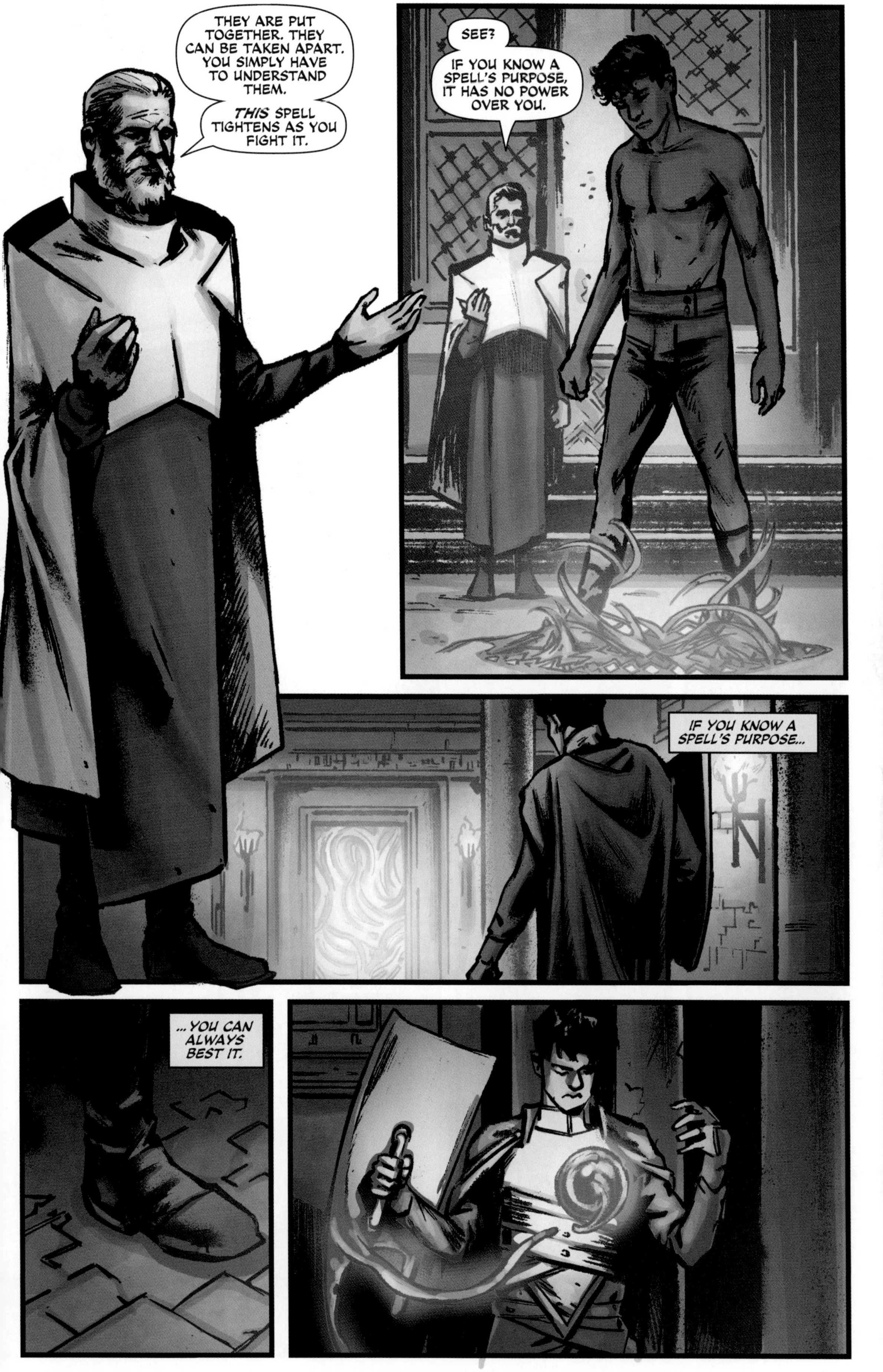
THEY ARE PUT TOGETHER. THEY CAN BE TAKEN APART. YOU SIMPLY HAVE TO UNDERSTAND THEM.
THIS SPELL TIGHTENS AS YOU FIGHT IT.
SEE?
IF YOU KNOW A SPELL'S PURPOSE, IT HAS NO POWER OVER YOU.
IF YOU KNOW A SPELL'S PURPOSE...
...YOU CAN ALWAYS BEST IT.

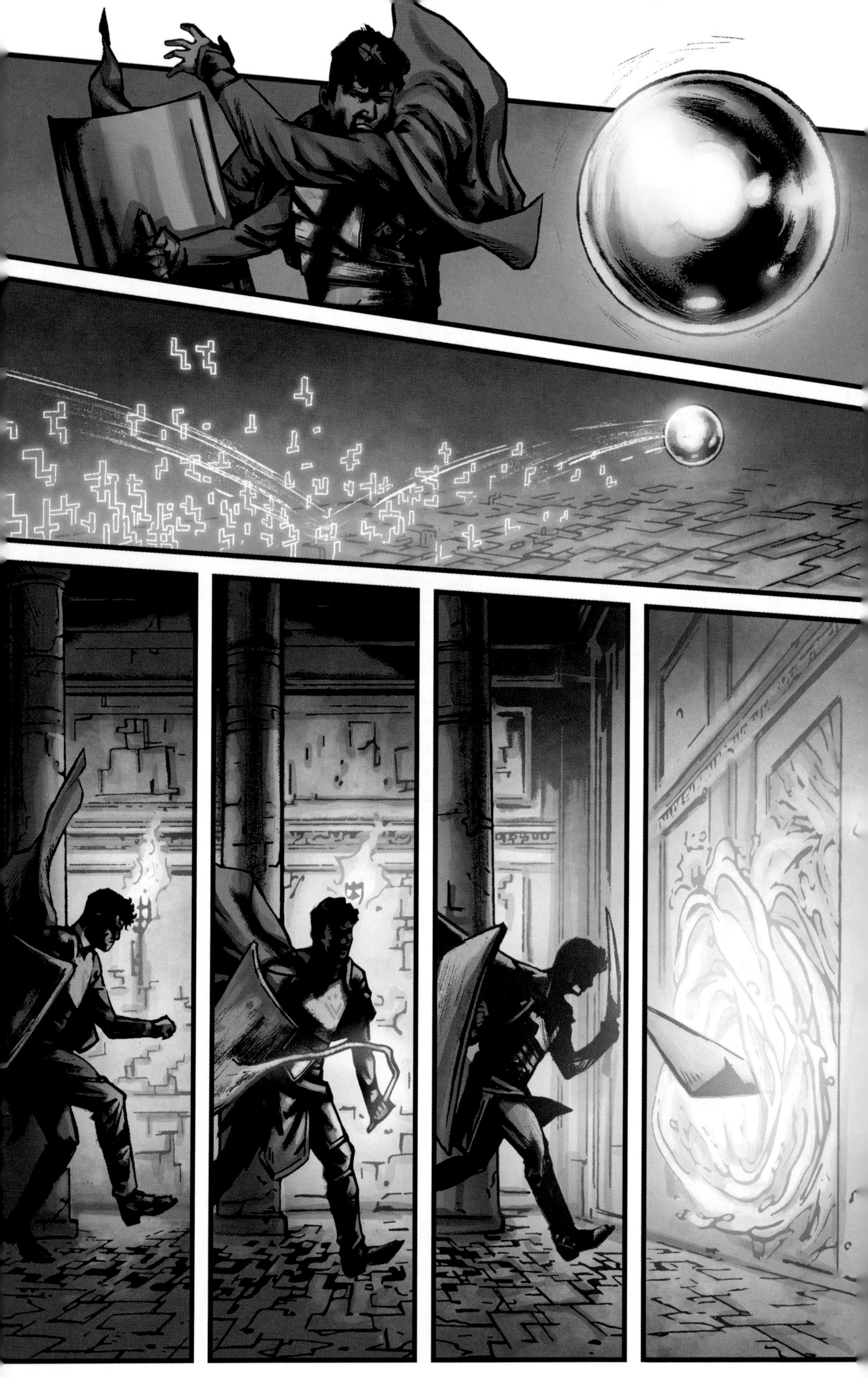

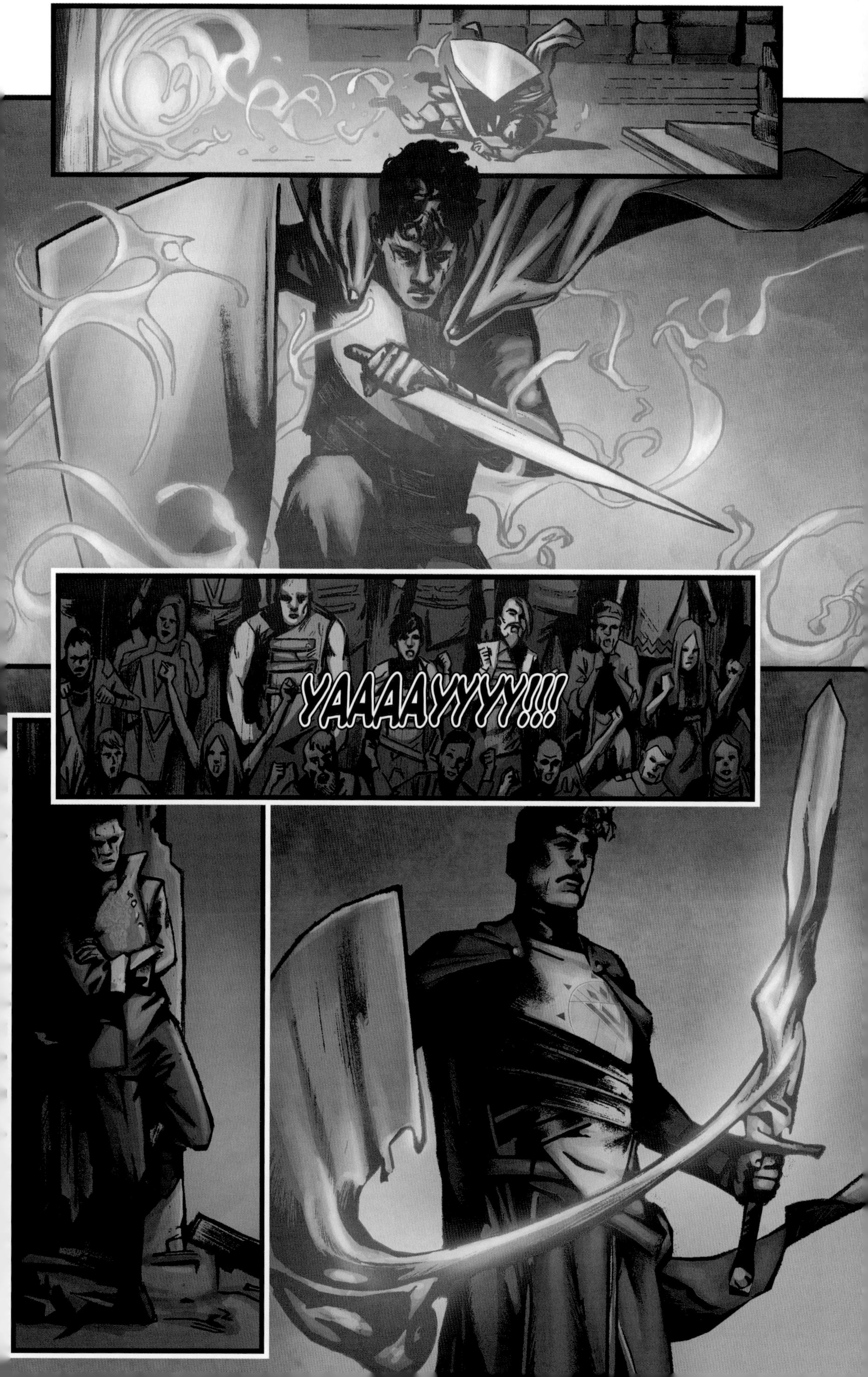
YAAAAYYYY!!!

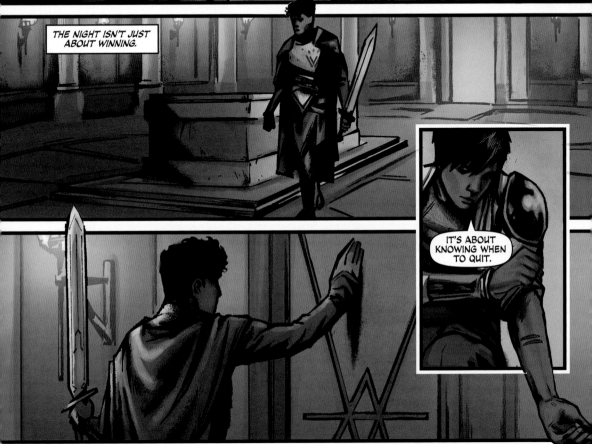

THE NIGHT ISN'T JUST ABOUT WINNING.

IT'S ABOUT KNOWING WHEN TO QUIT.

FOOL.

HAVE A LITTLE FAITH.

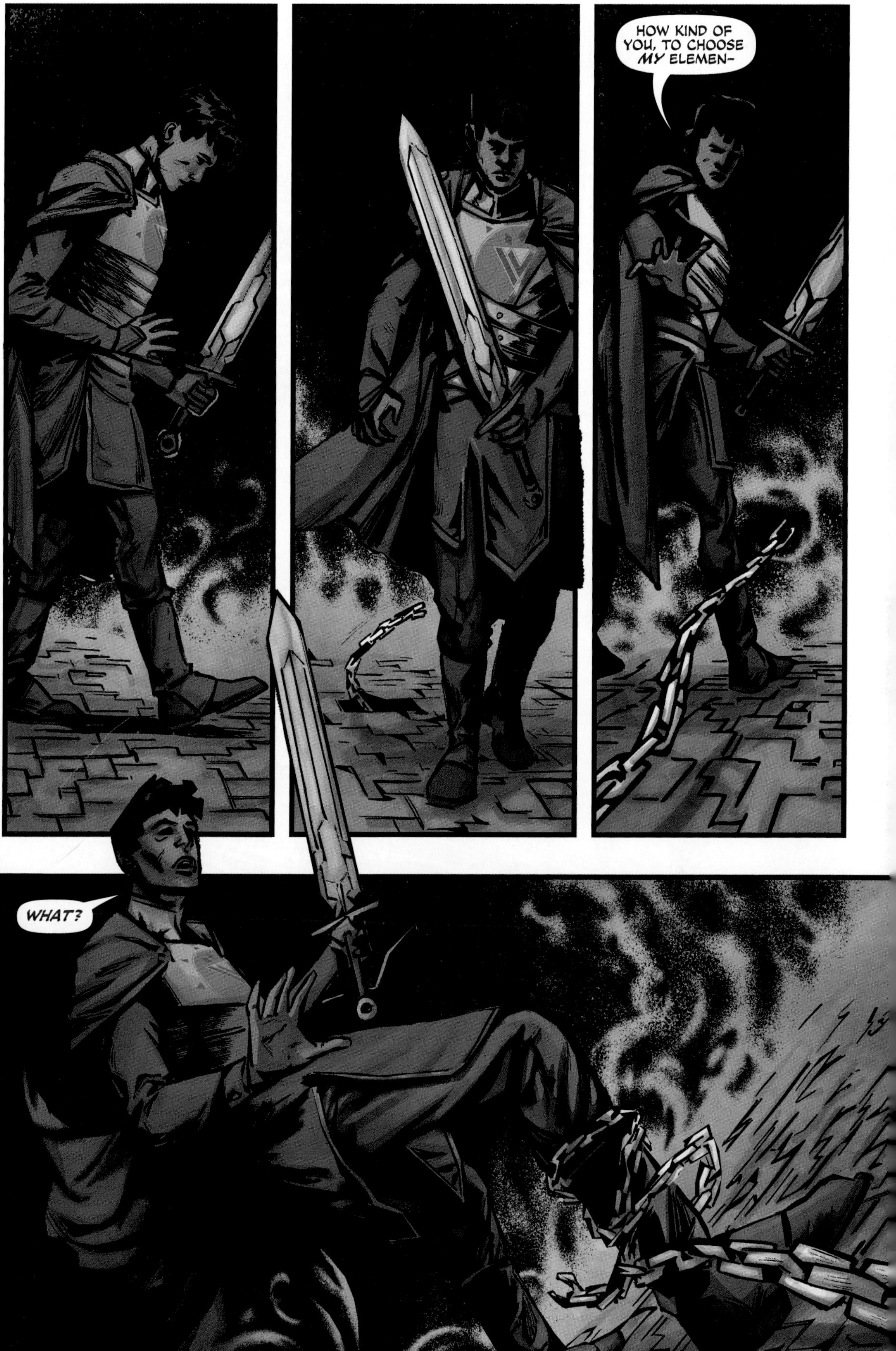
HOW KIND OF YOU, TO CHOOSE MY ELEMEN-
WHAT?

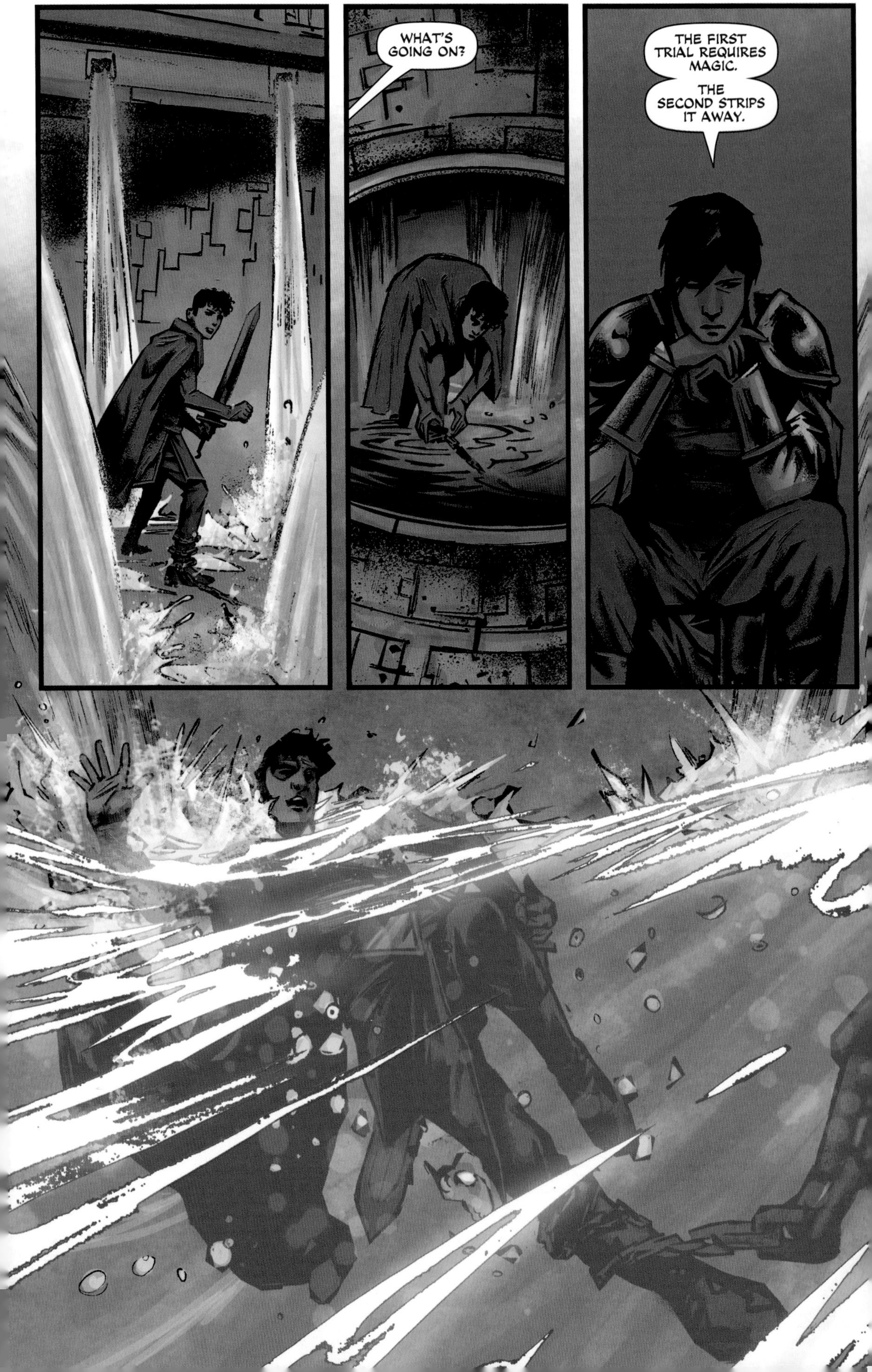
WHAT'S GOING ON?
THE FIRST TRIAL REQUIRES MAGIC.
THE SECOND STRIPS IT AWAY.

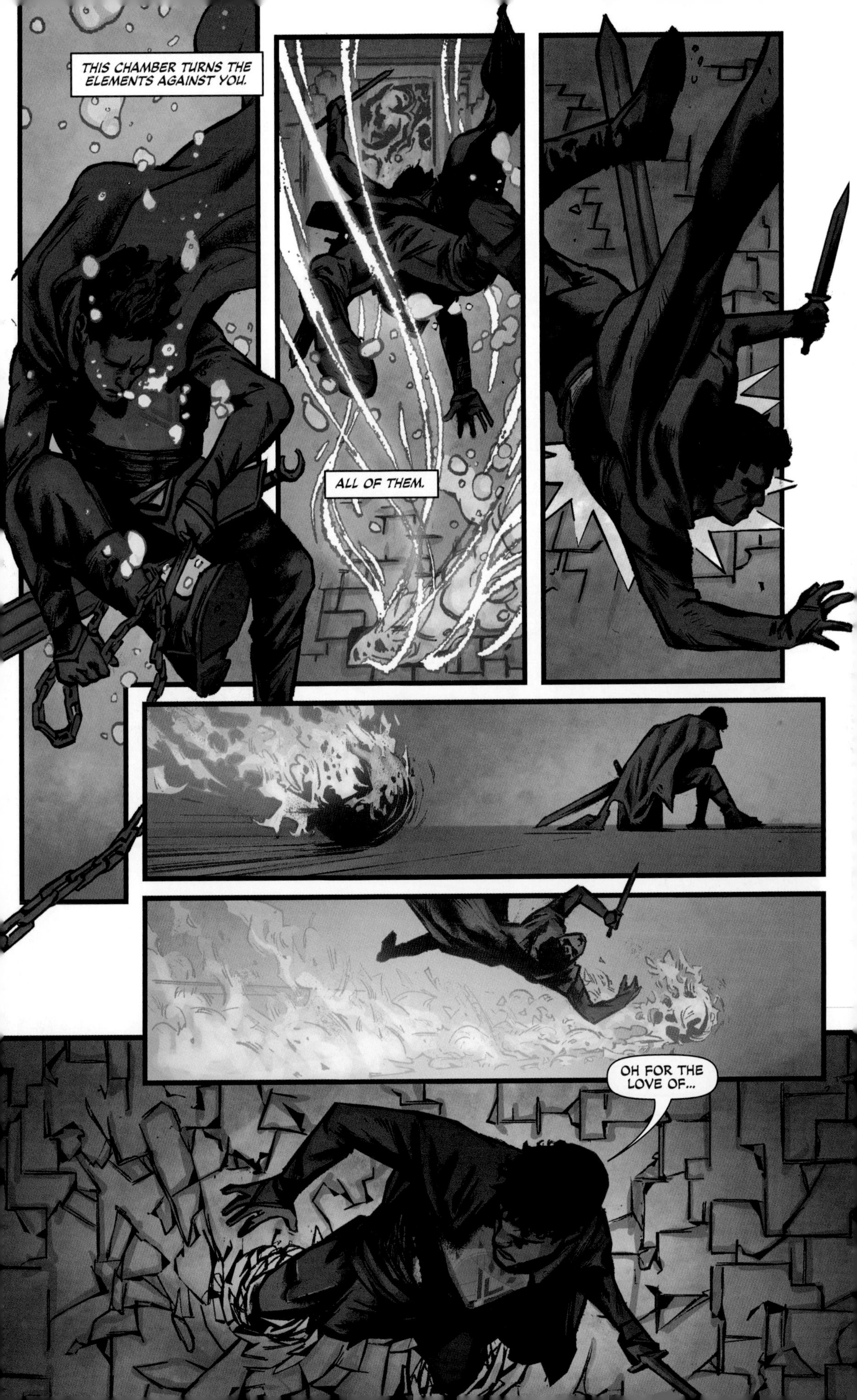
THIS CHAMBER TURNS THE ELEMENTS AGAINST YOU.
ALL OF THEM.
OH FOR THE LOVE OF...

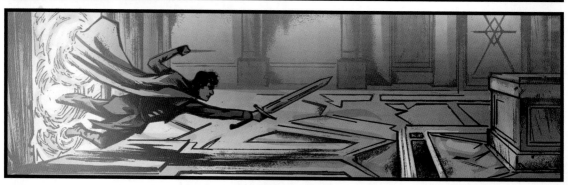

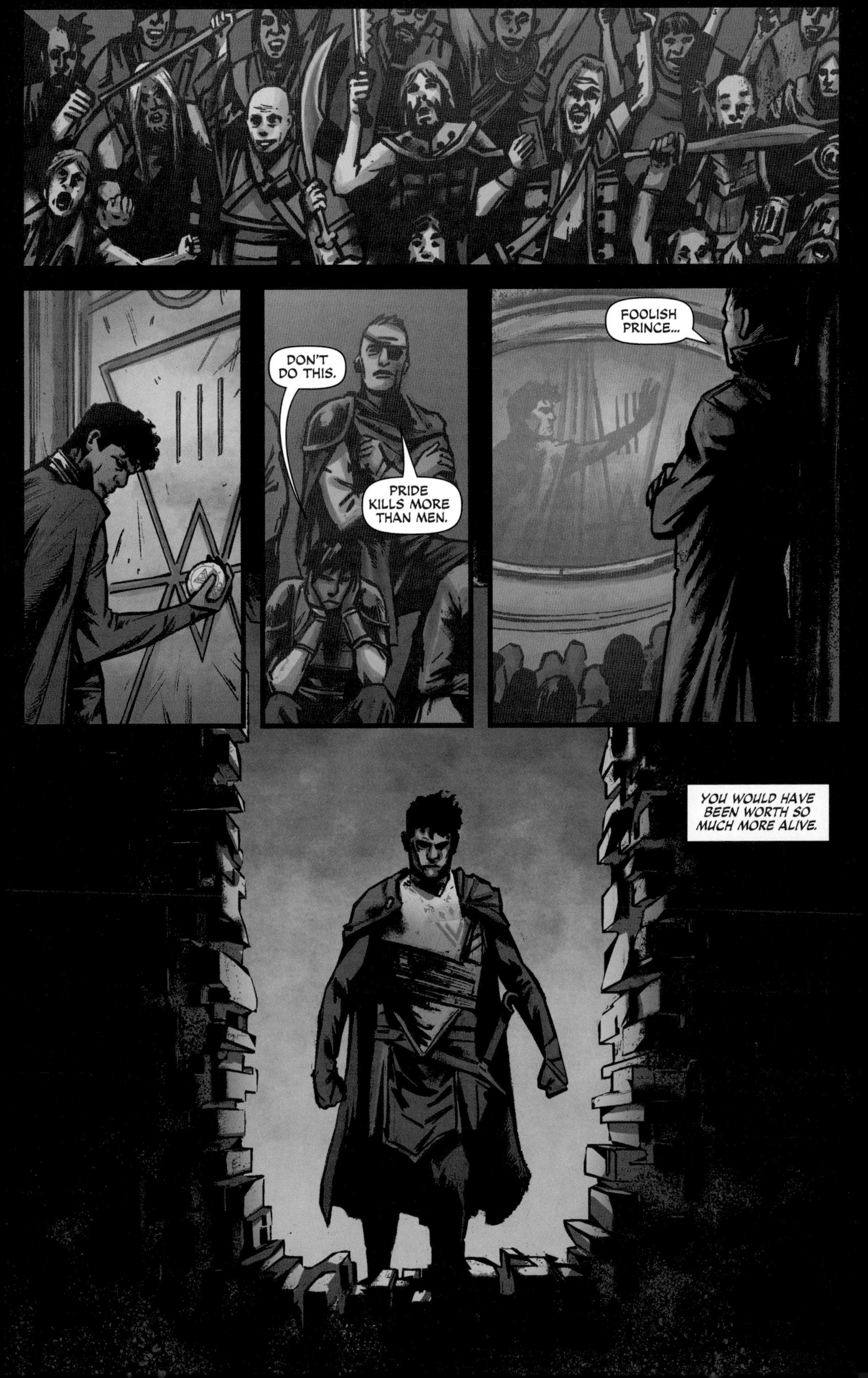

DON'T DO THIS.
PRIDE KILLS MORE THAN MEN.
FOOLISH PRINCE...
YOU WOULD HAVE BEEN WORTH SO MUCH MORE ALIVE.

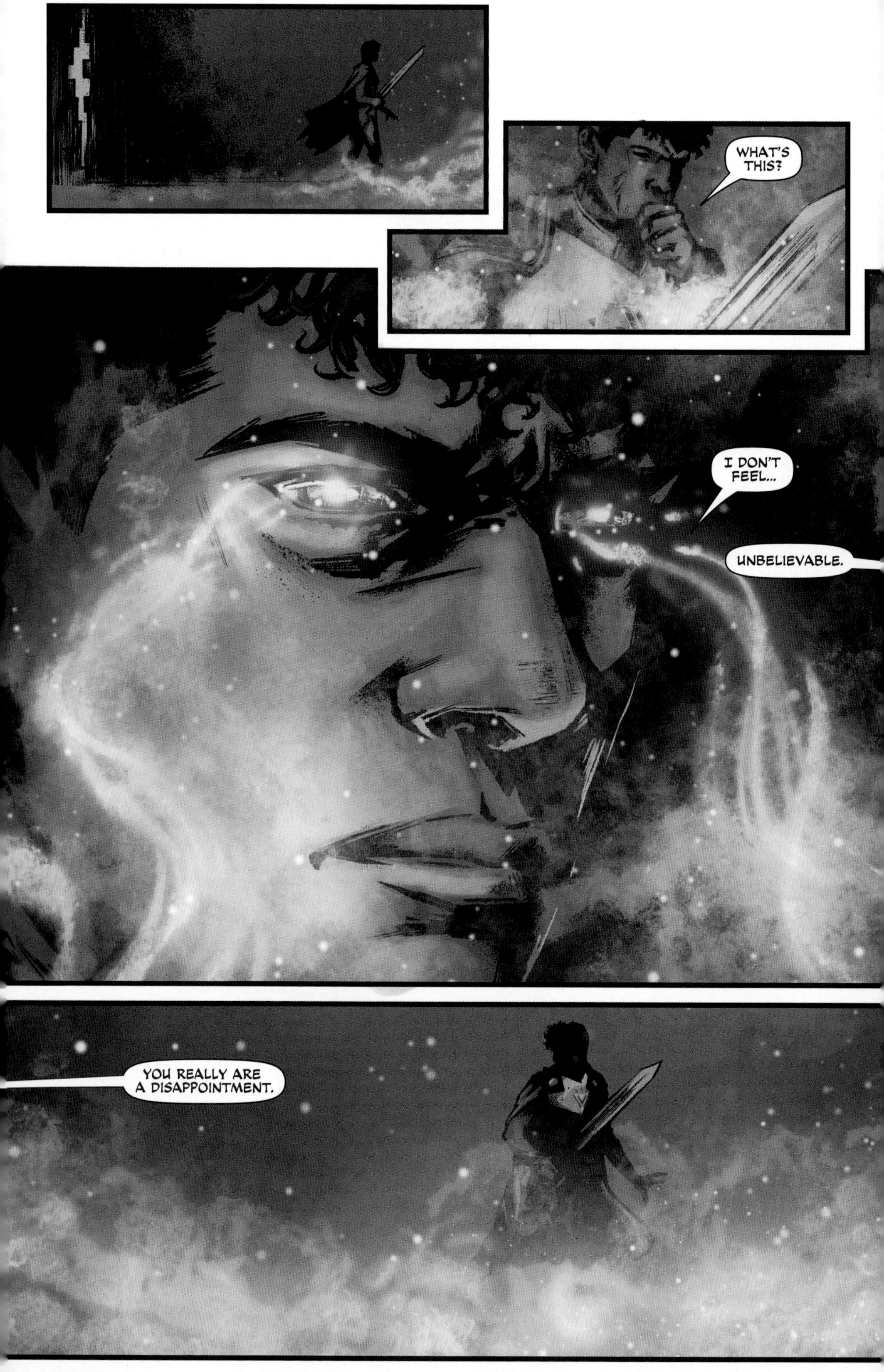
WHAT'S THIS?
I DON'T FEEL...
UNBELIEVABLE.
YOU REALLY ARE A DISAPPOINTMENT.

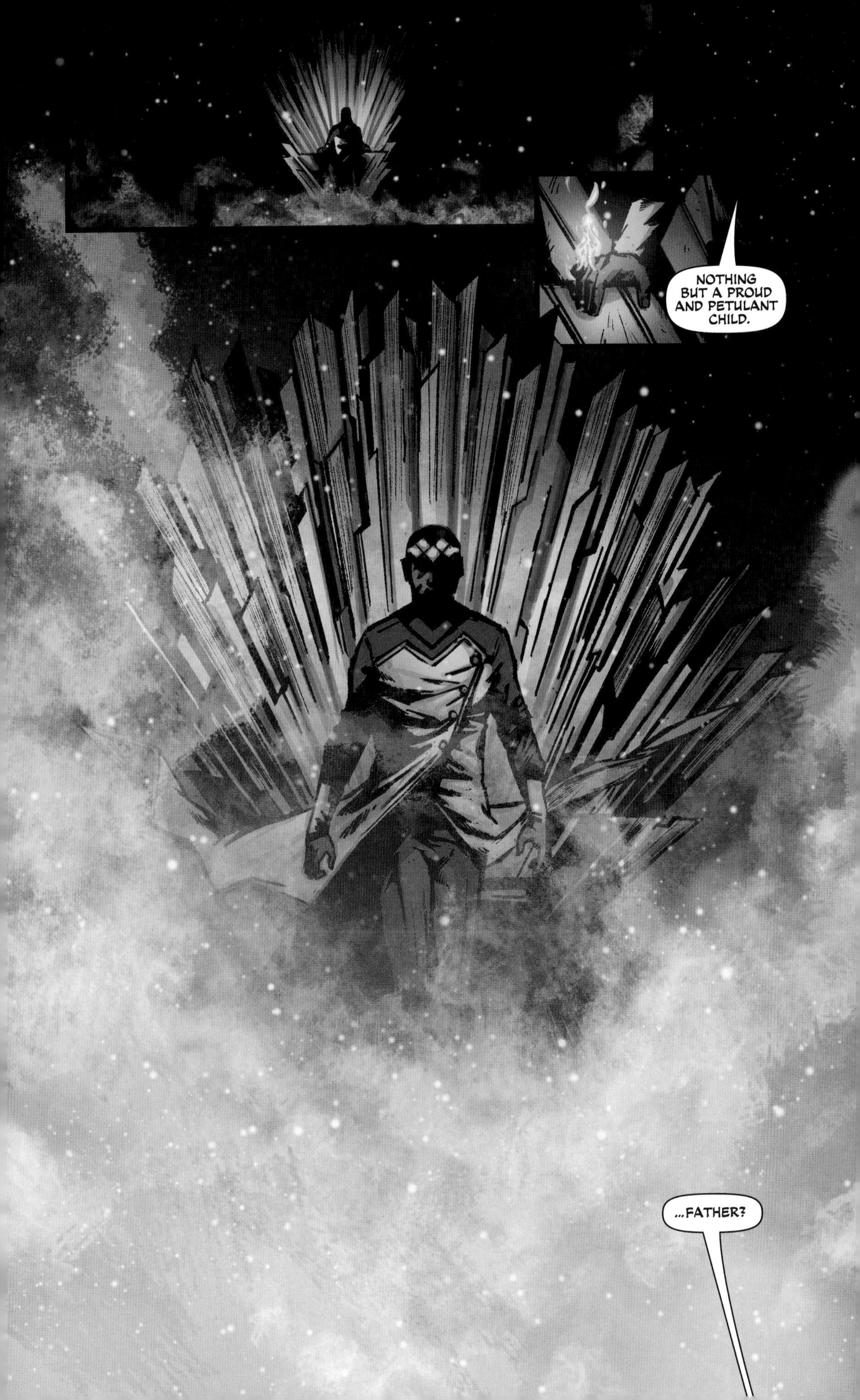
NOTHING BUT A PROUD AND PETULANT CHILD.
...FATHER?

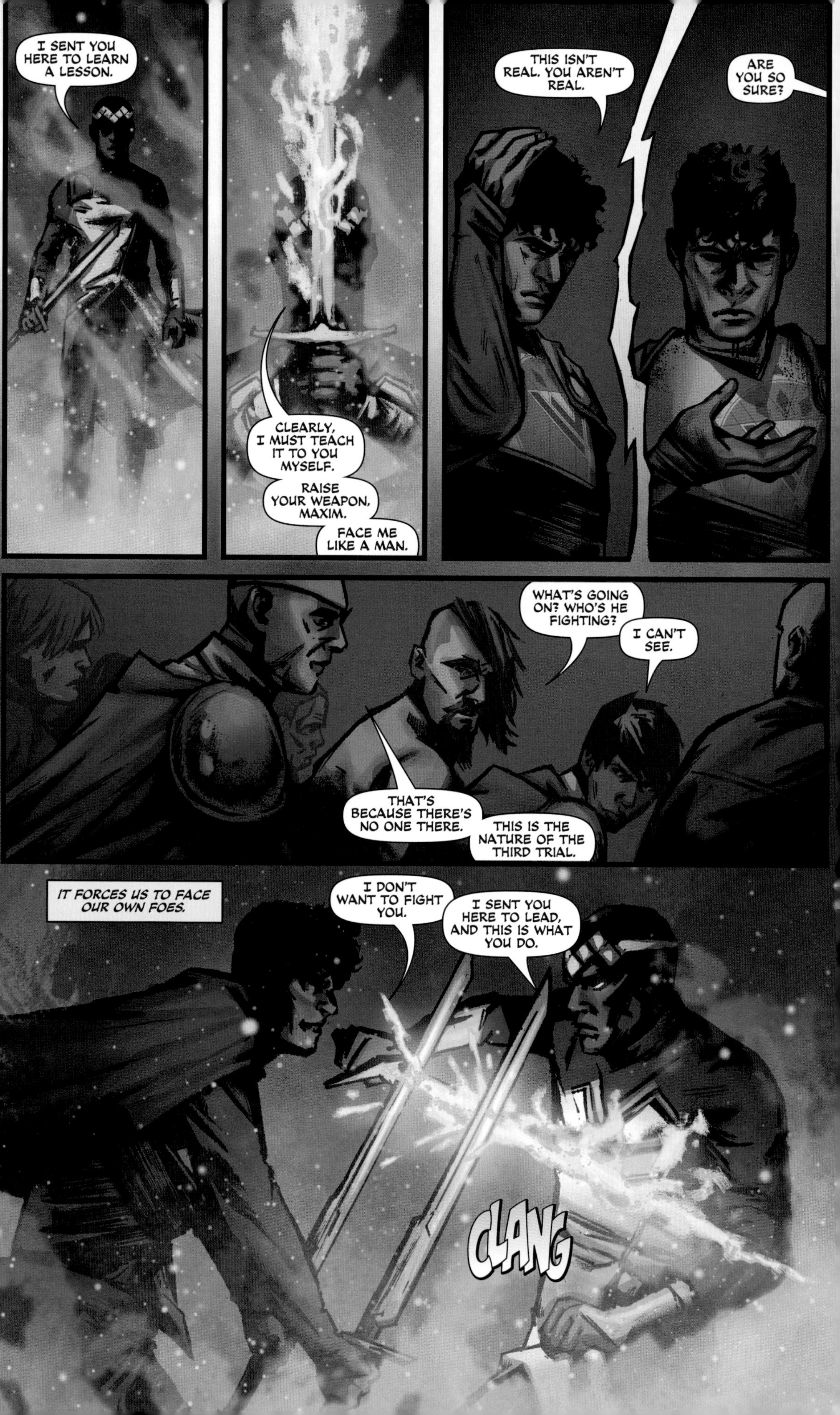
I SENT YOU HERE TO LEARN A LESSON.
CLEARLY, I MUST TEACH IT TO YOU MYSELF.
RAISE YOUR WEAPON, MAXIM.
FACE ME LIKE A MAN.
THIS ISN'T REAL. YOU AREN'T REAL.
ARE YOU SO SURE?
WHAT'S GOING ON? WHO'S HE FIGHTING?
I CAN'T SEE.
THAT'S BECAUSE THERE'S NO ONE THERE.
THIS IS THE NATURE OF THE THIRD TRIAL.
IT FORCES US TO FACE OUR OWN FOES.
I DON'T WANT TO FIGHT YOU.
I SENT YOU HERE TO LEAD, AND THIS IS WHAT YOU DO.
CLANG

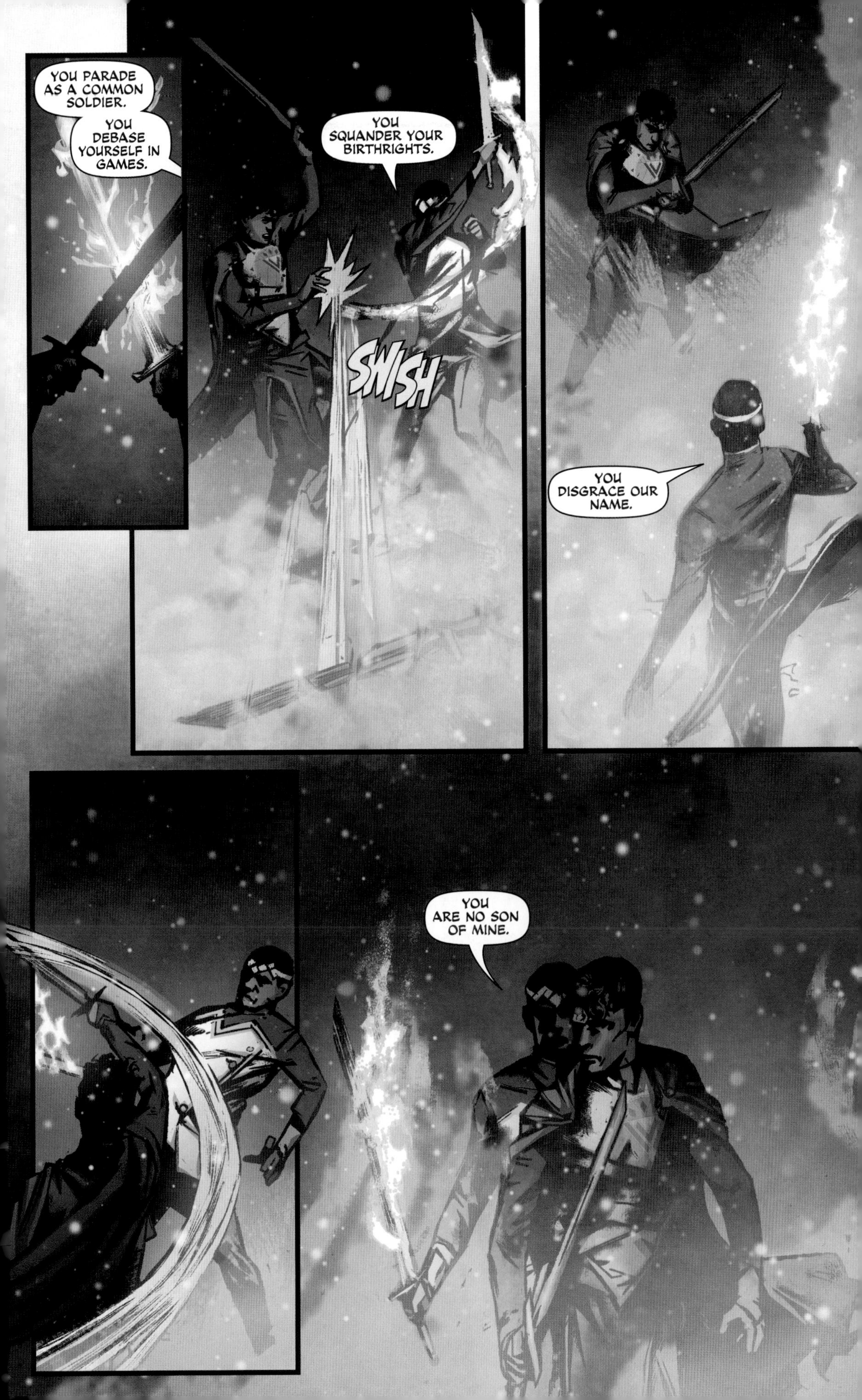
YOU PARADE AS A COMMON SOLDIER.
YOU DEBASE YOURSELF IN GAMES.
YOU SQUANDER YOUR BIRTHRIGHTS.
SWISH
YOU DISGRACE OUR NAME.
YOU ARE NO SON OF MINE.

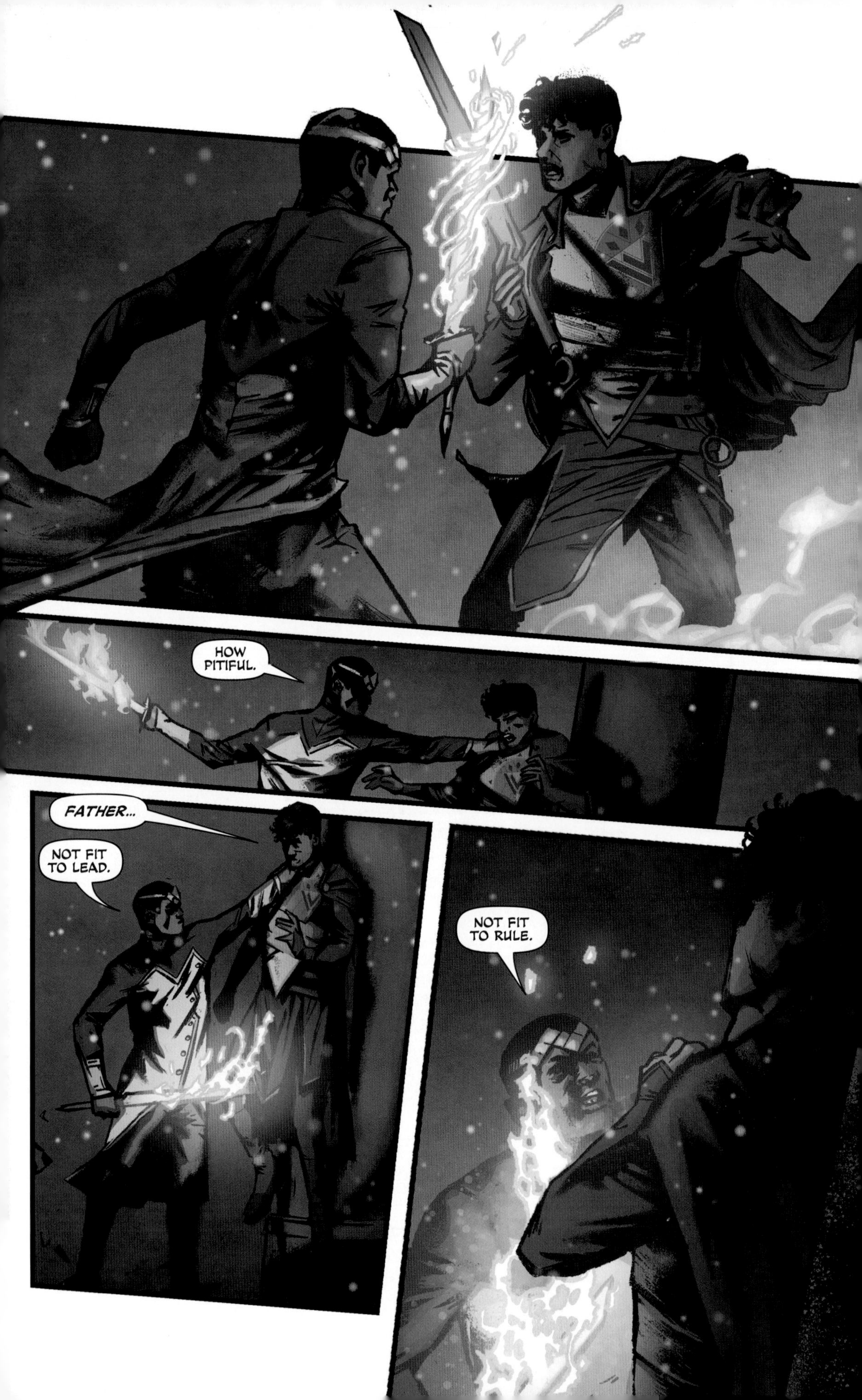
HOW PITIFUL.
FATHER...
NOT FIT TO LEAD.
NOT FIT TO RULE.

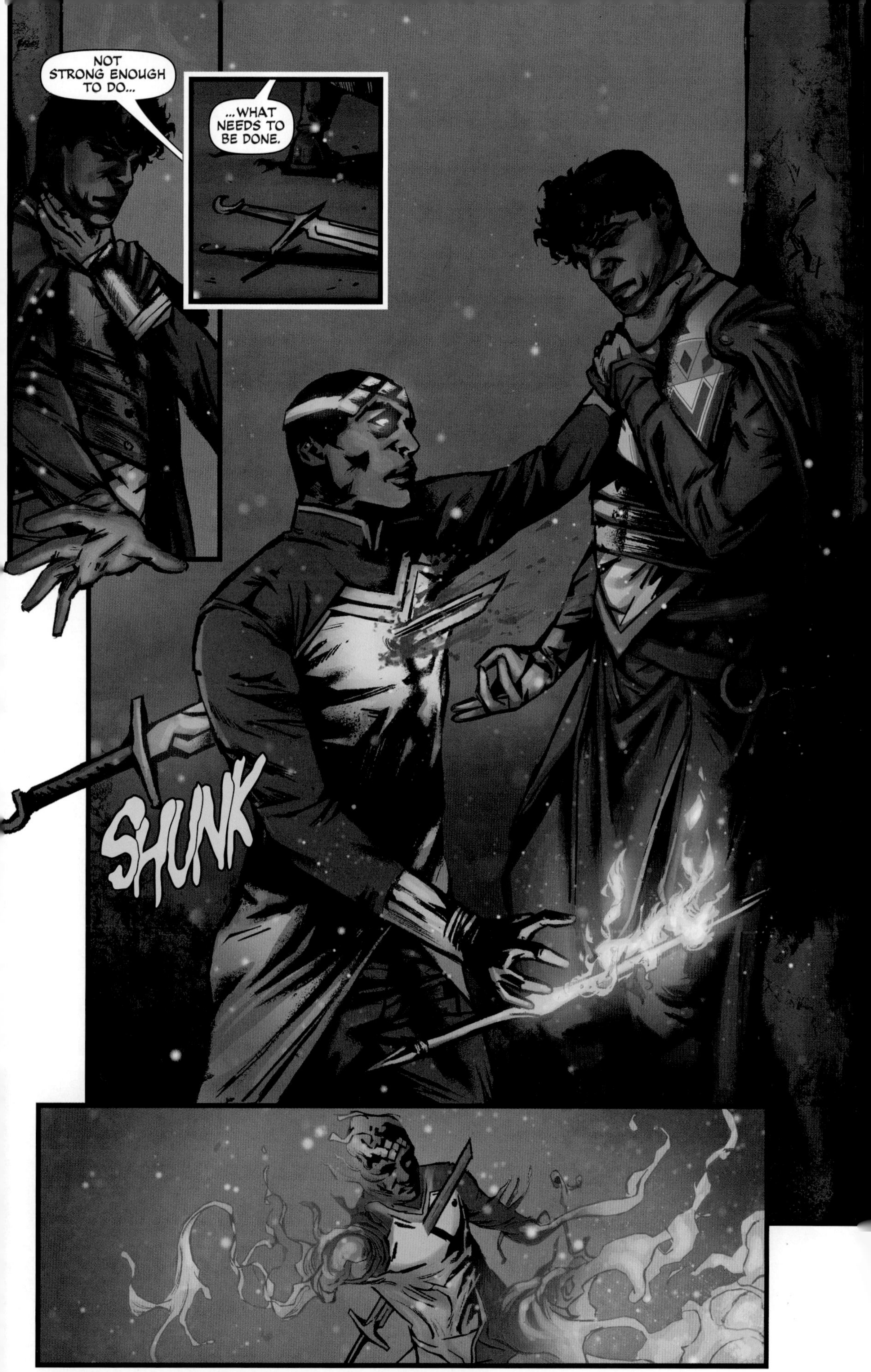
NOT STRONG ENOUGH TO DO...
...WHAT NEEDS TO BE DONE.
SHUNK

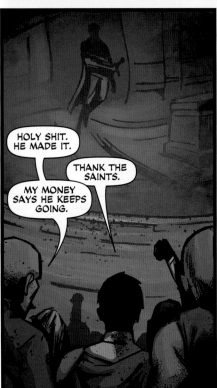

HOLY SHIT.
HE MADE IT.

THANK THE
SAINTS.

MY MONEY
SAYS HE KEEPS
GOING.

YOU BET
ON THE PRINCE'S
DEATH?

OF COURSE
NOT. I BET ON
HIS *PRIDE.*

WHAT IS HE DOING?

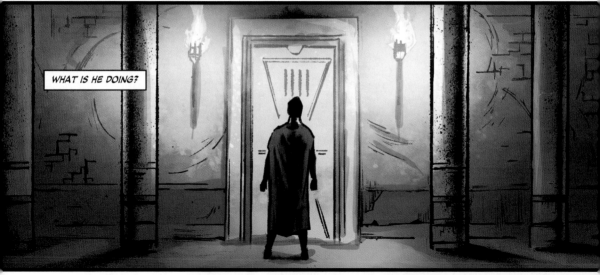

HE'S GOING THROUGH.

NO. NO, HE'S NOT.

YOU FUCKING PROMISED!

THE NIGHT ISN'T JUST ABOUT WINNING.

IT'S ABOUT KNOWING WHEN TO QUIT.

ENOUGH, MAXIM.

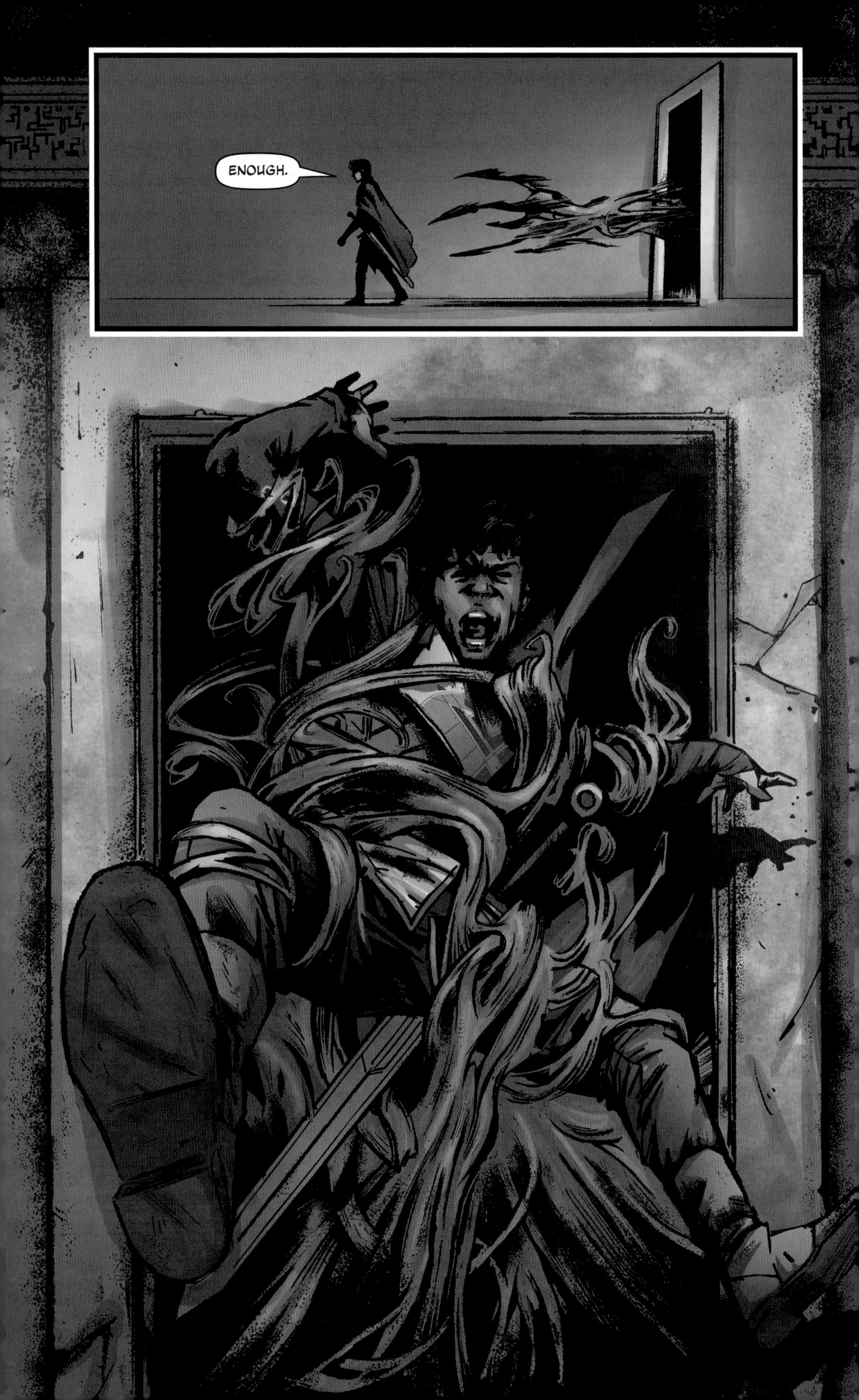
ENOUGH.

#4

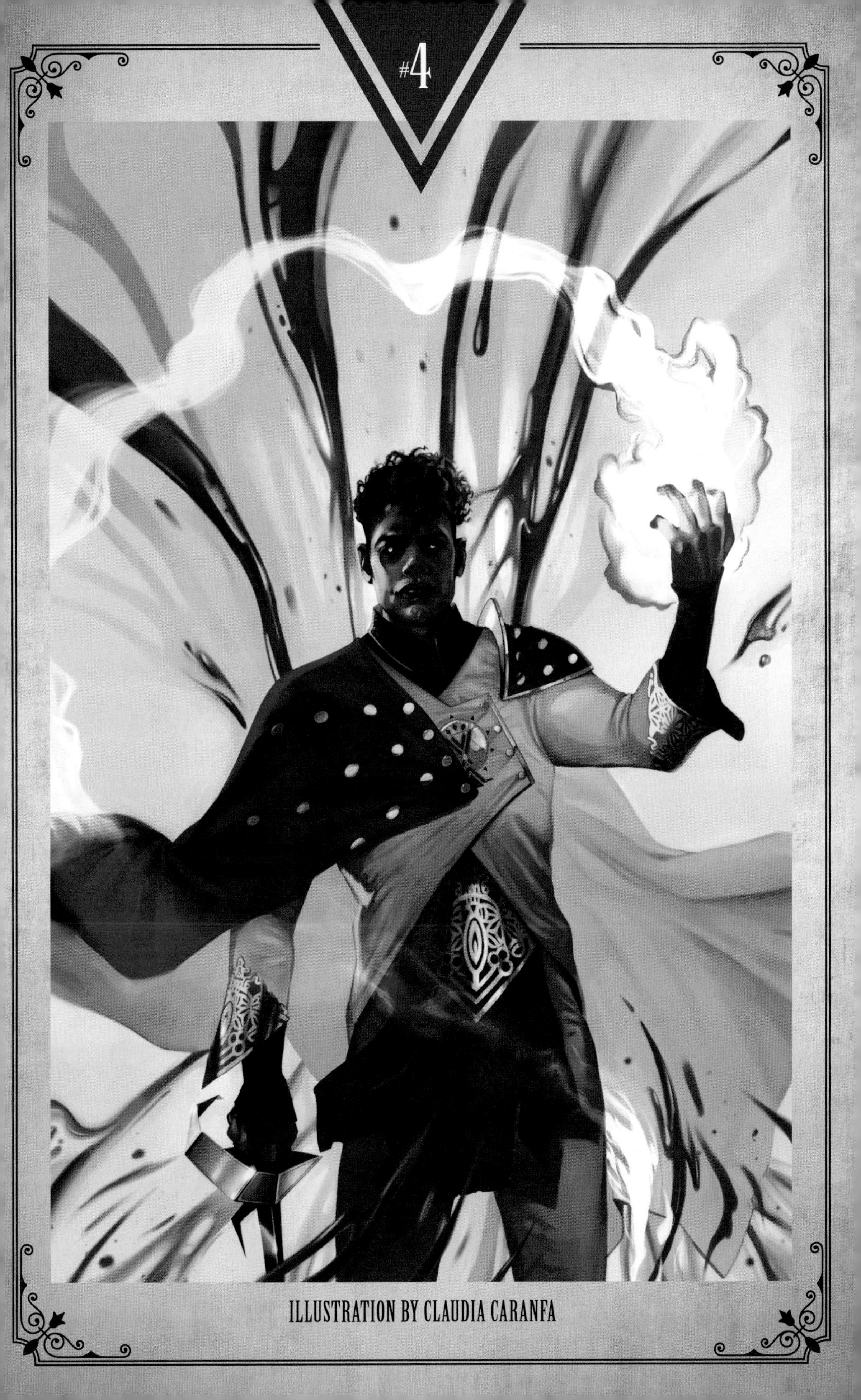

ILLUSTRATION BY CLAUDIA CARANFA

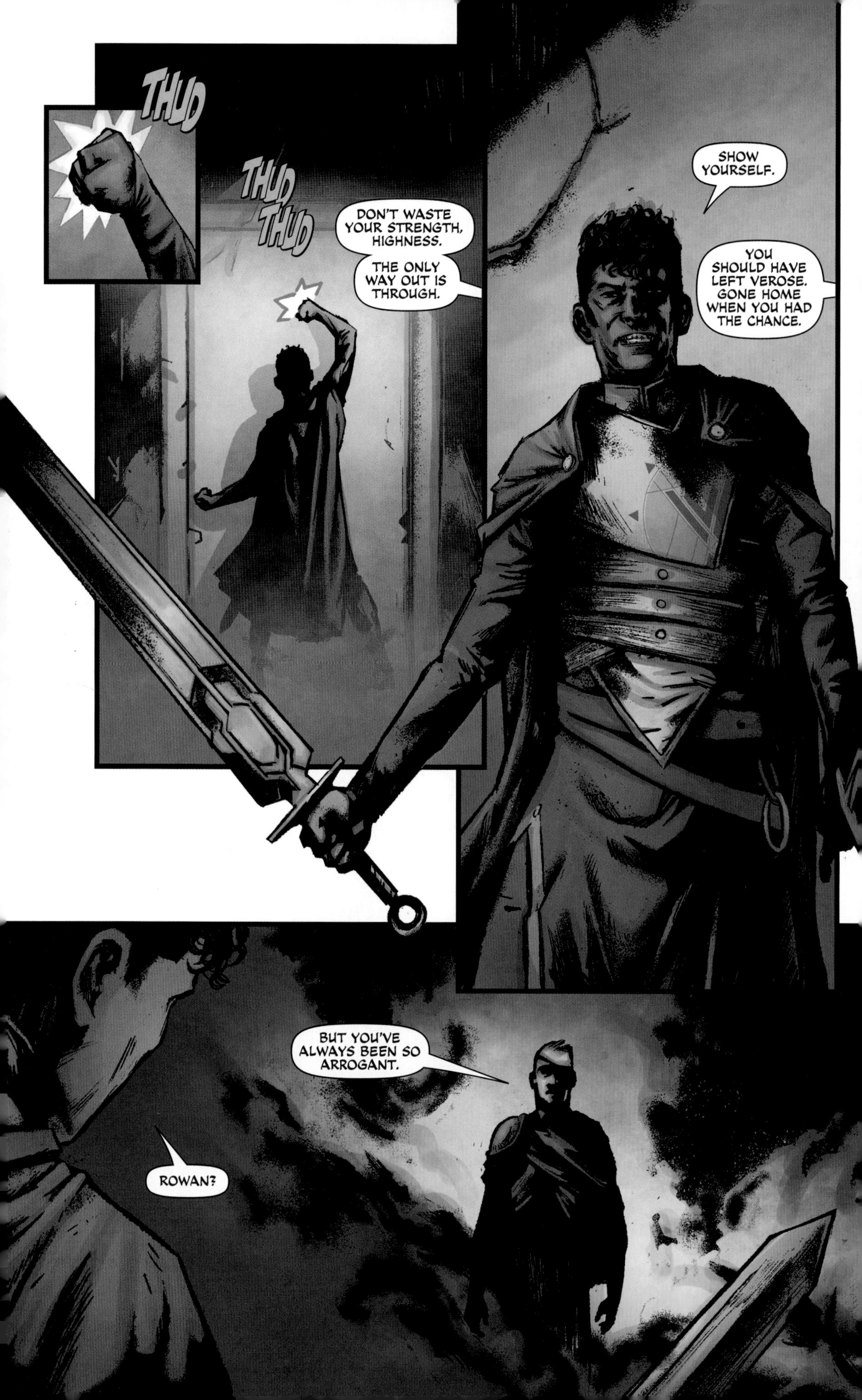
THUD
THUD THUD
DON'T WASTE YOUR STRENGTH, HIGHNESS.
THE ONLY WAY OUT IS THROUGH.
SHOW YOURSELF.
YOU SHOULD HAVE LEFT VEROSE. GONE HOME WHEN YOU HAD THE CHANCE.
BUT YOU'VE ALWAYS BEEN SO ARROGANT.
ROWAN?

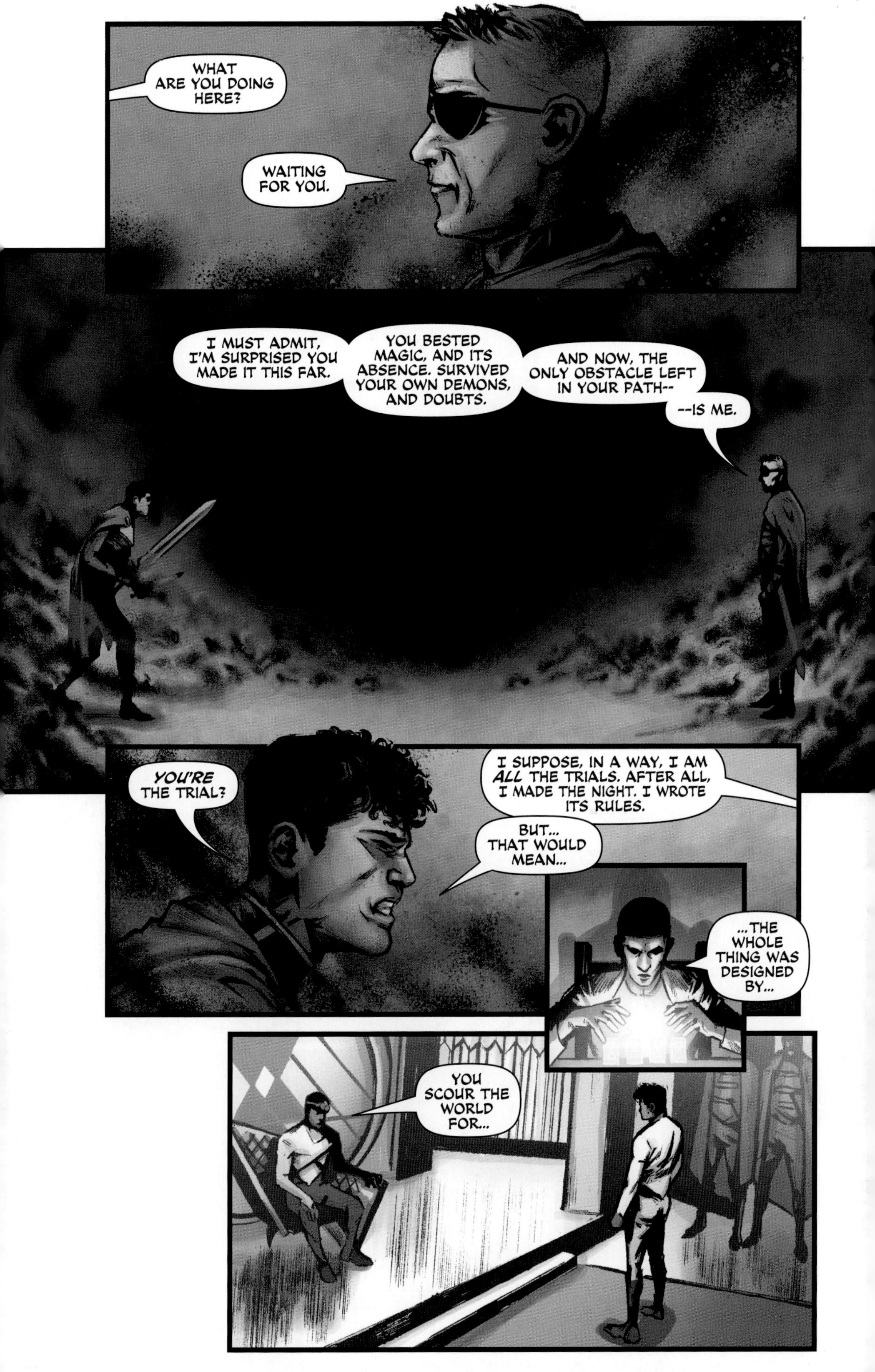
WHAT ARE YOU DOING HERE?
WAITING FOR YOU.
I MUST ADMIT, I'M SURPRISED YOU MADE IT THIS FAR.
YOU BESTED MAGIC, AND ITS ABSENCE. SURVIVED YOUR OWN DEMONS, AND DOUBTS.
AND NOW, THE ONLY OBSTACLE LEFT IN YOUR PATH--
--IS ME.
YOU'RE THE TRIAL?
I SUPPOSE, IN A WAY, I AM *ALL* THE TRIALS. AFTER ALL, I MADE THE NIGHT. I WROTE ITS RULES.
BUT... THAT WOULD MEAN...
...THE WHOLE THING WAS DESIGNED BY...
YOU SCOUR THE WORLD FOR...

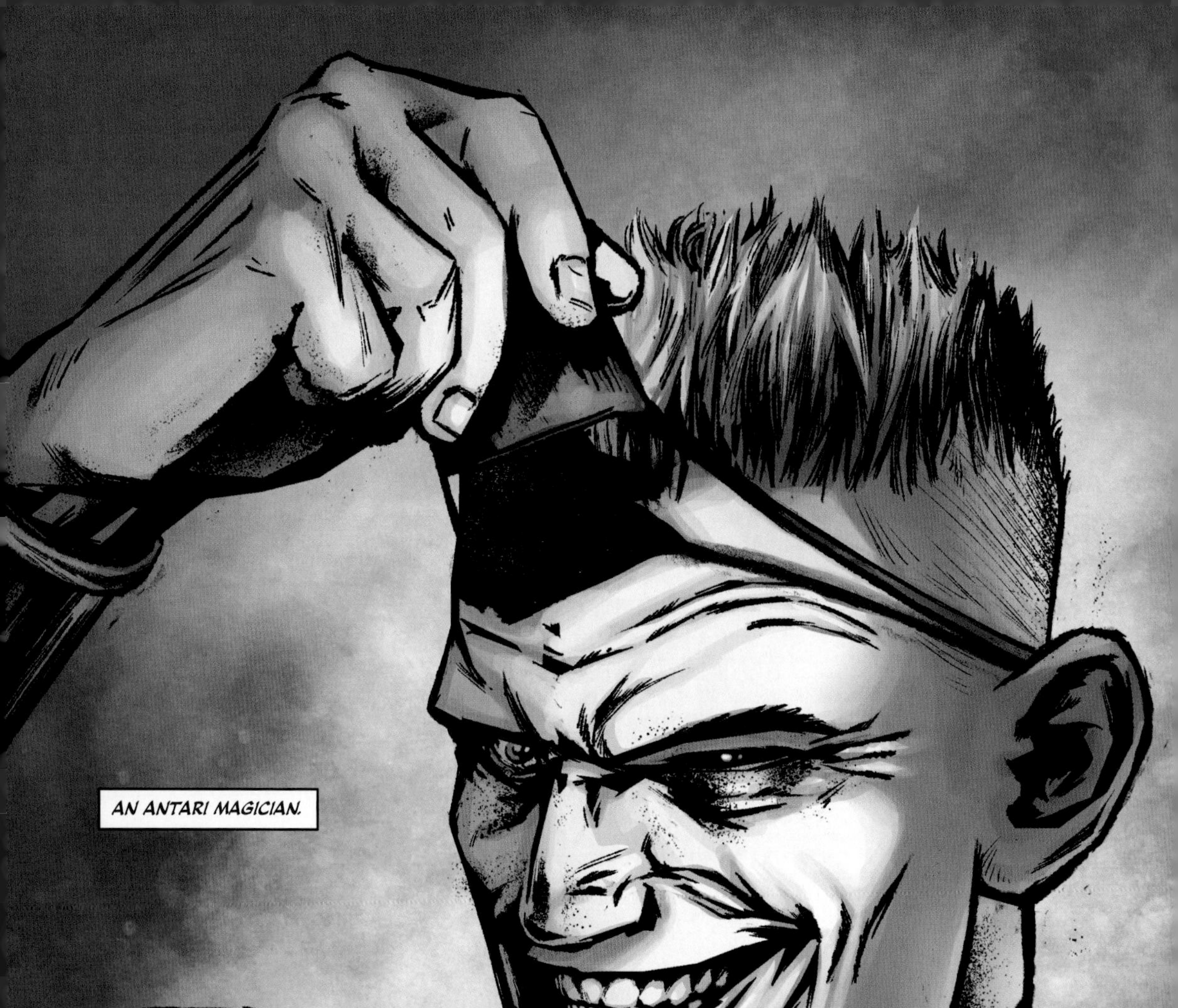
AN ANTARI MAGICIAN.

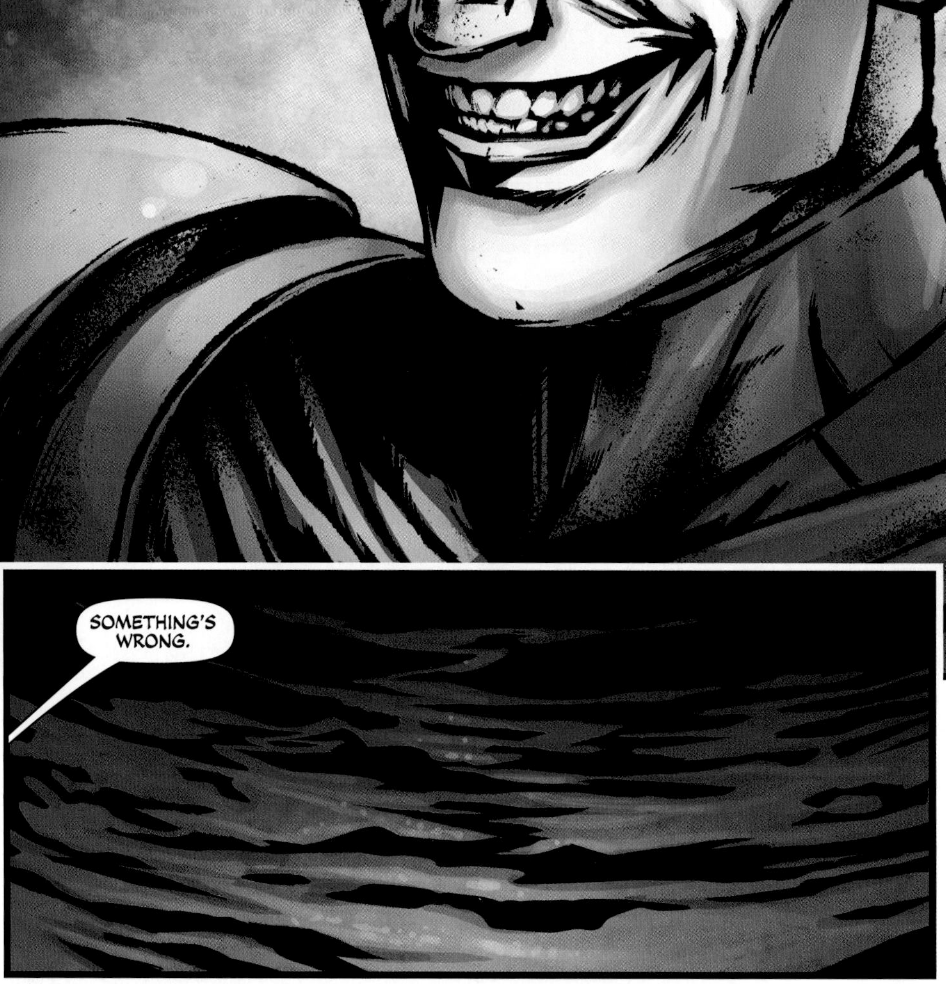
SOMETHING'S WRONG.

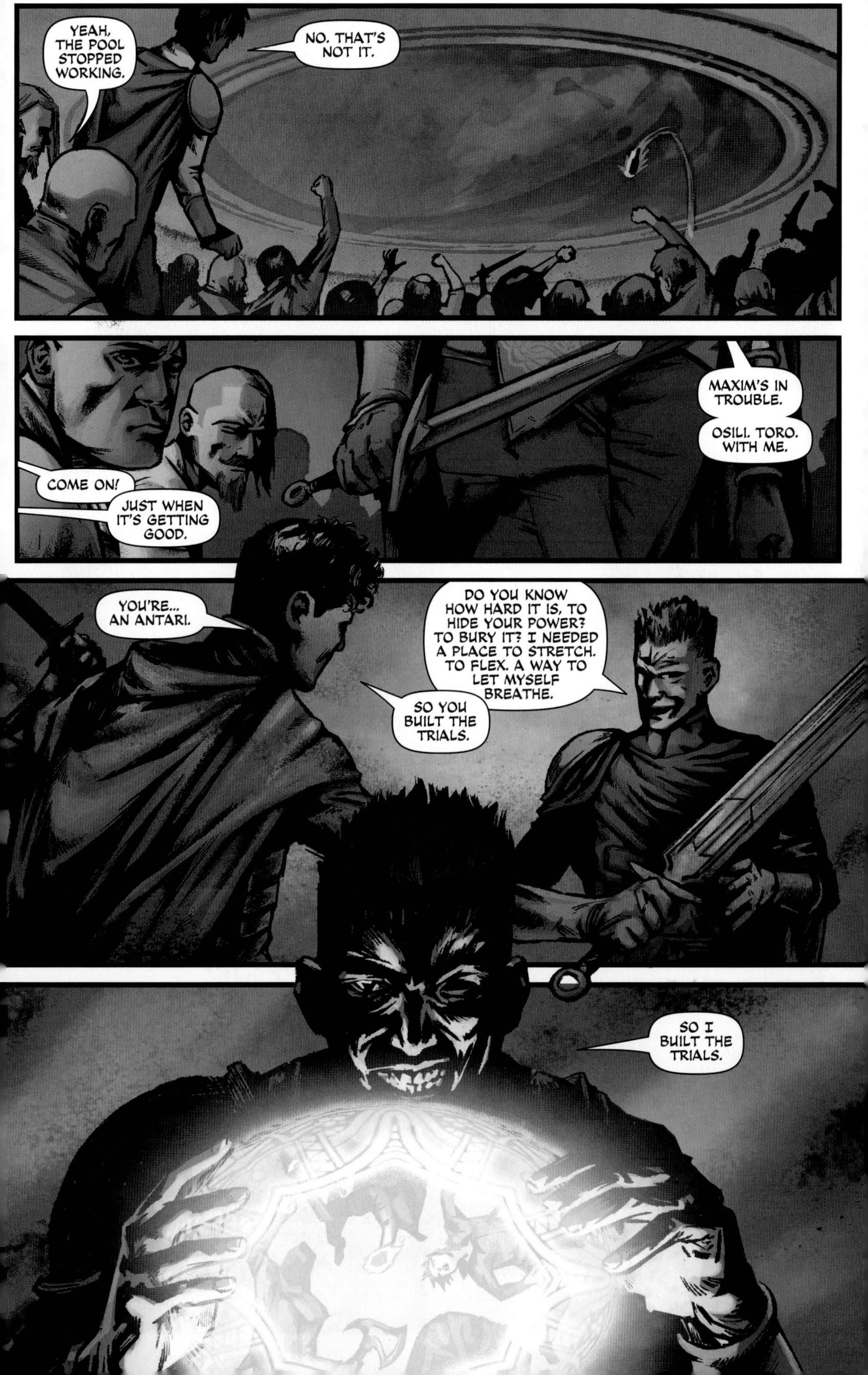

YEAH, THE POOL STOPPED WORKING.
NO. THAT'S NOT IT.
MAXIM'S IN TROUBLE.
OSILI. TORO. WITH ME.
COME ON!
JUST WHEN IT'S GETTING GOOD.
YOU'RE... AN ANTARI.
DO YOU KNOW HOW HARD IT IS, TO HIDE YOUR POWER? TO BURY IT? I NEEDED A PLACE TO STRETCH. TO FLEX. A WAY TO LET MYSELF BREATHE.
SO YOU BUILT THE TRIALS.
SO I BUILT THE TRIALS.

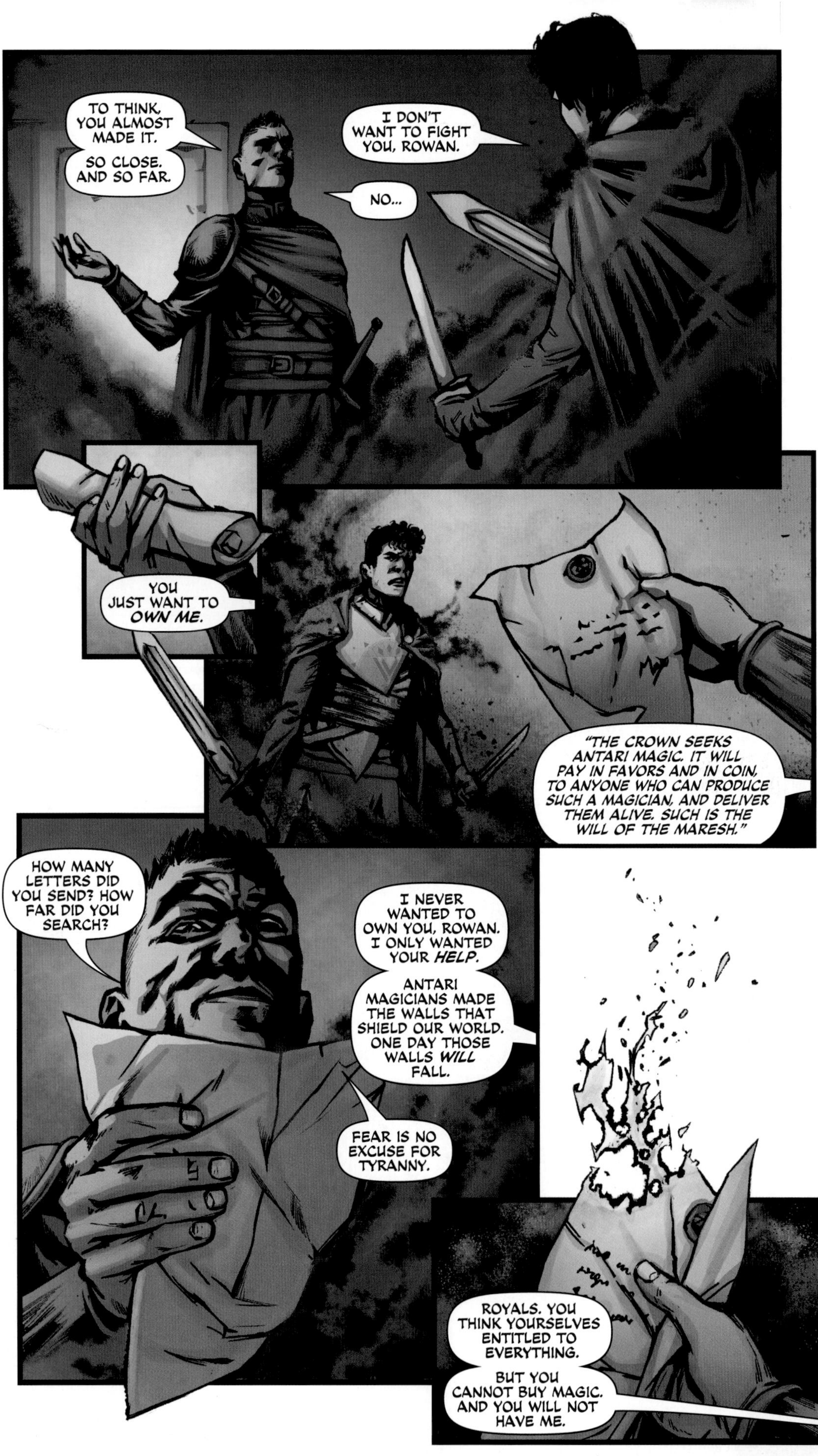

TO THINK, YOU ALMOST MADE IT.
SO CLOSE. AND SO FAR.
I DON'T WANT TO FIGHT YOU, ROWAN.
NO...
YOU JUST WANT TO *OWN ME.*
"THE CROWN SEEKS ANTARI MAGIC. IT WILL PAY IN FAVORS AND IN COIN, TO ANYONE WHO CAN PRODUCE SUCH A MAGICIAN, AND DELIVER THEM ALIVE. SUCH IS THE WILL OF THE MARESH."
HOW MANY LETTERS DID YOU SEND? HOW FAR DID YOU SEARCH?
I NEVER WANTED TO OWN YOU, ROWAN. I ONLY WANTED YOUR *HELP*.
ANTARI MAGICIANS MADE THE WALLS THAT SHIELD OUR WORLD. ONE DAY THOSE WALLS *WILL* FALL.
FEAR IS NO EXCUSE FOR TYRANNY.
ROYALS. YOU THINK YOURSELVES ENTITLED TO EVERYTHING.
BUT YOU CANNOT BUY MAGIC. AND YOU WILL NOT HAVE ME.

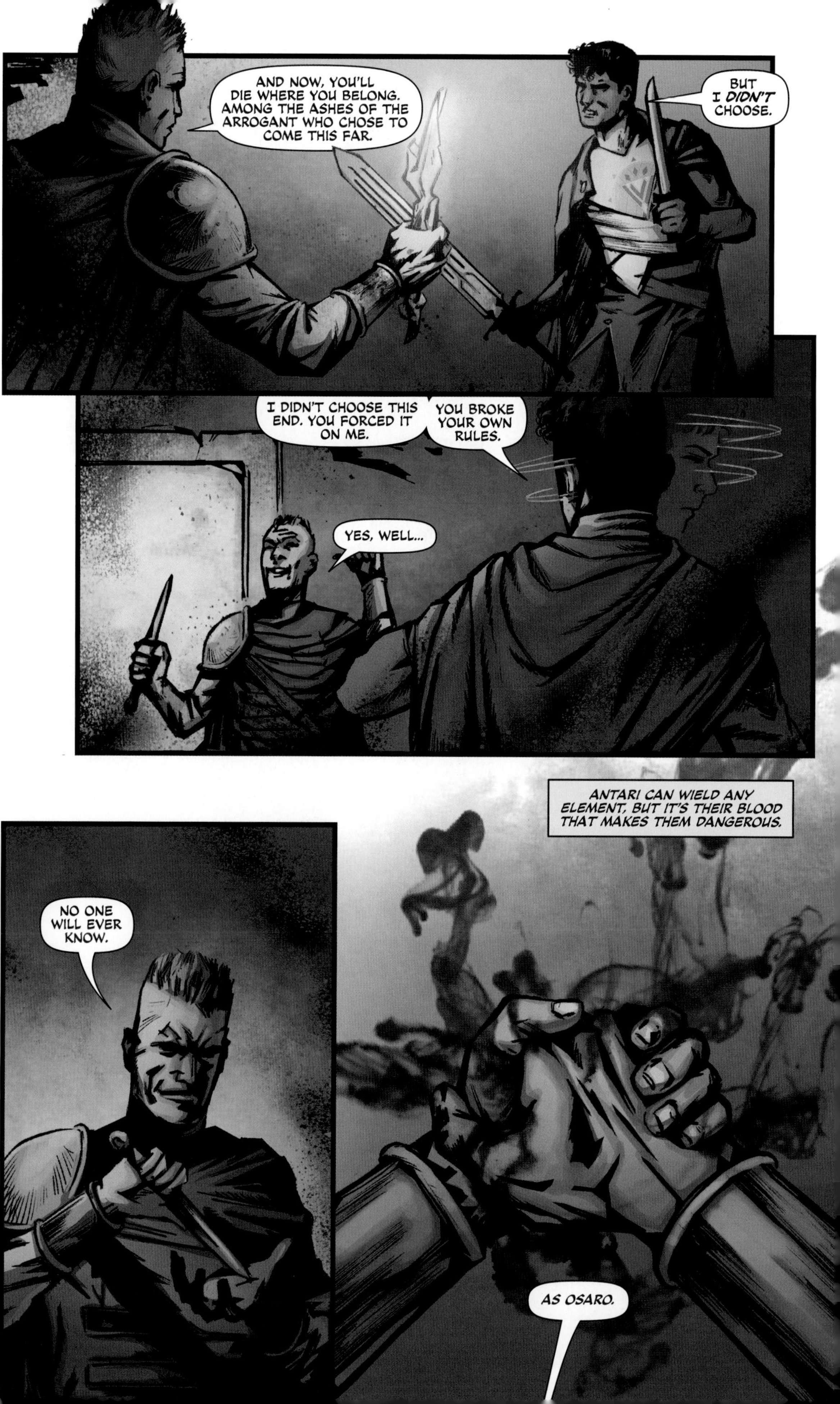
AND NOW, YOU'LL DIE WHERE YOU BELONG. AMONG THE ASHES OF THE ARROGANT WHO CHOSE TO COME THIS FAR.
BUT I *DIDN'T* CHOOSE.
I DIDN'T CHOOSE THIS END. YOU FORCED IT ON ME.
YOU BROKE YOUR OWN RULES.
YES, WELL...
NO ONE WILL EVER KNOW.
ANTARI CAN WIELD ANY ELEMENT, BUT IT'S THEIR BLOOD THAT MAKES THEM DANGEROUS.
AS OSARO.

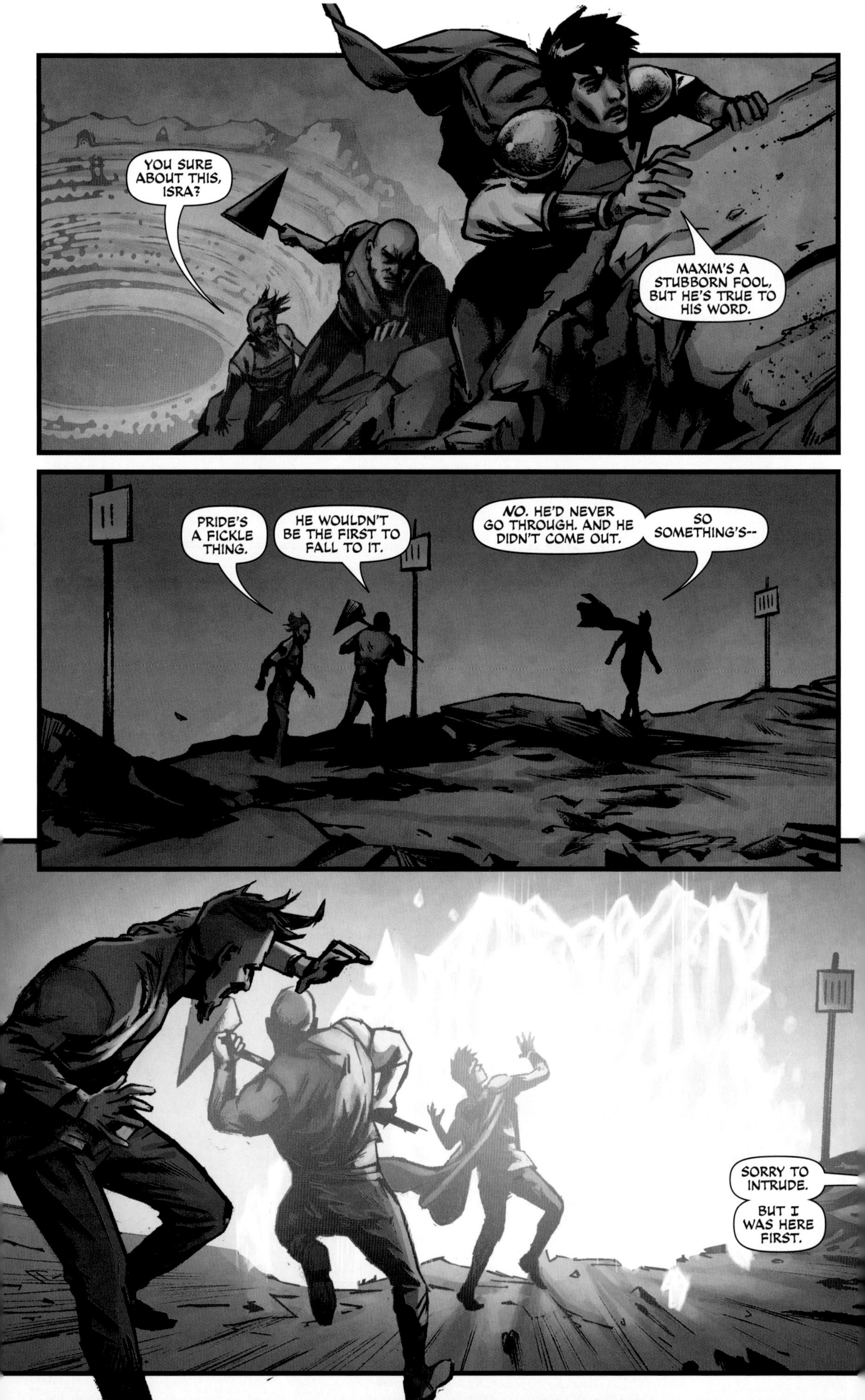
YOU SURE ABOUT THIS, ISRA?
MAXIM'S A STUBBORN FOOL, BUT HE'S TRUE TO HIS WORD.
PRIDE'S A FICKLE THING.
HE WOULDN'T BE THE FIRST TO FALL TO IT.
NO. HE'D NEVER GO THROUGH. AND HE DIDN'T COME OUT.
SO SOMETHING'S--
SORRY TO INTRUDE.
BUT I WAS HERE FIRST.

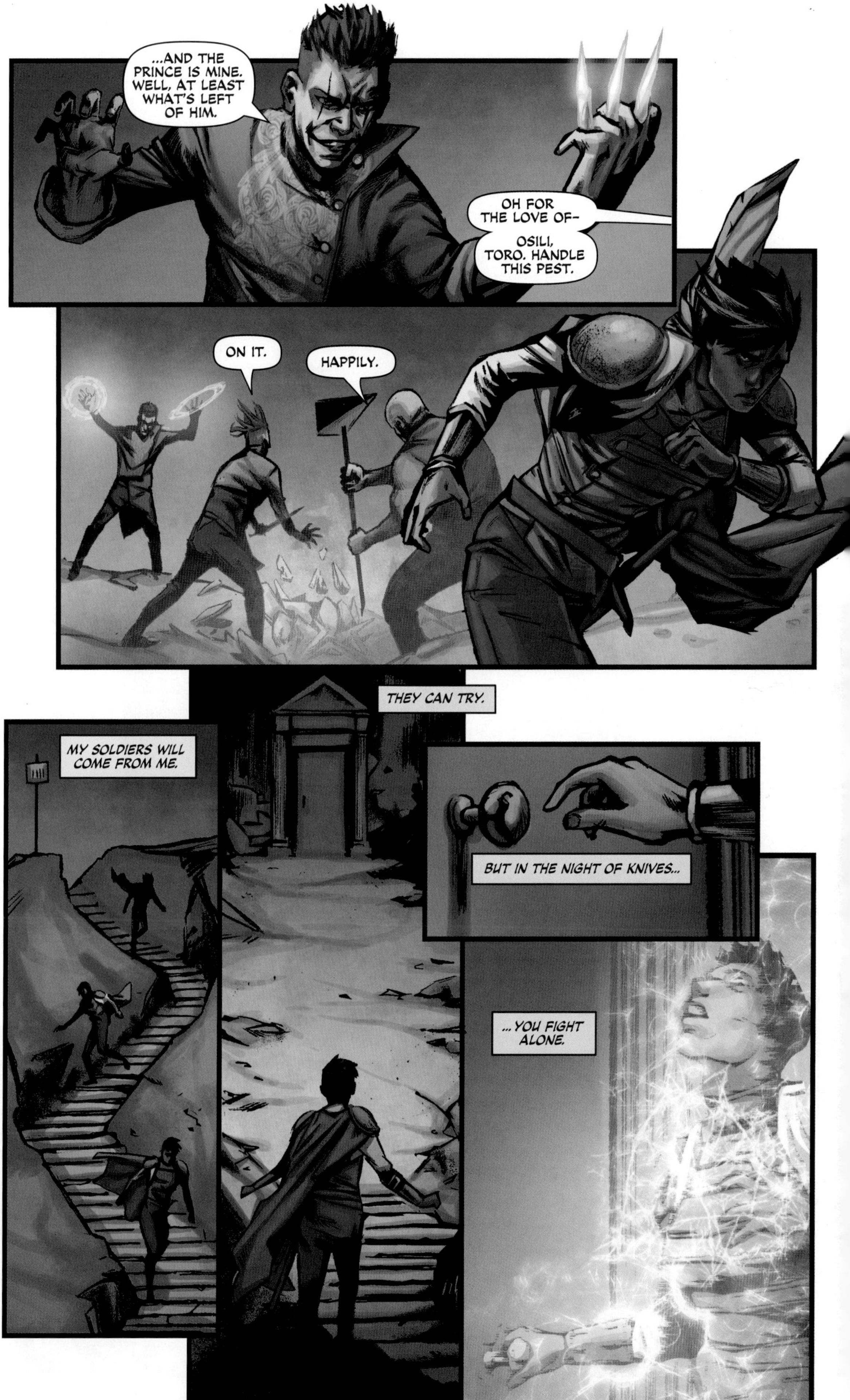
...AND THE PRINCE IS MINE. WELL, AT LEAST WHAT'S LEFT OF HIM.
OH FOR THE LOVE OF-
OSILI, TORO. HANDLE THIS PEST.
ON IT.
HAPPILY.
THEY CAN TRY.
MY SOLDIERS WILL COME FROM ME.
BUT IN THE NIGHT OF KNIVES...
...YOU FIGHT ALONE.

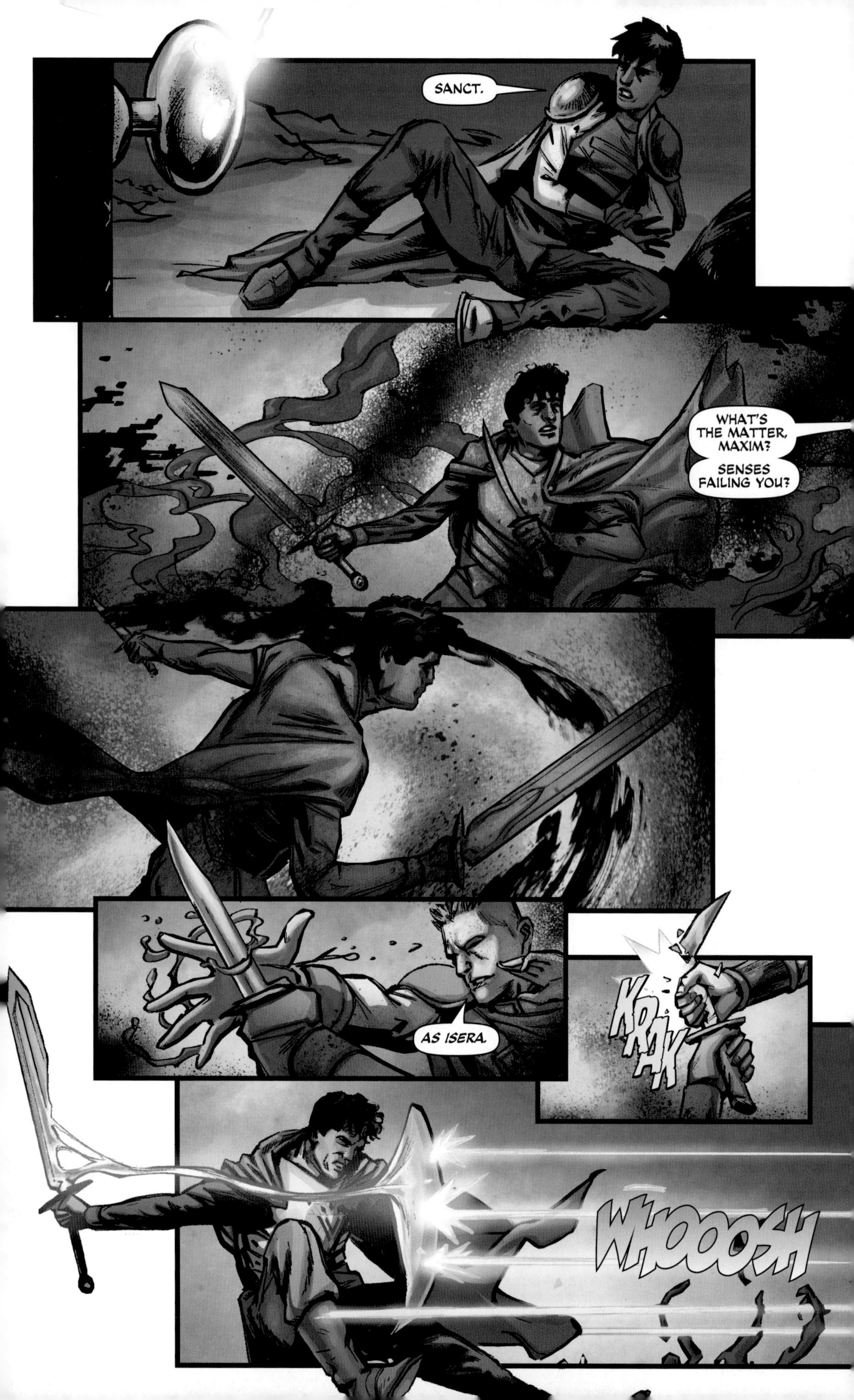
SANCT.
WHAT'S THE MATTER, MAXIM?
SENSES FAILING YOU?
AS ISERA.
KRAK
WHOOOSH

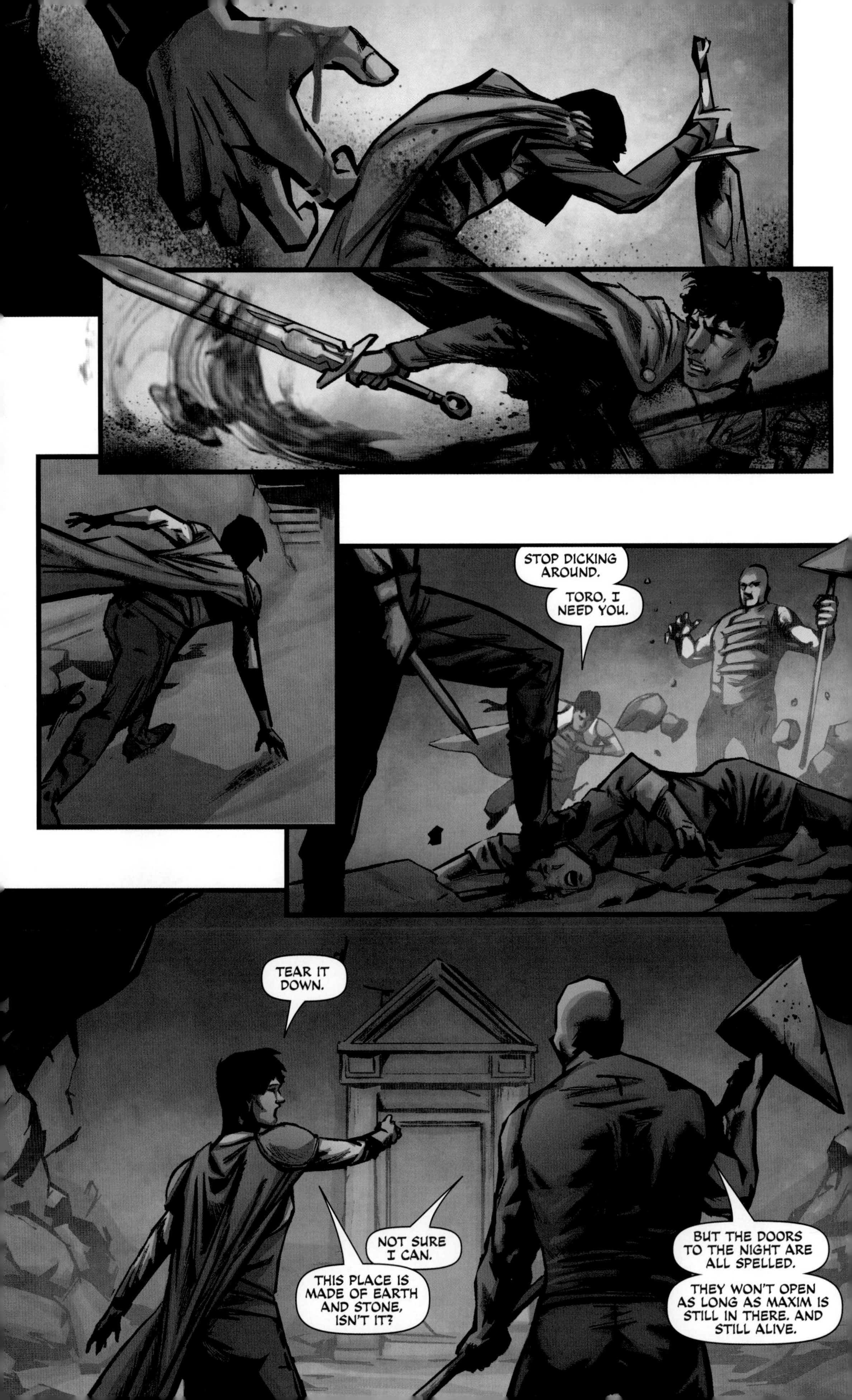
STOP DICKING AROUND.
TORO, I NEED YOU.
TEAR IT DOWN.
NOT SURE I CAN.
THIS PLACE IS MADE OF EARTH AND STONE, ISN'T IT?
BUT THE DOORS TO THE NIGHT ARE ALL SPELLED.
THEY WON'T OPEN AS LONG AS MAXIM IS STILL IN THERE. AND STILL ALIVE.

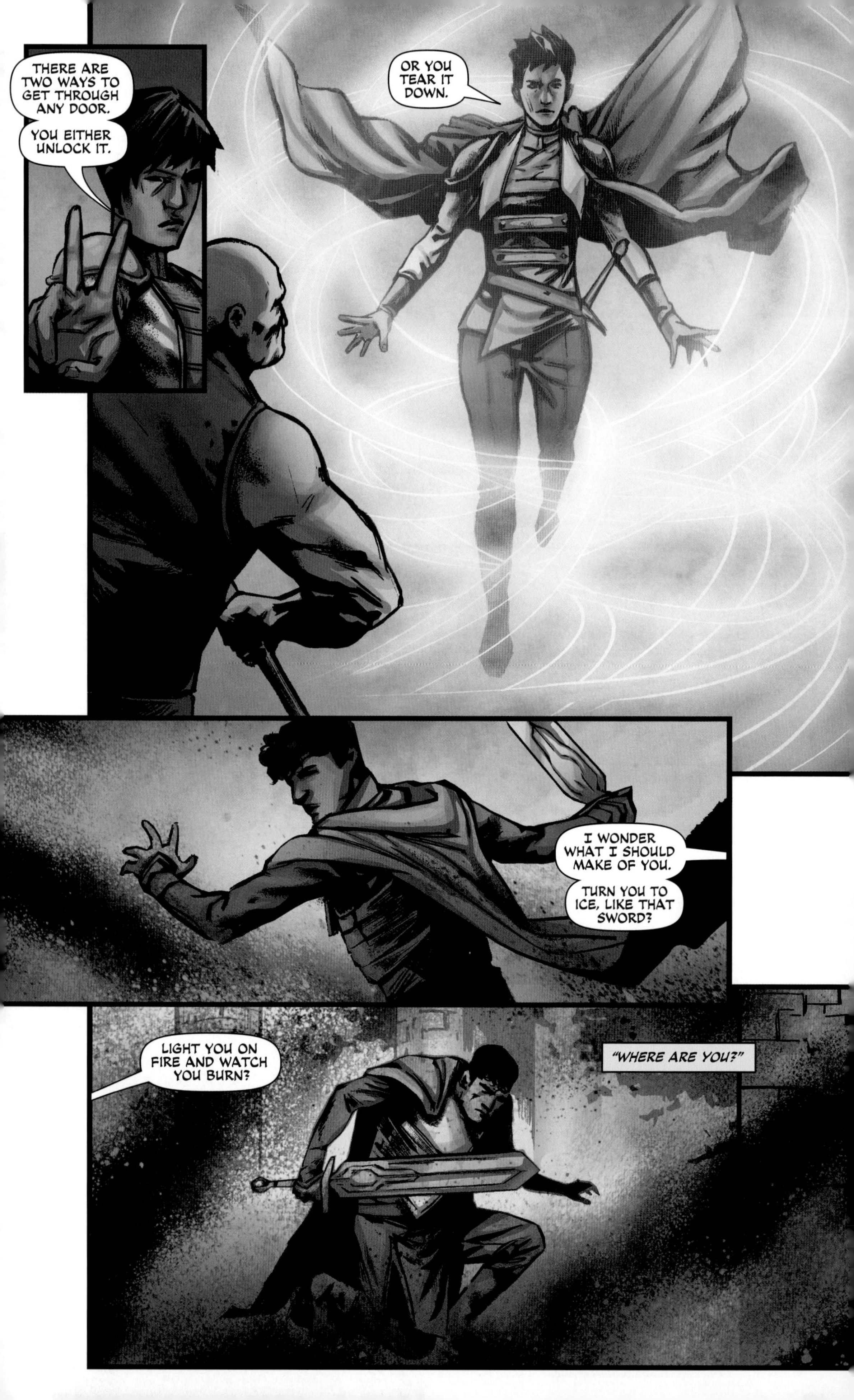
THERE ARE TWO WAYS TO GET THROUGH ANY DOOR.
YOU EITHER UNLOCK IT.
OR YOU TEAR IT DOWN.
I WONDER WHAT I SHOULD MAKE OF YOU.
TURN YOU TO ICE, LIKE THAT SWORD?
LIGHT YOU ON FIRE AND WATCH YOU BURN?
"WHERE ARE YOU?"

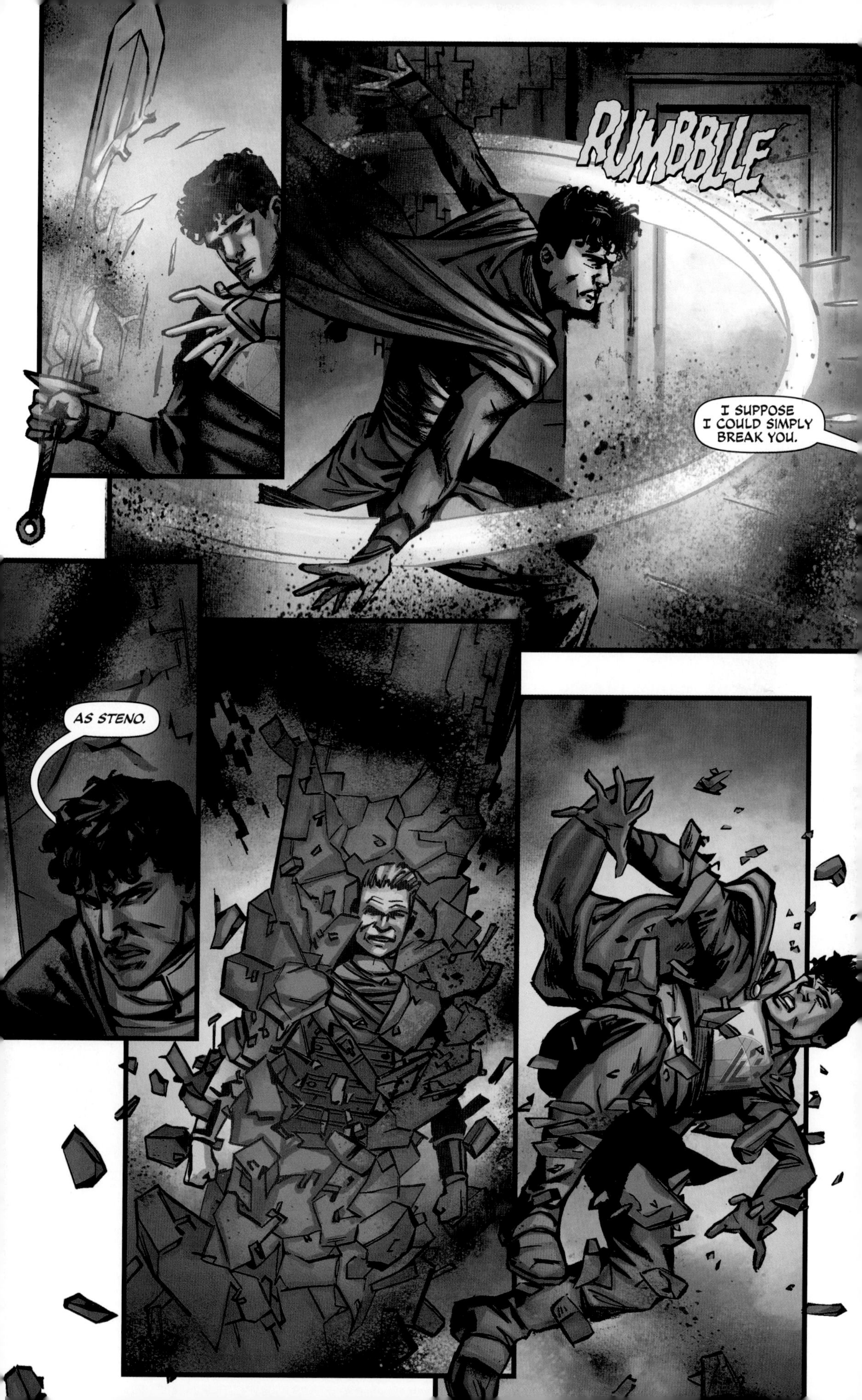
RUMBBLLE
I SUPPOSE I COULD SIMPLY BREAK YOU.
AS STENO.

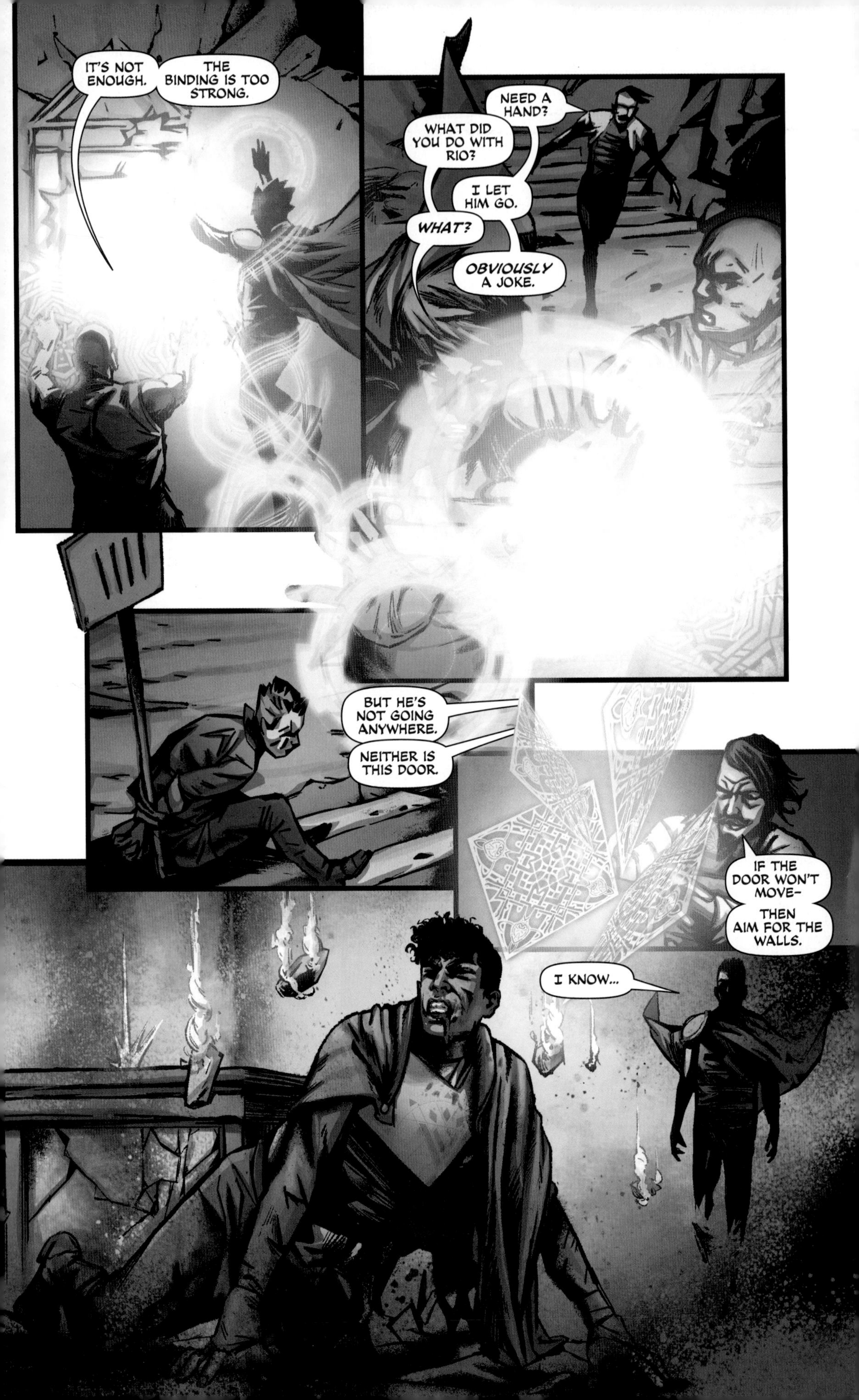
IT'S NOT ENOUGH.
THE BINDING IS TOO STRONG.
NEED A HAND?
WHAT DID YOU DO WITH RIO?
I LET HIM GO.
WHAT?
OBVIOUSLY A JOKE.
BUT HE'S NOT GOING ANYWHERE.
NEITHER IS THIS DOOR.
IF THE DOOR WON'T MOVE–
THEN AIM FOR THE WALLS.
I KNOW...

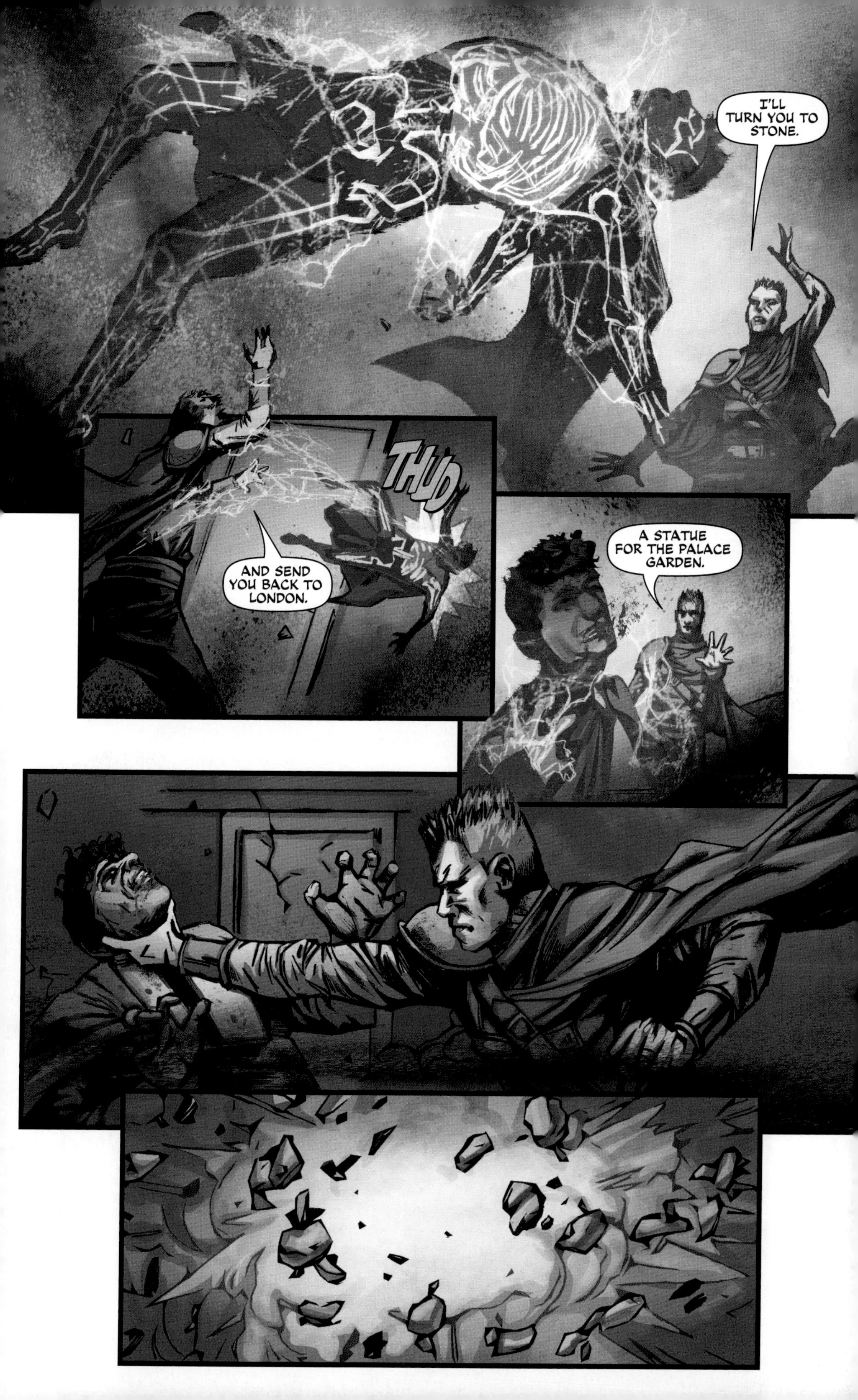

I'LL TURN YOU TO STONE.
THUD
AND SEND YOU BACK TO LONDON.
A STATUE FOR THE PALACE GARDEN.

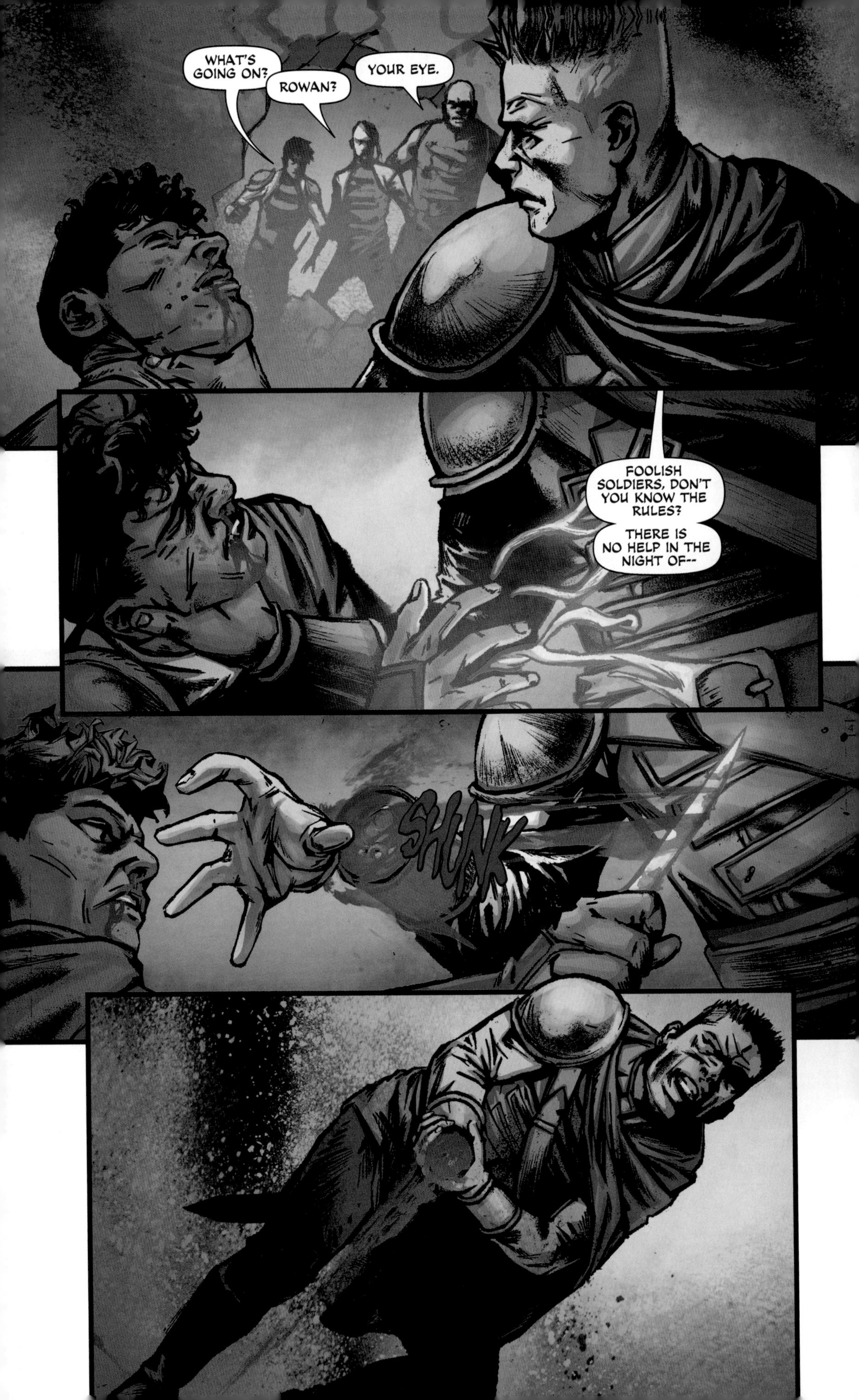
WHAT'S GOING ON?
ROWAN?
YOUR EYE.
FOOLISH SOLDIERS, DON'T YOU KNOW THE RULES?
THERE IS NO HELP IN THE NIGHT OF--
SHUNK

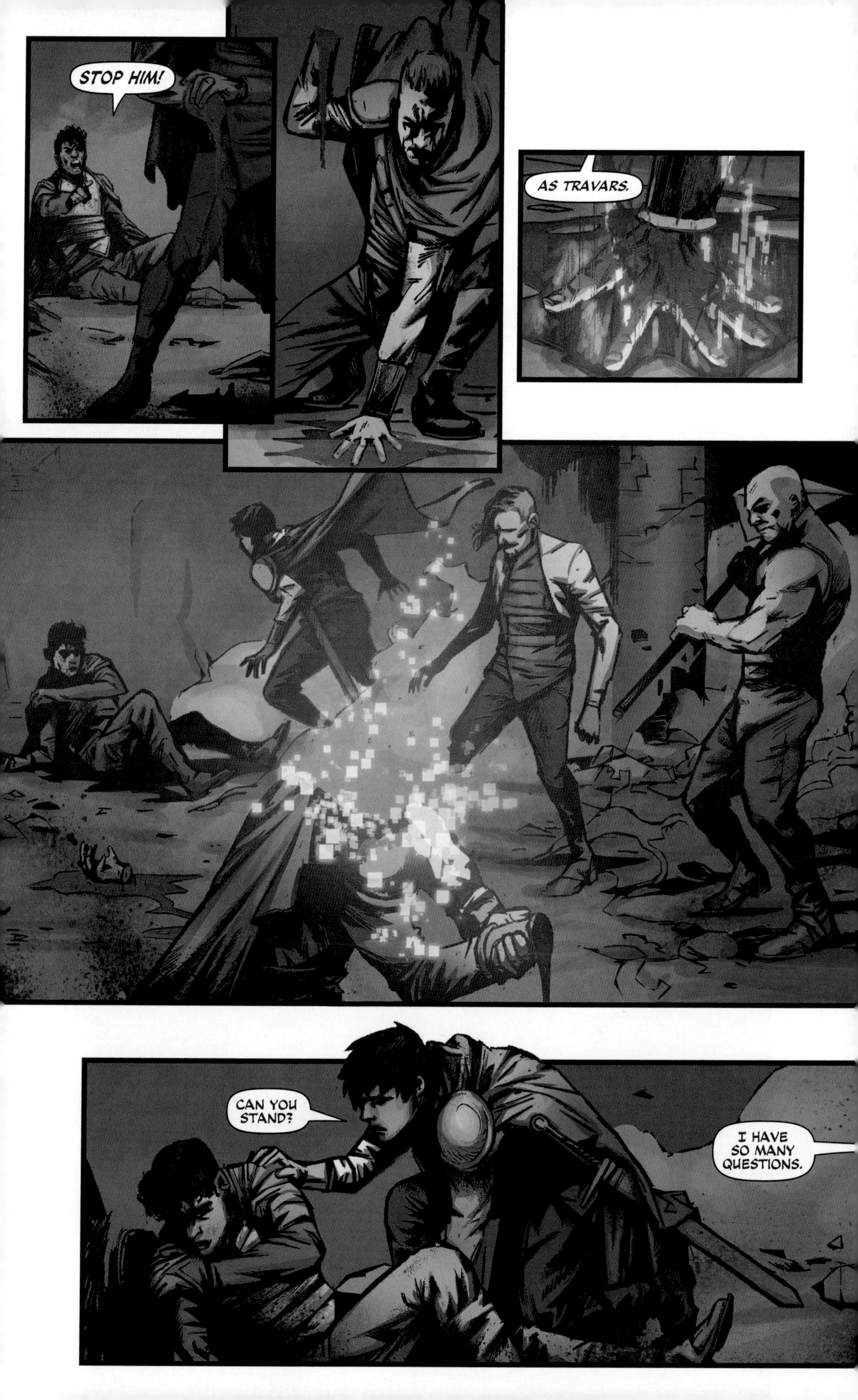
STOP HIM!
AS TRAVARS.
CAN YOU STAND?
I HAVE SO MANY QUESTIONS.

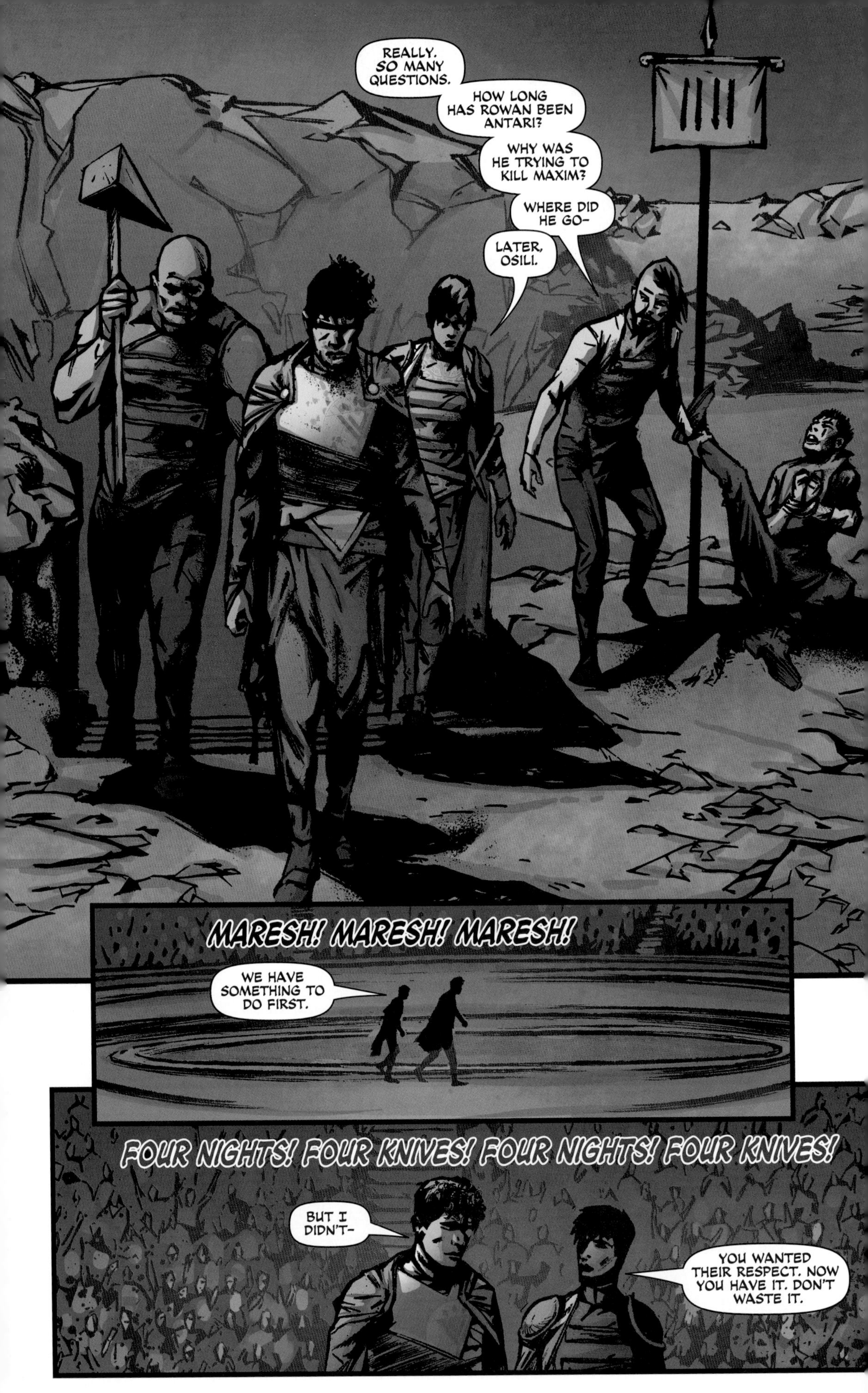

REALLY. SO MANY QUESTIONS.
HOW LONG HAS ROWAN BEEN ANTARI?
WHY WAS HE TRYING TO KILL MAXIM?
WHERE DID HE GO-
LATER, OSILI.
MARESH! MARESH! MARESH!
WE HAVE SOMETHING TO DO FIRST.
FOUR NIGHTS! FOUR KNIVES! FOUR NIGHTS! FOUR KNIVES!
BUT I DIDN'T-
YOU WANTED THEIR RESPECT. NOW YOU HAVE IT. DON'T WASTE IT.

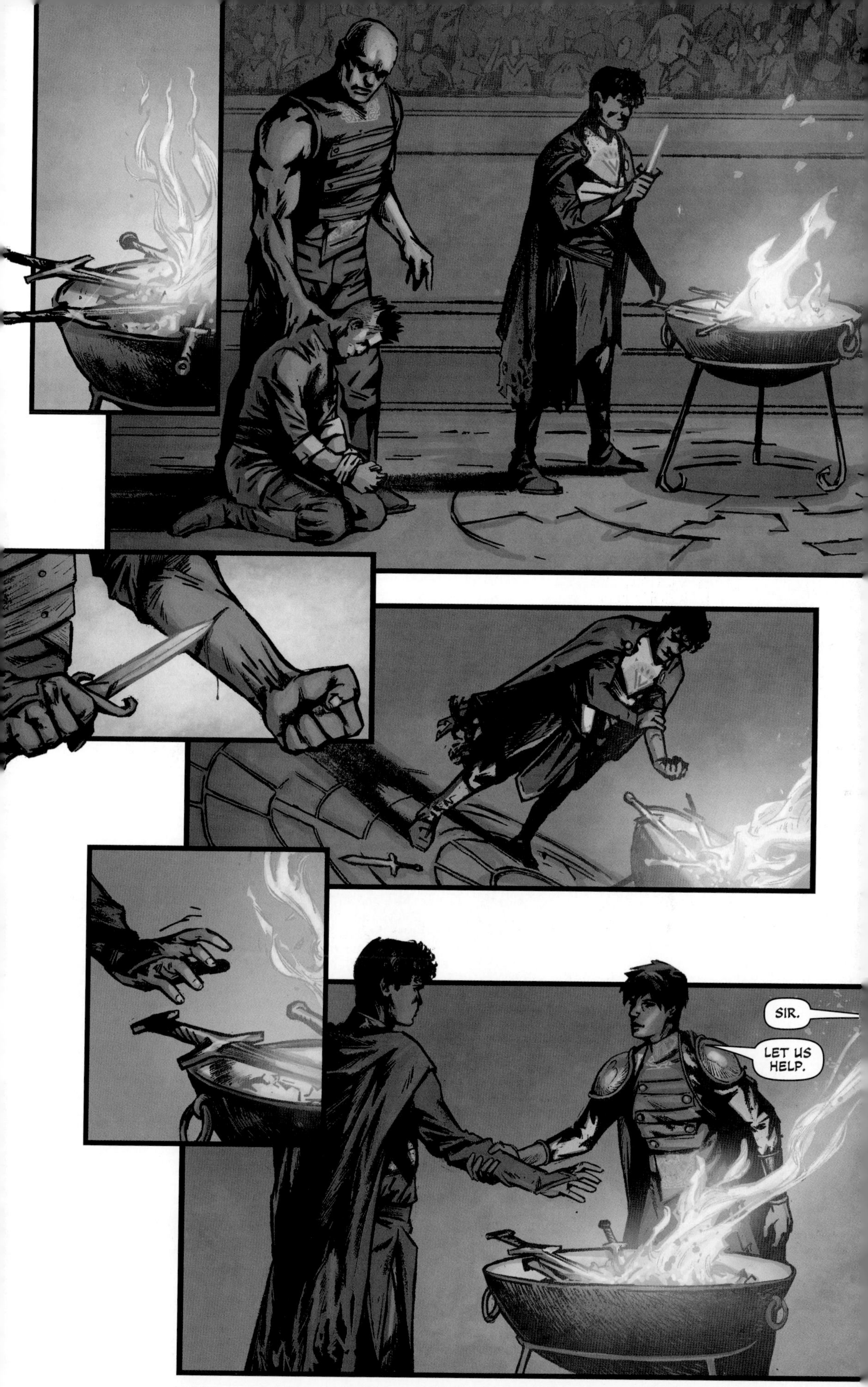
SIR.
LET US HELP.

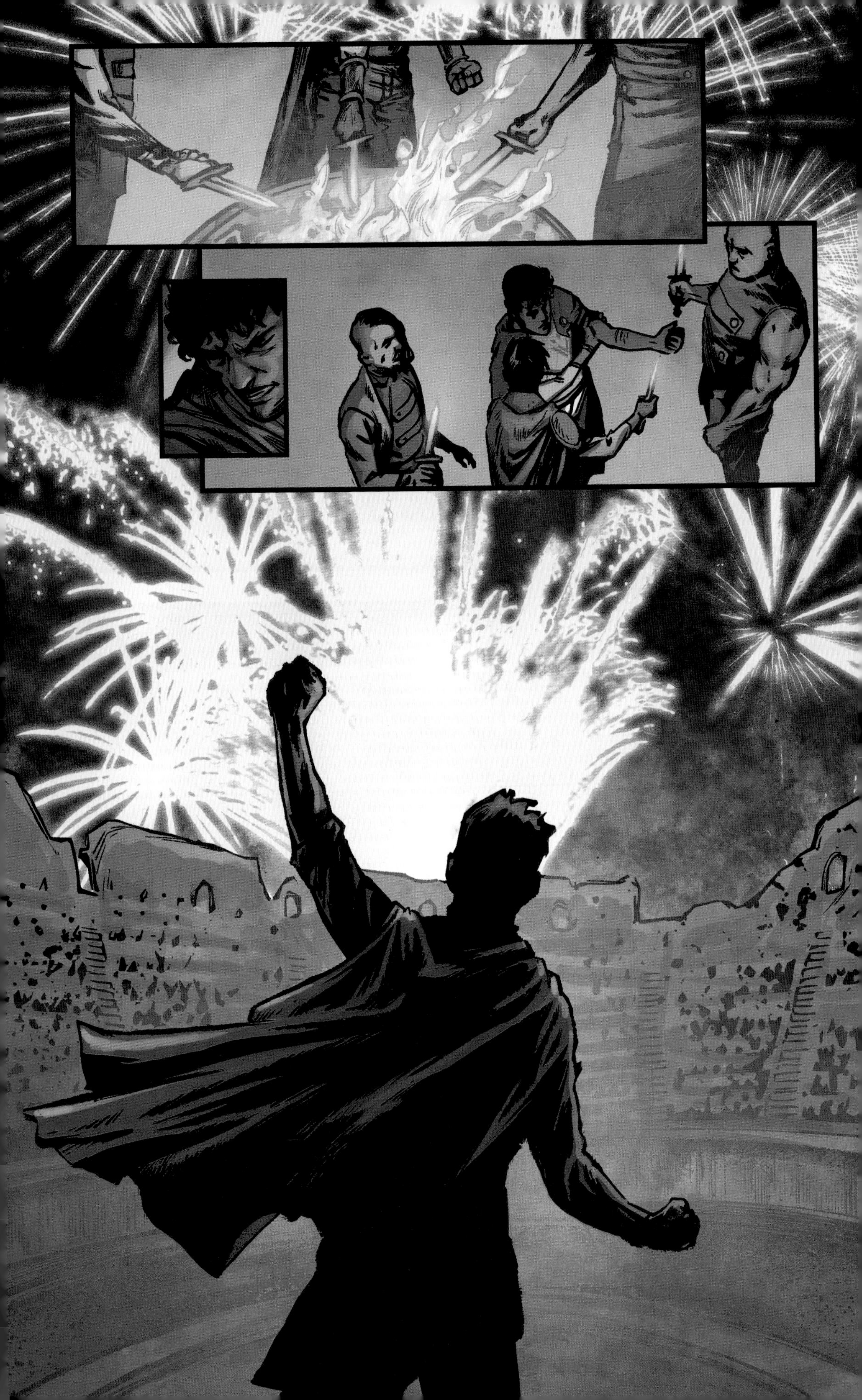

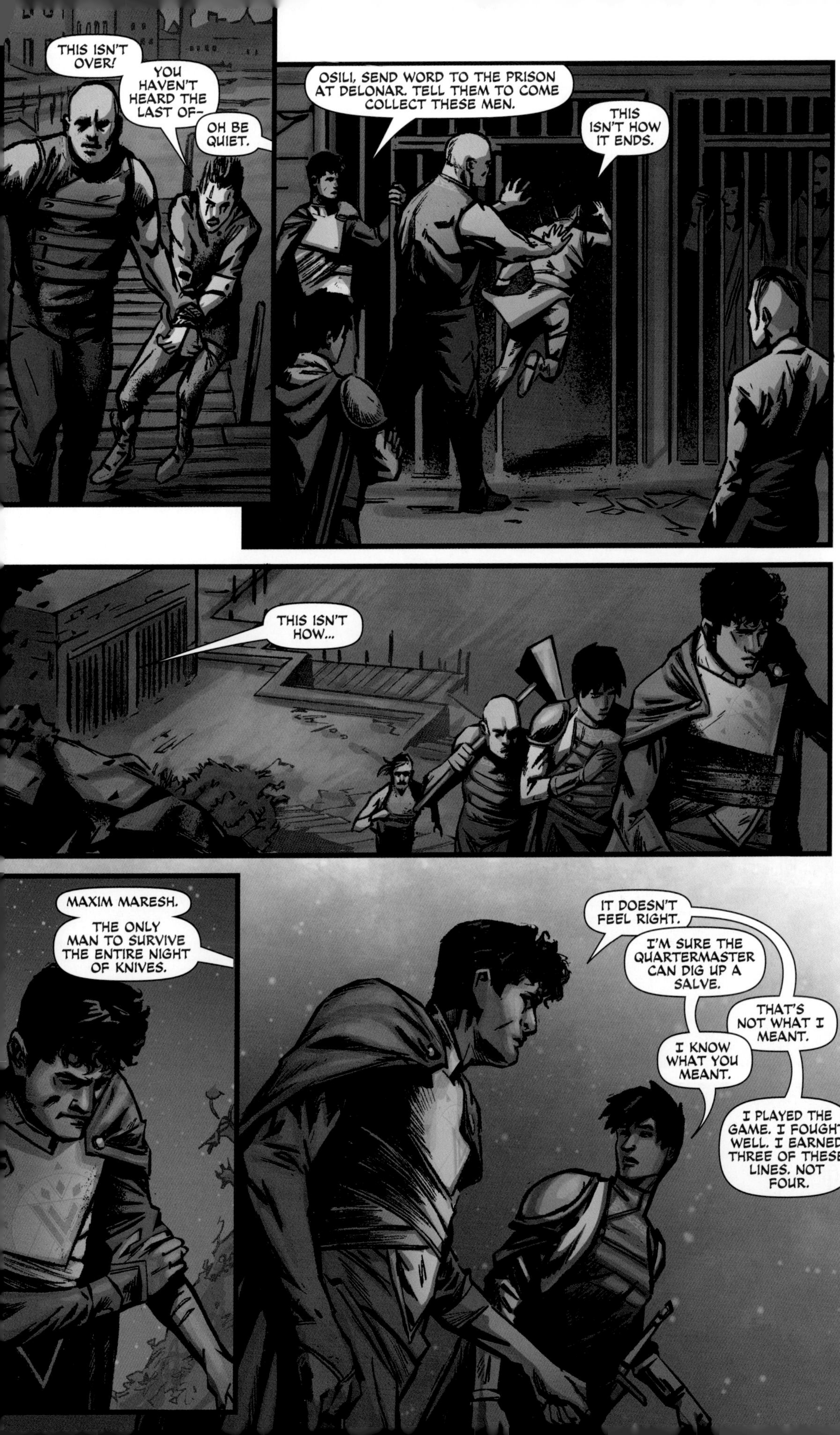
THIS ISN'T OVER!
YOU HAVEN'T HEARD THE LAST OF-
OH BE QUIET.
OSILI, SEND WORD TO THE PRISON AT DELONAR. TELL THEM TO COME COLLECT THESE MEN.
THIS ISN'T HOW IT ENDS.
THIS ISN'T HOW...
MAXIM MARESH.
THE ONLY MAN TO SURVIVE THE ENTIRE NIGHT OF KNIVES.
IT DOESN'T FEEL RIGHT.
I'M SURE THE QUARTERMASTER CAN DIG UP A SALVE.
THAT'S NOT WHAT I MEANT.
I KNOW WHAT YOU MEANT.
I PLAYED THE GAME. I FOUGHT WELL. I EARNED THREE OF THESE LINES. NOT FOUR.

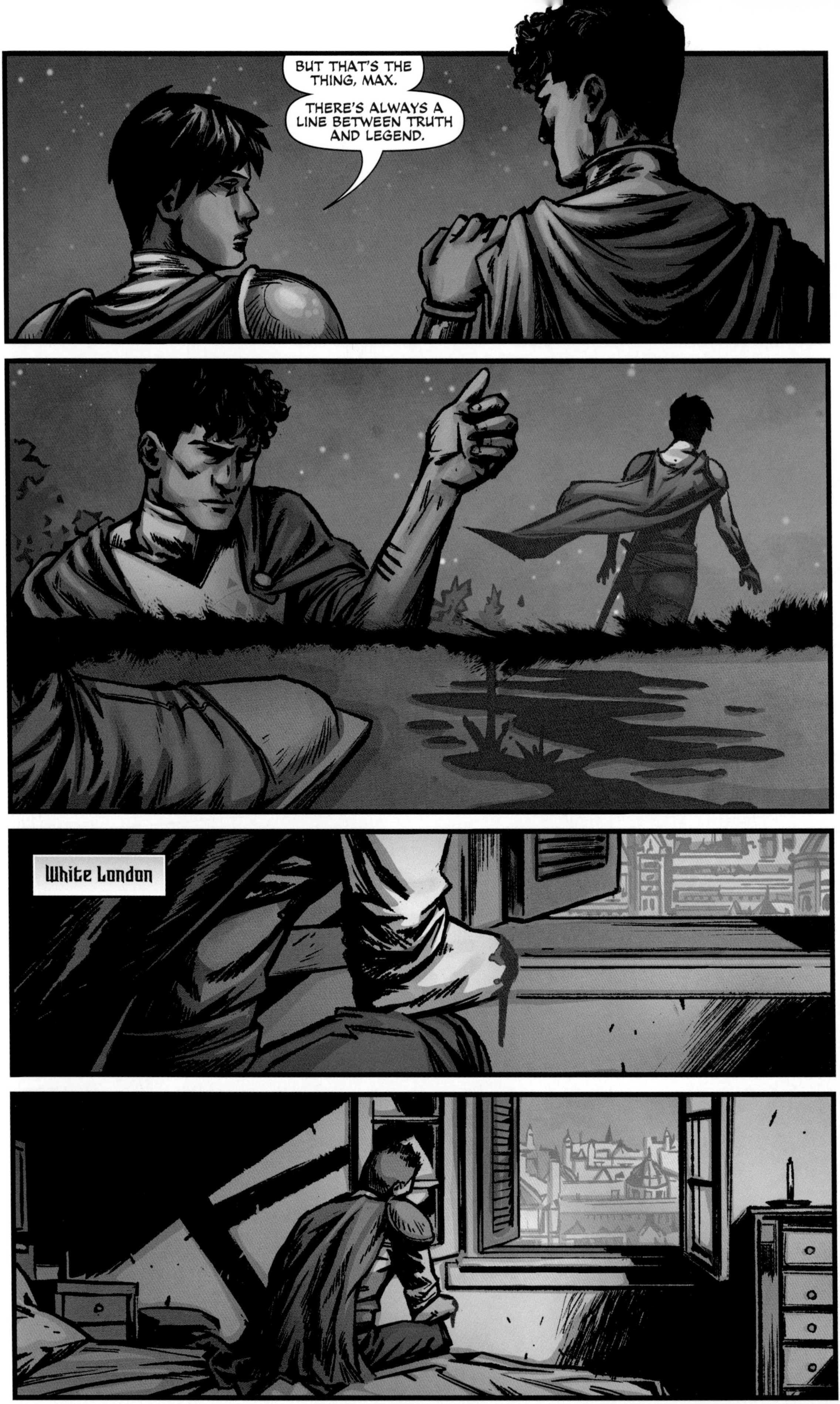
BUT THAT'S THE THING, MAX.
THERE'S ALWAYS A LINE BETWEEN TRUTH AND LEGEND.
White London

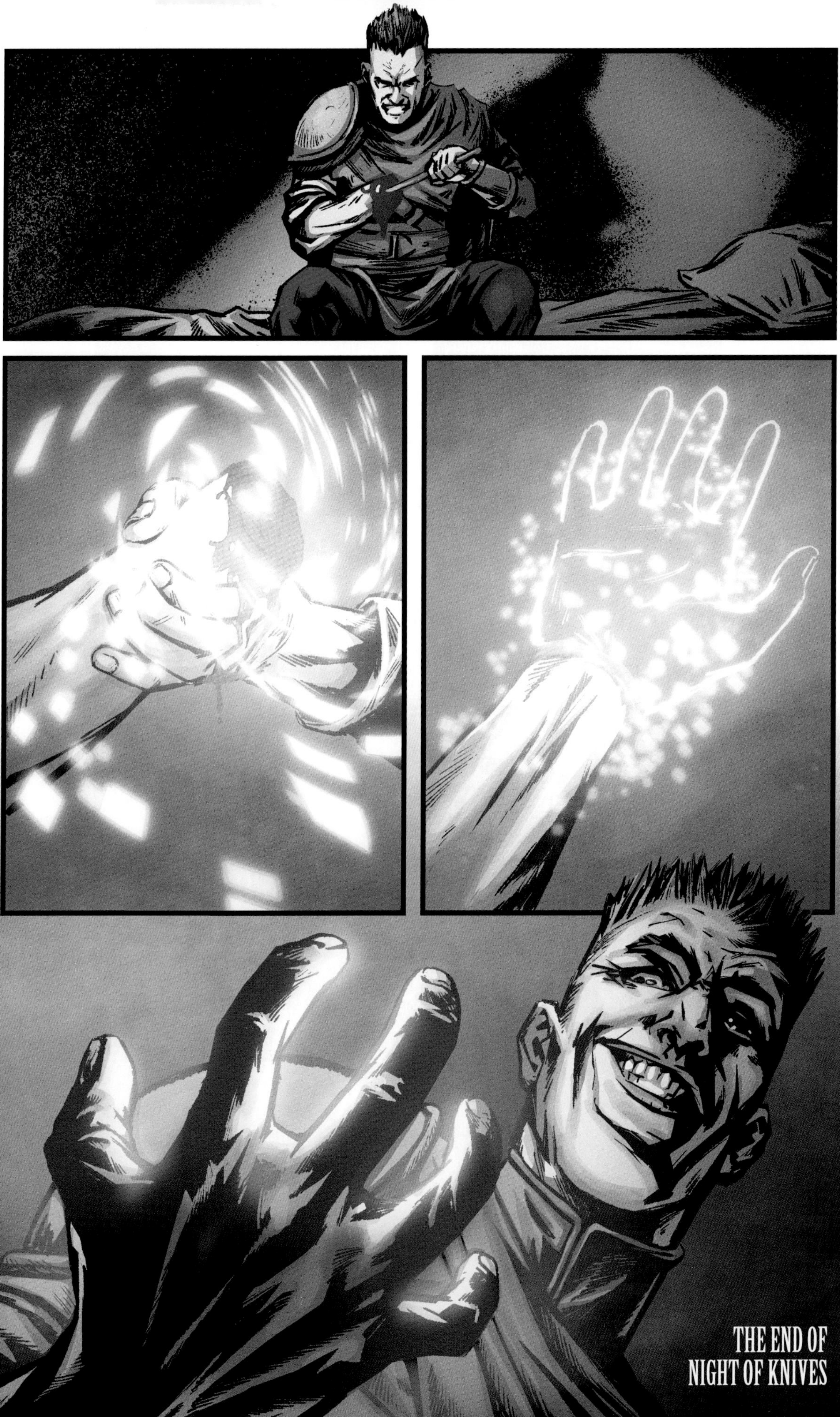
THE END OF
NIGHT OF KNIVES

COVER GALLERY

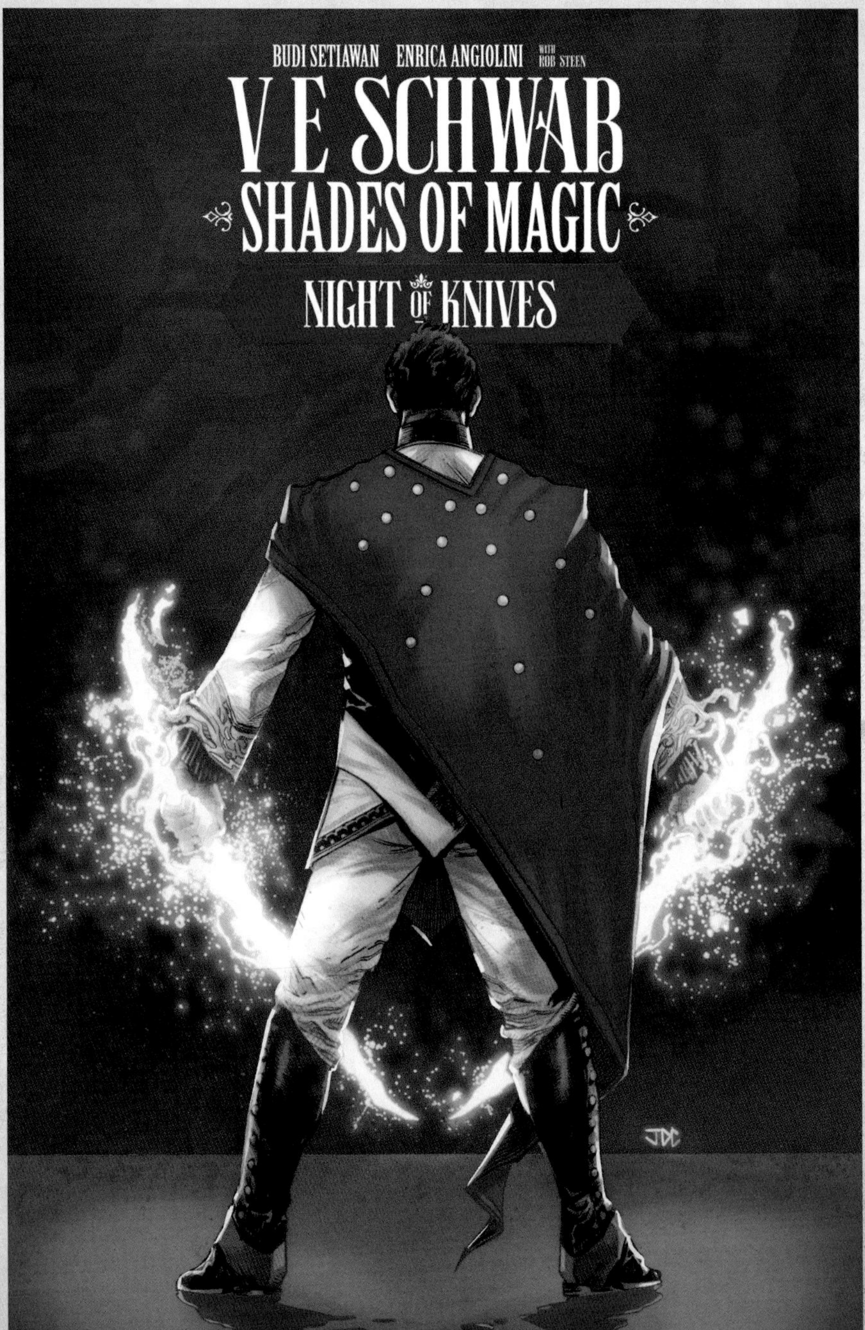
BUDI SETIAWAN ENRICA ANGIOLINI WITH ROB STEEN
V E SCHWAB
SHADES OF MAGIC
NIGHT OF KNIVES
JDC

ISSUE 5 / COVER B - JOSH CASSARA

BUDI SETIAWAN | ENRICA ANGIOLINI | WITH ROB STEEN

V. E. SCHWAB
SHADES OF MAGIC
NIGHT OF KNIVES

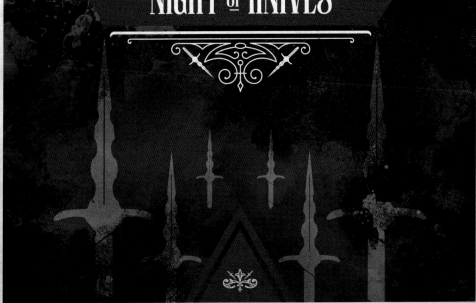

ISSUE 5 / COVER C - ANDREW LEUNG

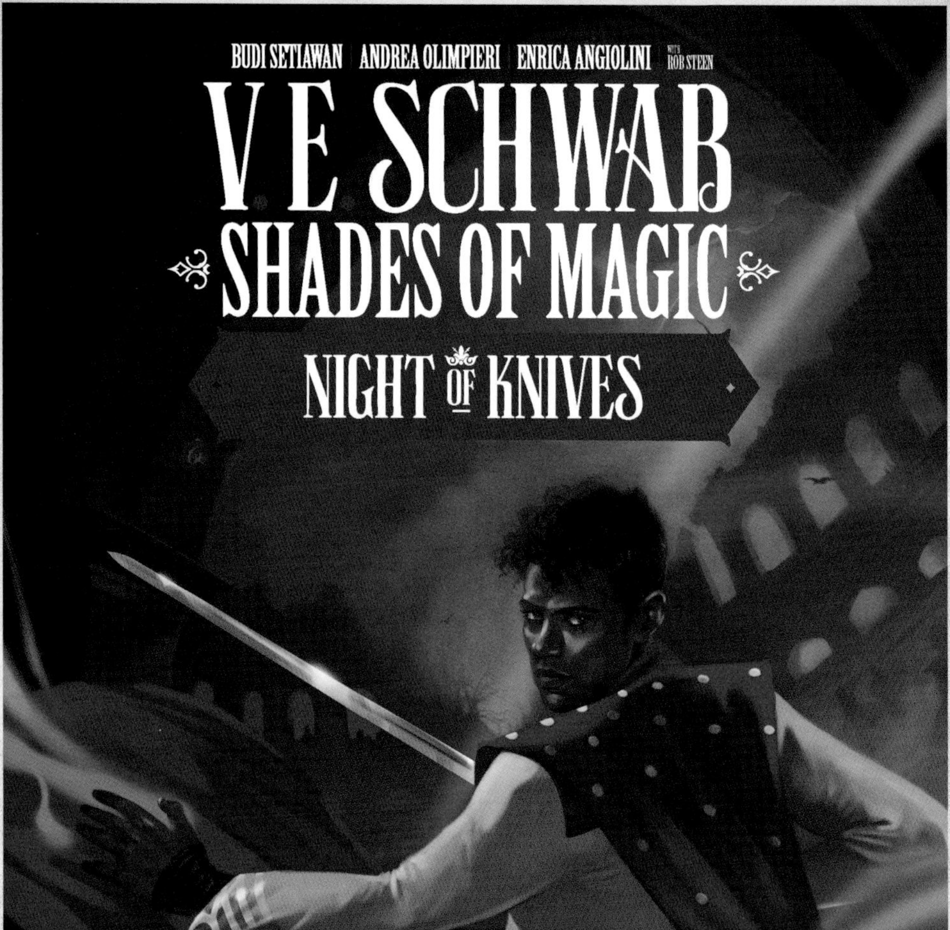

BUDI SETIAWAN   ANDREA OLIMPIERI   ENRICA ANGIOLINI   WITH ROB STEEN

V E SCHWAB
SHADES OF MAGIC
NIGHT OF KNIVES

ISSUE 6 / COVER B - CLAUDIA CARANFA

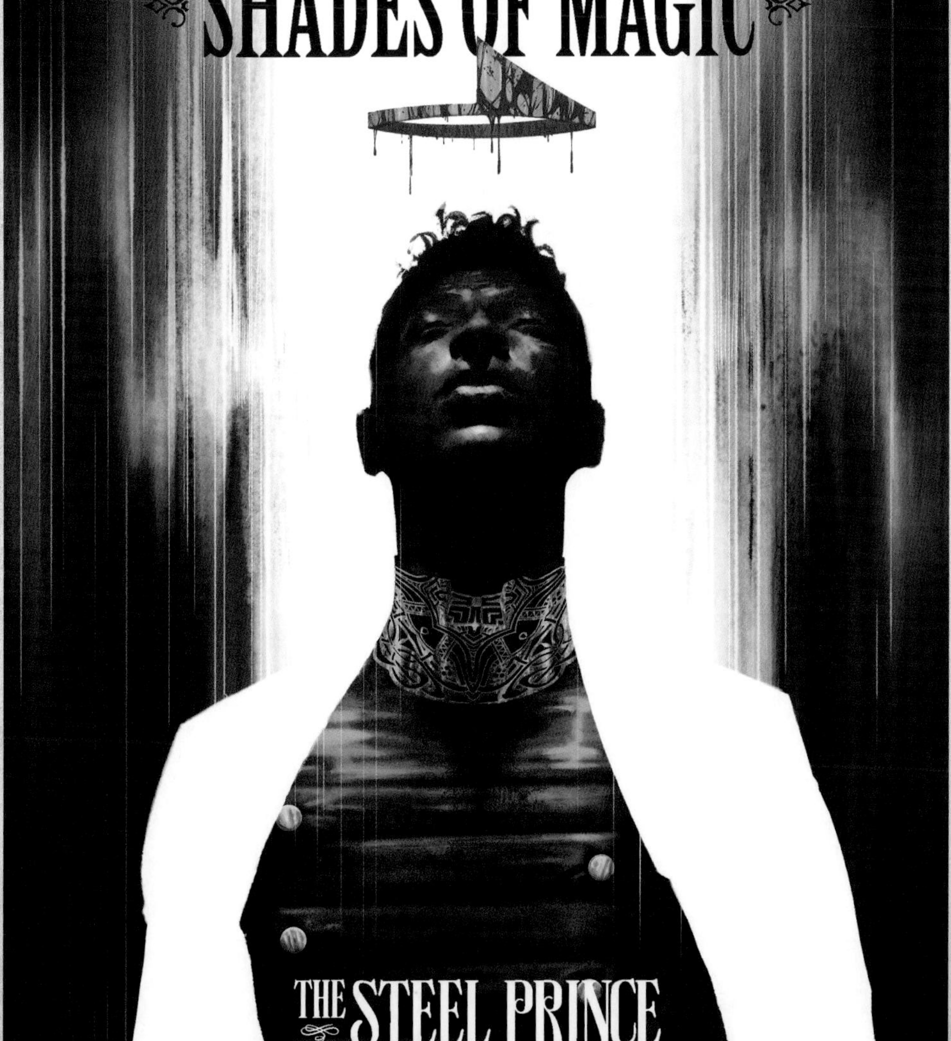

BUDI SETIAWAN | ANDREA OLIMPIERI | ENRICA ANGIOLINI | WITH ROB STEEN

V. E. SCHWAB
SHADES OF MAGIC

THE STEEL PRINCE
NIGHT OF KNIVES

ISSUE 7 / COVER B - ANDREA OLIMPIERI

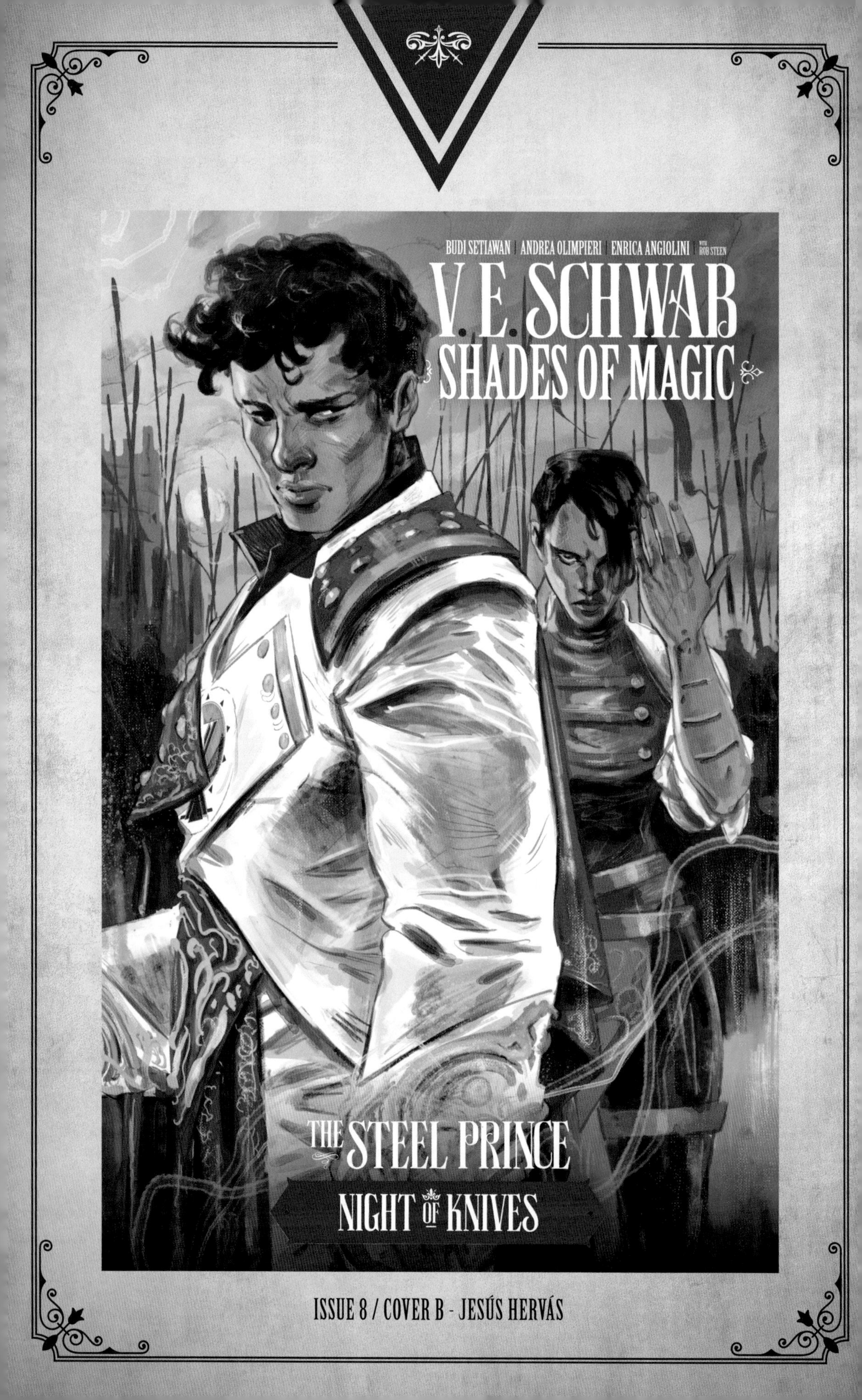
BUDI SETIAWAN | ANDREA OLIMPIERI | ENRICA ANGIOLINI | WITH ROB STEEN
V.E. SCHWAB
SHADES OF MAGIC
THE STEEL PRINCE
NIGHT OF KNIVES

ISSUE 8 / COVER B - JESÚS HERVÁS

AN INTERVIEW WITH
V. E. SCHWAB

Can I start by asking you what it feels like to be finishing off the second book of your three-arc Steel Prince saga?
VES: It's surreal, but incredibly satisfying. I have really enjoyed being able to deepen and expand the narrative, and explore a different facet of Maxim's growing mythology. It's also a relief, because the second of any three-part narrative is inherently a bit daunting. The story needs to be its own, while also transporting us from the introductions of arc 1 to

the conclusions of arc 3. But I'm really proud of the final product.

Do you enjoy watching your scripts being transformed into comics?
VES: It's a process of such immediate gratification. When you write novels, it might be years before you get to see your characters/story interpreted into other media, usually in an unofficial, though flattering, capacity, like fan art. But with this, the process is so much more collaborative. I'm such a visual thinker – I really do see what I write as a movie in my head –

and getting to see it translated from script to comic as I work is thrilling.

What aspect of writing comics do you find the most challenging and exciting? And does it give you the same buzz as writing books?
VES: If anything, I struggle most with the constraints of the format. Not so much on a page by page basis, because as a comic reader and fan I know what I want in terms of flow, but simply the length of the issues. In a novel, a chapter can take as long as it needs to. Here, the arc

must equal 22 pages. Sometimes, I would really love to have 21 or 23 or 30. But the brevity of the form is also part of what makes it so exciting. The short serialization gives the creator a sense of satisfaction that would take months or years in a longer format.

Do you have any one particular sequence or scene that stands out as your favorite in this new series?
VES: I loved designing the challenges Maxim faces in the Night of Knives, and my favorite one was probably the third, where Maxim has to face his own demons. I'm a fan of that trope in any medium, but getting to see it come to life in a visual one was so pleasing.

What would you say would attract readers to this Steel Prince series?
VES: I would describe the books and the comics as grown-up *Harry Potter* meets *Avatar: The Last Airbender*. I think if you enjoy magic, and combat, and adventure, then these should hold some appeal for you.

You've now written eight comic books. Is it safe to say it's been a bit of a learning curve when it comes to working in comics?
VES: Oh, absolutely. I mean, I'm used to working in novel format, and while there's an awareness of length, you're not bound to it in this way. It's a completely different wavelength to think about things in terms of a 22-page issue and also where each page breaks and how much content to put on each page… it's a completely different way of thinking about a story. It's been a from-scratch-education. I've been very fortunate to have the opportunity to do it, but it's absolutely been a learning curve.
    Night of Knives is a continuation of the same narrative.

There's three episodes, if you will, but I'm hoping that I'll become more confident as it goes on, and there'll be less learning, less planning, less revision. I'm getting a better feel for how much should go on any given page, or how much content to fit into any given issue. It's definitely been a trial by fire, but I am hoping that the more I do of it, the more familiar I become with that gut sense of how something will work.

How have the fans responded? Have you been pleased by the reaction?
VES: Yeah! From what I've seen everyone has really enjoyed it. *Shades of Magic* fans are incredibly voracious, and they always like anything art-based – fan-art, merchandise, things like that – so I think for a large portion of fans this is a really cool gift, because it allows them to see characters and see this world that we imagine in a way that

> "I LOVED DESIGNING THE CHALLENGES MAXIM FACES IN THE NIGHT OF KNIVES."

they haven't before. And it's really exciting to see readers who have not read *Shades of Magic*, and are starting with the comics, and who have a different doorway into this world. It's very exciting!

A lot of reviews have said *The Steel Prince* was a very accessible story. Given that *Night of Knives* is a sequel of sorts, is that something you're going to be focusing less on, or are you trying to make sure every issue is a good entry point?
VES: I think everything will be a fairly good entry point. Obviously my hope is that readers will read the volumes in order, as with most comics, but I think that you shouldn't have any difficulty entering at any point you want. It's designed to be accessible, in the same way as my fantasy novels.

I think for a long time, accessibility was regarded as a negative in genre fiction. It was almost seen as a bad word. Historically, I think the exclusivity was a matter of pride for hardcore genre fans. I think there's been a shift, because for my generation, I want readers to be able to drop into a story, fall into it, with ease and feel consumed by it. I don't want to gatekeep that process in any way or, say, leave hardcore fans behind. My great interest is in making stories, fantastic stories, that are accessible for the broadest audience possible.

Can you describe the origin of the story for *Shades of Magic: The Steel Prince: Night of Knives*?
VES: All three arcs of *The Steel Prince* are based on a piece of conversation that happens in one of the novels, where we learn that Maxim Maresh, the King of Red

London, garnered a reputation as the Steel Prince when he was the crown prince and he earned this reputation through three extraordinary feats. When I was writing this conversation I wasn't thinking about the feats themselves, I was just thinking "well, what would sound cool?"

So I wrote, just off-hand, without thinking about what might actually be the events behind the scenes, the Steel Prince and the Pirate Queen, which was our first arc, and the Steel Prince and the Night of Knives, which is our second arc, and the Steel Prince and the Rebel Army, which will be our third. The problem is that I didn't actually think about what those things might be referring to, until I sat down to write the comics and found myself in this position!

The Rebel Army was fairly straightforward, as was the Pirate Queen. That left me with the Night of Knives, which I had written just because it sounded so damn cool! And I was just, like… oh, hell, what is the Night of Knives? And so I had to go about it in reverse-fashion, figuring out what the Night of Knives is.

And what is the Night of Knives?
VES: What it actually is, is a trial that both criminals and royal guard and anyone and anything in between can choose to undergo in this very lawless community of Verose where the story is set. And it's actually a series of trials, a series of challenges, and it's called the Night of Knives because you get a marking, you get a scar, for each challenge you survive. The problem is that no-one has actually survived all of the trials. So it's also

a challenge of when to stop, a test of wisdom; you have to know when you can take on the next level, and when you need to bow out. And so it's a way that members of the royal army and thugs and criminals and pirates gain a little bit of cred, a little bit of respect among their own and among the others. So Maxim has decided that in order to gain respect among his soldiers, who think that he is just a prince playing soldier, and to gain a little bit of respect among the citizens of Verose, who see him as just a target, he is going to undertake the trials of the Night of Knives.

Having read *The Steel Prince*, I can imagine someone telling Maxim that no-one survives the Night of Knives… and him responding with a blank look: "Don't you know who I am?!"
VES: So often in my novels – and now in my comics – it's not about having power, it's about knowing what to do with it. It's about knowing how to understand your own limitations and your own weaknesses, in order to make yourself stronger.

There is an inherent irony to proving that you're not just some arrogant callow youth who doesn't know his limits by… throwing yourself into a trial to the death. Not really proving anyone wrong, there…
VES: Maxim is a very proud, definitely arrogant and self-righteous character at the beginning of the comics, because he's never been under any duress before the comics started. He really did come into this as a royal prince, playing soldier. The comic series, all three arcs of it, are really about him learning that he has to really earn this reputation that's going to outlive him.

"SO OFTEN IN MY NOVELS – AND NOW IN MY COMICS – IT'S NOT ABOUT HAVING POWER, IT'S ABOUT KNOWING WHAT TO DO WITH IT."

And finally, what can you tell us about *The Steel Prince: The Rebel Army*? What awaits Maxim Maresh and are there any secrets you can tease us with?
VES: In the third and final arc of the *Steel Prince* saga, Maxim's dual identities as both prince and soldier collide, and a decision he made at the very beginning of the series comes back to haunt him. He has to face not only a threat to his family and the empire, but a very immediate danger in Verose, and a mysterious foe – one he might not be strong enough to defeat.

COMING SOON

ANDREA OLIMPIERI | ENRICA ANGIOLINI | WITH ROB STEEN

V. E. SCHWAB
SHADES OF MAGIC

THE STEEL PRINCE
THE REBEL ARMY

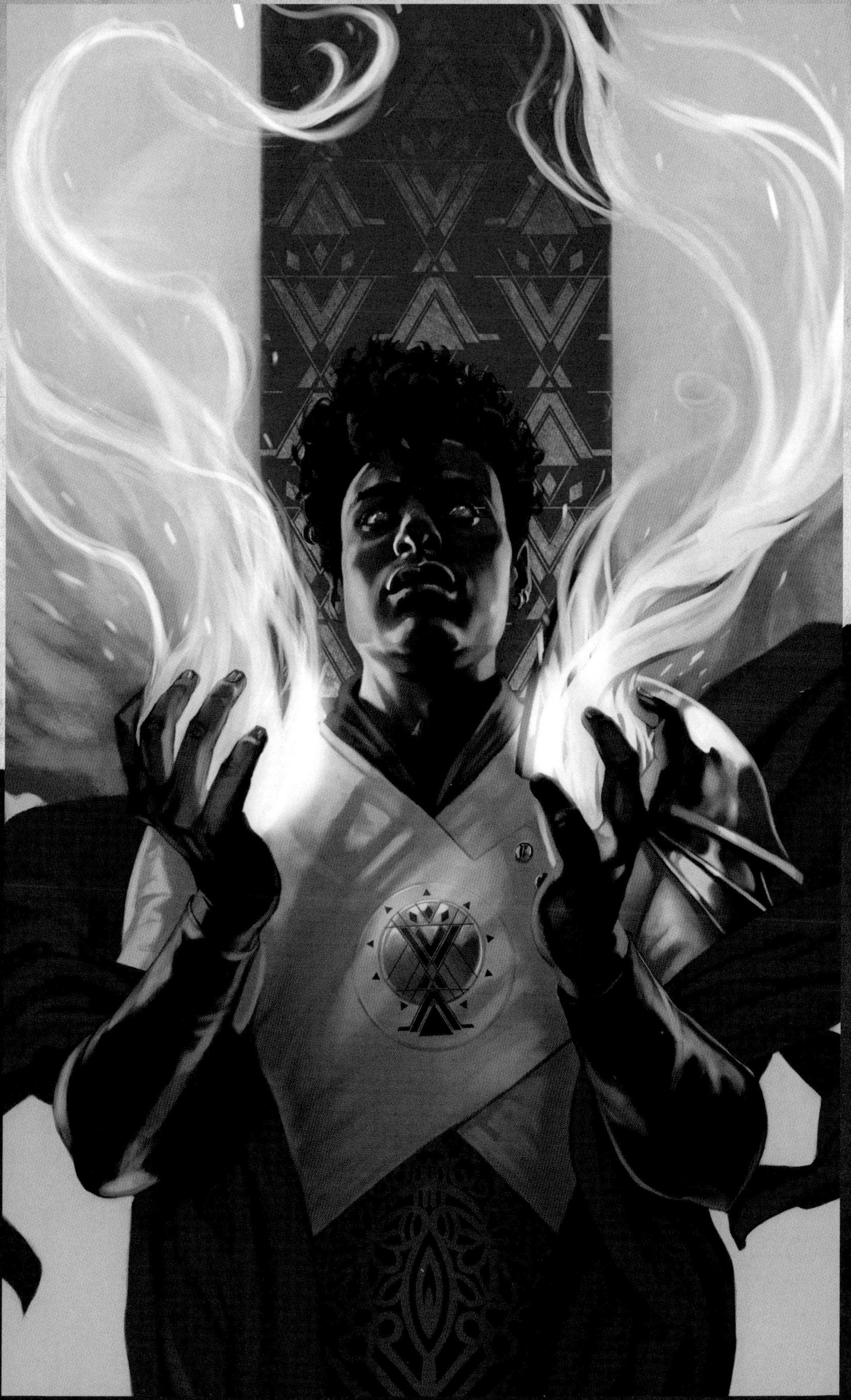

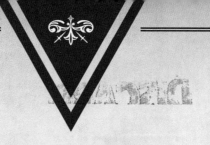

CREATOR BIOS

V. E. SCHWAB

Victoria "V.E." Schwab is the #1 NYT, USA, and Indie-bestselling author of more than a dozen books, including *Vicious*, the *Shades of Magic* series, and *This Savage Song*. Her work has received critical acclaim, been featured by *Entertainment Weekly* and *The New York Times*, been translated into more than a dozen languages, and has been optioned for TV and film. *The Independent* calls her the "natural successor to Diana Wynne Jones" and touts her "enviable, almost Gaimanesque ability to switch between styles, genres, and tones."

◆

BUDI SETIAWAN

Indonesian artist Budi Setiawan came to prominence in 2007 when he was nominated for the Russ Manning Most Promising Newcomer Award at the Harvey Awards. He has gone on to draw the *Road Kill Zoo* series for Novaris Entertainment, *Rex Royd* for Titan Comics and the critically acclaimed *The Raid* also for Titan Comics.

◆

ANDREA OLIMPIERI

Andrea is a comic book artist based out of Italy. He has been instrumental in creating the visual aesthetic for the *Shades of Magic* comic series. He has also contributed artwork to a number of high-profile titles, including *Monstri* and *True Blood* for IDW, and Titan Comics' *Dishonored*. He pencilled and inked *Shades of Magic: The Steel Prince* and inked issues 2 – 4 of *Night of Knives*.

◆

ENRICA EREN ANGIOLINI

A skilled colorist and an accomplished fencer, Enrica has colored for books such as *Doctor Who: The Thirteenth Doctor*, *Warhammer 40,000*, *Terminator*, and *The Order of the Forge*. She lives and works in Rome, Italy.

◆

ROB STEEN

Rob Steen is an experienced letterer, whose skilled calligraphy has enlivened the works of many comics, including *Arrowsmith*, *Astro City*, *Bloodshot*, *Harbinger*, *Wolverine*, *X-Men*, and Titan's own *Rivers of London* and *Warhammer 40,000* series.